Case White

The German Army in the Polish Campaign - September 1939

William Russ

THE NAFZIGER COLLECTION

2017

T0325494

Cover Art from wikipedia
Case White by William Russ
This edition published in 2017

Published by Winged Hussar Publishing
1525 Hulse Road, Unit 1
Point Pleasant, NJ 08742

ISBN 978-1-945430-40-4
LCN 2017958000

Bibliographical References and Index
1. World War II. 2. Germany. 3. Military

Contents

Introduction
and
Acknowledgments

In 1985, Hippocrene Books published the 'September Campaign' by Victor Madej and Steve Zaloga. It was the first book in English to cover in detail the German invasion of Poland in September 1939. The one disappointment of the book was its lack of information on the German forces. The authors stated in the introduction that there was plenty of information about the German Army in other sources, being the reason why it was not included. This however was not completely true. Information on the German Army could be found but it was scattered in different books and other forms. And even if one could bring all of this together, it still would not be as comprehensive as their book was for the Polish forces. Hence, the reason for this book. I felt there should be a companion book to theirs so any reader could get a comparative whole to the campaign. I hope this book fills that need. There is still a gap that needs to be filled and that is for the Luftwaffes contribution to the German effort. Hopefully, someone will write on that subject one day.

I may have written this book alone, but without the help and support of many individuals, I could not have finished it. First and foremost, I want to thank George Nafziger for encouraging me to write this book. Without his help (and great editing skills) this book would have never been published. My research on the maps was greatly facilitated by Ross Taylor, assistant Map Librarian at the University of South Carolina. Because of his help, I found the right base maps for the strategic maps. I want to thank Mr. Holland and his staff at the National Archives at College Park, Maryland for their assistance in my research through the microfilm library. They made all my trips to the National Archives a very pleasant one. For some critical translations of German documents, Leo Niehorster was of immense help. His vast knowledge of the German Army was particularly helpful on questions I had on order of battle and organizational matters. I spent dozens of hours scanning microfilm rolls at the Richland Public Library and want to thank their staff, in particular Debbie Bloom, for putting up with me. Last, but not least I want to thank my wife Lois. Her proofreading and editing skills made this a better book. Her patience in putting up with this book and me in general were extraordinary.

In the end, I take full responsibility for any errors in this book. If there are any questions on the material in this book, please write me in care of the publisher and I will try and answer them.

Terrain Symbology Key

Strategic Maps

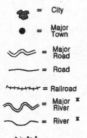

- = City
- = Major Town
- = Minor Town
- = Major Road
- = Railroad
- = River˟
- = Border

Operational Maps

- = City
- = Major Town
- = Major Road
- = Road
- = Railroad
- = Major River ˟
- = River ˟
- = Forest

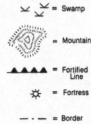

- = Swamp
- = Mountain
- = Fortified Line
- = Fortress
- = Border

˟ All rivers, lakes, seas and other bodies of water are italicized.

Abbreviations for Maps and Charts

Polish

Krak	=	Krakow
Kra	=	Krakowska
Karp	=	Karpathian
Kres	=	Kresowa
Mas	=	Mazowiecka
NG	=	National Guard
Now	=	Nowogrodska
Podl	=	Podlaska
Pom	=	Pomorska
Suw	=	Suwalska
War	=	Warsaw
Wiel	=	Wielkopolska
Wil	=	Wilenska
Wol	=	Wolynska
Zako	=	Zakopane

German

AA	=	Anti–Aircraft
AFV	=	Armored Fighting Vehicles
Art	=	Artillery
AT	=	Anti–Tank
Auf	=	Aufklarung (reconnaissance)
Aufkl	=	" "
BG	=	Borderguard
bn	=	battalion
Div	=	Division
Eber	=	Eberhardt
Erz	=	Ersatz
Ff	=	Fliegerfuhrer (air command)
Ft	=	Fortress
g	=	gun (artillery)
h	=	howitzer (artillery)
Hvy	=	Heavy
JG	=	Jagd Geschwader (fighter wing)
KG	=	Kampf Geschwader (bomber wing)
KuflGr	=	Kustenflieger Gruppe (coastal air group)
KusG	=	Kusten Geschwader (coastal wing)
LAH	=	Liebstandarte Adolf Hitler
Ldw	=	Landwehr (reservists)
Lds	=	Landesschutzen (local defence)
LG	=	Lehr Geschwader (training wing)
LK	=	Luftgau Kommando (area air command)
Lt	=	Light
LW	=	Luftwaffe (air force)

Misc.	=	Miscellaneous
Mcy	=	Motorcycle
MG	=	machinegun
Pol	=	Police
Pz	=	Panzer
Reg	=	Regiment
Sdkfz	=	Sonderkraftfahrzeug (special motor vehicle)
Sec	=	Security
Sl	=	Slovak
SS	=	Schutz Staffel (protection echelon)
StG	=	Sturzkampfflugzeug Geschwader (divebomber wing)
zbv	=	zur besonderen verwendung (for special use)
ZG	=	Zerstorer Geschwader (destroyer wing)

Military Symbology Key
Strategic and Operational Maps

German

- = Infantry
- = Cavalry
- = Armor
- = Motorized Infantry
- = Armored Cavalry
- = Mountain
- Bdr = Border Guard
- Pol = Police
- = Army Headquarters
- XIX Corps = Numbered Corps

Polish

- = Infantry
- = Cavalry
- = Armor
- = Naval Infantry
- = National Guard
- = Army Headquarters
- = Corps Headquarters

Slovak

- = Infantry
- = Motorized Infantry

Unit Size:
(Common to map symbols and order of battle charts and organizational charts.)

Army Group	= xxxxx
Army	= xxxx
Corps	= xxx
Division	= xx
Brigade	= x
Regiment	I I I
Battalion	I I
Company or Battery	= I

German:
- xxxxx ——— = Army Group Boundary
- xxxx ——— = Army Boundary
- xxx ——— = Corps Boundary

Order of Battle and Organizational Charts

Ground Units:

- = Infantry
- = Mountain Infantry
- = Marine
- = Naval Infantry
- = Motorized Infantry
- = Armor
- = Cavalry
- = Armored Cavalry* or Recon
- = Motorized Artillery
- = Artillery
- = Anti-tank (motorized)
- = Anti-Aircraft (motorized)

- = Mortar (motorized)
- = Machinegun (motorized)
- = Motorcycle
- = Machinegun
- = Engineer (motorized)
- = Engineer
- = Construction Engineer
- = Bridge Construction
- = Road Construction
- BOR = Borderguard
- LDS = Landesschutzen
- LDW = Landwehr
- = Ersatz Infantry

- Ft = Fortress
- Sec = Security
- NG = National Guard
- Pol. = Police
- = Signal
- DS = Divisional Services
- = Einsatzgruppen

Air Units:

- = Single engine Fighter
- = Two engine Fighter
- = Single engine Ground Support
- = Two engine Bomber
- = Reconnaissance
- = Torpedo Bomber

Headquarter and Command Units:
(Any units that are italicized are headquarter or command units.)

- xxx VIII = Corps Headquarters (Sample shown: Eighth Corps)
- xxxx 4 = Army Headquarters (Sample shown: Fourth Army)
- xxxxx A = Army Group Headquarters (Sample shown: Army Group A)

*The Light divisions are considered armored cavalry. All other units are reconnaissance units.

Poland 1938 By Halibutt - Own work; based on an earlier raster map made in 2005, as well as similar maps made by myself in 2004 (see below). In preparation of this map I used many other maps as sources and backup. Among them were: a German roadmap of Poland printed in 1938 (colours and the shape of East Prussian border) and (shape of Czechoslovakia) (Polish and German rivers)(parts of German shoreline and borders(Austria)(Sweden and Norway, parts of Denmark)and perhaps a dozen others., CC BY-SA 3.0, https://commons.wikimedia.org/w/index.php?curid=3703674

Chapter 1
Plans and Preparations

After the occupation of what was left of Czechoslovakia in early March 1939, Hitler turned his attention to his next target - Poland. Hitler's pretext for an attack on Poland was the German nations desire to regain the territories lost to the Polish nation after World War One. These territories included the Polish part of Silesia, the Polish Corridor and the city of Danzig. The area of Polish Silesia had many mining and industrial complexes that would help bolster Germany's growing rearmament industries. Danzig was economically important as a seaport and trade center on the Baltic Sea. Even though the Germans and Poles 'shared' the city of Danzig's economy, all German goods had to be shipped by sea around the Polish Corridor and therefore lessened it value to the Germans. The German government began negotiations with Poland in late 1938 by making proposals for the return of these territories to the Reich, though without offering the Poles much compensation for what they would lose. Hitler certainly knew that the Poles would rebuff these overtures and with their final refusal in early 1939 he issued an order by late March for plans to be drawn up by OKW (Oberkommando Wehrmacht) for invasion plans. On 3 April 1939 OKW issued a directive to all three armed services to prepare such plans under the code name Case White (Fall Weiss).

The Army's planning for Case White fell under the responsibility of General Franz Halder, Oberkommando de Heeres (OKH's) chief of staff. Halder gave the task of accessing Poland's military capabilities and for selecting the best operational plan to use against Poland to General Karl von Stülpnagel, Chief of OKH Operations; Colonel Hans von Greiffenberg, Chief of OKH Operations section and General Kurt von Tippelskirch, then Chief of the Military Intelligence section.

The three factors that became obvious to the planners for the overall strategy were: 1) the German ability to concentrate a number of superior forces against the Poles, 2) Poland's long frontier made her vulnerable to wide encirclements beyond her western frontiers and 3) a hostile Soviet regime with territorial grievances of its own.

The Polish armed forces, if fully mobilized, could present a considerable problem for the Germans. After full mobilization, the Polish army would consist of forty-one infantry divisions, two mountain divisions, three mountain brigades, eleven cavalry brigades and fifty-one non-divisional combat battalions. Combine this with the first-class reservists that could be called up and this would give the Polish army a total of 2.1 million men under arms. This would give the Polish army, a numerical advantage in comparison to the German army's estimated strength of 1.5 million men. If the fighting stretched into months this gave Allies (the French and British) time to mobilize and attack the German's weak western front. On the plus side for the Germans, the Polish armies were armed with much older equipment, the Polish motorized forces were tiny by comparison to the German forces and the Polish air force was also small and had many obsolescent aircraft. Since the Poles relied on telephone landlines for most of her communications systems, they were vulnerable to air attack and disruption. The Germans also used telephone lines for communications, but also had an extensive radio communications network used by all of the German armed forces.

The Poles long and exposed frontier offered the Germans many possible avenues for invasion. The country itself was relatively flat with very few terrain features that could offer much defense. Along its border with East Prussia in the north, there were some forests extending from the Masurian Lakes[1] and small rivers, which mostly run north to south, but these were not much of an obstacle. From the area of Silesia and on into Poland, the terrain was an open flat plain extending to the Vistula River and beyond, intersected only by some small rivers and forests. The largest natural barrier the Poles had were the Carpathian Mountains that ran along her southern border with Slovakia and some of the lands recently incorporated into Germany from Czechoslovakia. These mountains would certainly slow any German advance from this direction. The Vistula River, running from the Baltic Sea to the south of Poland, was another chief obstacle. Its advantage was largely negated by the fact that the Germans already had forces deployed on the east side of the river in East Prussia and in eastern Slovakia. As for man made obstacles the Poles had built very few fortifications. Because of limited funds in their military budget, fortifications had been built in a few strategic areas.

The basic German military doctrine of encirclement and destruction (in German *kesselschlacht*) meant that the Polish forces would have to be encircled west of the Vistula before to many Polish forces escaped across to the east side of the Vistula River. This would mean pinning down as many enemy troops as possible along the Polish frontier giving the motorized divisions a chance to get behind the Poles and cutting off their major axis of retreat. The Luftwaffe would also play an important part by interdicting major crossing points at rivers, attacking major communication centers and disrupting the flow of military traffic along road and rail lines.

General Halder and the OKH staff came up with the basic strategic plan of using two army groups. Army Group North would concentrate one army in Pomerania and one army in East Prussia, while Army Group South would have two armies in the Silesian region and one army in Slovakia arranged along the Carpathian Mountains (see OKH strategic plan map).

After briefing Hitler on the army's plan on 26-27 April, Hitler gave his approval for the strategic plan of attack and for the more intricate planning for the operational and tactical details to be worked out. On 1 May, OKH ac-

---

[1]The Masurian Lakes was the area where the great battle of Tannenberg was fought in 1914.

tivated two army group headquarters. The 1st, Army Group North (under it's cover name of *Heeresgruppen Kommando 1*) was given command to General Feodor von Bock and General Hans von Salmuth was assigned as his chief of staff. Command of Army Group South (under it's cover name *Arbeitstab Rundstedt*) was given to General Gerd von Rundstedt and assigned as his chief of staff was General Erich von Manstein. Both army group staffs sent appropriate orders to the peacetime commands that would form their army headquarters to initiate planning at the operational and tactical levels. By late May both army group staffs, with the approval of both Bock and Rundstedt, submitted their comments and recommendations to OKH. Both staffs recommended a wargame to explore the possibilities of Germany's strategic options. This was refused by Hitler for security reasons and because it might endanger ongoing diplomatic negotiations.

Generals Rundstedt and Bock had some dissenting opinions of the OKH plan. Rundstedt thought the 10th Army, Army Group South's largest army, should destroy the Polish forces on its front before advancing on to Warsaw. He was afraid he would have to divert to many of his infantry divisions to guard the 10th Army's flanks and this would weaken the 10th Army's spearhead. He was told that the 8th Army would be adequate for the flank protection, but the SS Adolf Hitler Motorized Regiment was added to the 8th Army order of battle to help in this mission. Bock felt that any attacks toward Warsaw from the west would have a much harder time advancing and suggested that the 3rd Army should engage in a wider flank attack east of Warsaw. Bock was granted some latitude on how to use his forces in this regard by OKH, but OKH remained skeptical that the limited forces he had in East Prussia could accomplish it.

On 15 June 1939 OKH directed both working staffs to continue working out the finer details of their plans. The target date to have all of the details worked out (including those of the Luftwaffe and Kriegsmarine) was set for 20 July. Both army groups had attached to them the commands of the active Army that would form the army headquarters on mobilization, and the corps, divisions and supporting troops considered necessary to accomplish their missions.

By the first week in July, the basic outline of the order of battle for both army groups had taken shape. Army Group North would control the 3rd Army under General Georg von Küchler and the 4th Army under the command of General Günther von Kluge. The 3rd Army had under its command the I Army Corps with the 1st, 11th and 12th Infantry Divisions and one panzer division, the XXI Army Corps with the 21st and 228th Infantry Divisions, the 1st Cavalry Brigade and in reserve the 61st, 206th and 217th Infantry Divisions. The 4th Army had under its command the II Army Corps with the 3rd and 32nd Infantry Divisions, the III Army Corps with the 23rd Infantry Division, the XIX Motorized Corps with the 3rd Panzer Division, the 2nd Motorized Division and one third of the 20th Motorized Division, the 1st Border Command with the 207th Infantry Division and in reserve two thirds of the 20th Motorized Division. Army Group North had two infantry divisions in reserve, the 208th and 218th.

Army Group South would control the 8th Army under the command of General Johannes Blaskowitz, the 10th Army under the command of General Walter von Richenau, and the 14th Army under the command of Generaloberst Wilhelm List. The 8th Army had under its command the X Army Corps with the 24th and 30th Infantry Divisions and the XIII Army Corps with the 10th and 17th Infantry Divisions. The 10th Army had under its control the IV Army Corps with the 46th Infantry Division, the XI Army Corps with the 19th and 31st Infantry Divisions, the XIV Motorized Corps with the 1st Light Division and 18th Infantry Divisions, the XV Motorized Corps with the 2nd Light Division and 4th Infantry Division and the XVI Motorized Corps with the 1st Panzer Division, 3rd Light Division and the 14th Infantry Division. The 10th Army held the 13th and 29th Motorized Divisions in its reserve. The 14th Army had under its command the VIII Army Corps with the 5th Panzer Division and the 8th and 28th Infantry Divisions, the XVII Army Corps with the 2nd Panzer Division and the 44th and 45th Infantry Divisions and the XVIII Army Corps with the 4th Light Division, the 7th Infantry Division and the 2nd and 3rd Mountain Divisions. Army Group South had in reserve the VII Army Corps with the 27th and 68th Infantry Divisions, the XXII Army Corps with the 62nd, 213th, 221st and 239th Infantry Divisions and the 1st Mountain Division in general reserve. Over the next two months this order of battle would change according to operational adjustments, perceived changes in the strength and location of Polish units and to try and deceive the Polish intelligence services (for the final order of battle see the 1 September 1939 order of battle charts for the German Army).

Meanwhile, mobilization of the army had already begun. The mobilization plans for 1938 and early 1939 had proven to be unsatisfactory and by the summer of 1939 the system had been greatly refined. To conceal any aggressive intentions against Poland, the deployment was disguised as maneuvers, exercises and refresher training in carefully installed phases. In the first phase, between 26 June and 4 August, all of the pre-war divisions including thirty-five first wave infantry divisions (the 1st, 3rd -12th, 14th-19th, 21st-28th, 30th-36th and 44th-46th), three mountain divisions (the 1st-3rd), seven panzer divisions (the 1st-5th, 10th and Kempf), four motorized infantry divisions (the 2nd, 13th, 20th and 29th), four light divisions (the 1st-4th), and the 1st Cavalry Brigade were to be filled out to full strength. Also included in the first mobilization phase were the activation of army group, army and most of the army corps headquarter staffs. In the second phase, the second wave divisions were to be formed and brought up to strength. This was started in early August after issuance of orders to start the second phase. These divisions included the 52nd, 56th-58th, 61st, 62nd, 68th, 69th, 71st, 73rd, 75th, 76th, 78th, 79th, 86th and 87th infantry divisions. Also included were the headquarter staffs for the XXI, XXII,

XXVII and XXX army corps. In this period, the first phase units were to move up to their pre-invasion assembly areas by 19 August. In the third and final phase, all of the pre-war divisions were to move into their pre-invasion positions. The third wave divisions (including the 206th-209th, 211th-218th, 221st, 223rd, 225th, 227th, 228th, 231st, 239th and 246th infantry divisions) and the fourth wave divisions (including the 251st-258th, 260th, 262nd, 263rd and 267th-269th infantry divisions) were to be mobilized six days after the beginning of general mobilization. The second, third and fourth wave divisions were to be echeloned to the rear of the first phase divisions as reinforcements.

By comparison, the Polish mobilization process had not proceeded as smoothly as the German mobilization. After the breakdown of negotiations in March 1939, the Poles initiated the first part of their mobilization plan. This phase of the general mobilization order called for twenty-four infantry divisions (the 1st, 2nd, 4th-6th, 10th, 12th-20th, 23rd, 25th-30th), two mountain divisions (the 21st and 22nd), all eleven cavalry brigades, the 10th Motorized Brigade and the three mountain brigades to be mobilized within twenty-four to sixty hours of the issuance of the order. The second mobilization wave consisted of the Warsaw Motorized Brigade, three infantry divisions (the 3rd, 38th and 55th) and portions of four other divisions (the 5th, 33rd, 36th and 41st). These units were formed two to four days after general mobilization had begun. This gave the Poles a total of 500,000 men under arms. The third and final phase of mobilization had been delayed until 27 August 1939 because of Polish and British fears that full mobilization might disrupt ongoing diplomatic negotiations between Britain, Germany, Poland and the Soviet Union and provoke the Germans into an invasion. The final phase would take place between the fifth and seventh day of mobilization forming the three remaining divisions (the 39th, 44th and 45th) as well as the partially formed divisions. Only about one-third of the first phase units had already been mobilized by 27 August. By 1 September, only 600,000 of the anticipated 2.1 million men were under arms as compared to 1.5 million German. For logistics, the German army's preparations were made much easier because of the extensive rail network at or near the borders with Poland. Part of this network also ran through much of Poland, since most of it was built by the Germans under the regime of Kaiser Wilhelm II. This would help the German army advance their railheads much more rapidly and keep the advancing armies in good supply.

The only real fear the Germans had were the plans of France and England if they declared war on Germany. OKH made calculations on the speed of the Allied mobilization and deployment of forces based on what intelligence they had on the Allies. It was calculated that the French army could have forty-seven divisions available for offensive purposes after the first four days of mobilization. The Germans only had thirty-three weak infantry divisions to defend from any kind of threat against Germany's western frontier. Depending on how much resistance the Poles would put up, units were to be transferred as rapidly as possible from the Polish front to shore up the West Wall defenses. Of course, attacks by the Allies were limited by the areas along the French-German border that an offense could be reasonably carried out. The border between the Swiss frontier north to Saarbrücken had the West Wall fortifications and the rough terrain of the Black Forest region behind it, which made this area easily defensible. The area between Saarbrücken and Trier promised better offensive possibilities since the land between these two points and then northeasterly to Mainz was more open. North of this area the rough terrain of the Eifel region would seem to preclude any offensive possibilities and this would also mean violating the neutrality of Luxemburg and Belgium. In a meeting with Hitler on August 14, General Halder presented Hitler with all of the above possibilities and he agreed in general with all the hypotheses put forth. Hitler voiced his opinion that the Allies would probably not intervene anyway given that they had acceded to every demand made on them in the past few years. However, it was agreed to accelerate the mobilization of the reserve divisions to help shore up the western defense forces. The only question left was the Soviet Union's position in relation to Poland. During the summer, the Allies and the Germans had been seperately negotiating with the Soviets to try and sign a new military alliance with them. The Allies were trying to entice the Soviets to make an agreement to support their efforts to guarantee Poland's security against any German aggression by offering them substantial offers of economic aid. The Germans themselves were also offering economic aid with the addition of splitting Polish territory between Germany and the Soviet Union. All Allied efforts to reach an agreement were doomed to fail because one of the conditions the Soviets placed was to be able to move their ground forces into Poland which the Poles themselves would never agree to. By late August the Germans and Russians signed a non-aggression pact which included trade agreements, and under secret protocol, the partitioning of Poland between both nations. With this signing Hitler told his generals that the Soviet Union would not be a problem in the coming invasion but he gave no details why. Halder and the OKH staff did not learn of the details until after the Russians invaded Poland on 17 September. The invasion was still to be launched on 26 August as planned.

However, two events on 25 August caused Hitler to postpone the attack set for the next day. First, Mussolini had proposed one last attempt for a peace conference to all parties concerned to avert a conflict as he had done in the previous year at Munich. Mussolini's reason for wanting to prevent war at this stage was because he knew Italy was not ready for an armed conflict in the immediate future. On Hitler's part, he was counting on Italy's military support if Britain and France did try to intervene. The second event was news that Britain and Poland had signed a military alliance. This alliance had been held up during the summer over the negotiations with Soviet Russia. When it was announced, it was an incredible shock to Hitler, who had thought Chamberlain incapable of such an act. Indeed, Chamberlain had decided to sign the treaty over a period of just 24 hours, despite the incredible difficulties of honoring the agreement. Direct aid to Poland, once at war with Germany was impossible because of German domination of the Baltic and Russia's apparent unwillingness to become involved in such a program. By this treaty, Britain had essentially committed itself to a war where it had no interest and was powerless to intervene directly.

Once this had failed there was no reason for further postponement. With this alliance Britain was hoping to dissuade Hitler from making any aggressive moves toward Poland. This new pact between Britain and Poland gave Hitler pause to think that he may have underestimated the Allies resolve to fight. But he regained his nerve a couple of days later and issued a new invasion date set for 1 September.

By the evening of 31 August, all units were in place and ready to go. OKH had moved to its forward command post in Zossen south of Berlin. The Germans had concentrated a total force of 1,516,000 men. Army Group North had in the 3rd Army 320,000 men, the 4th Army 230,000 men and 80,000 men in reserve. Army Group South had in the 8th Army 180,000 men, in the 10th Army 300,000 men, in the 14th Army 210,000 men and in reserve 196,000 men. Military operations were to commence at 4:45 AM on 1 September.

German Infantry Divisions

Table No. 1

Infantry Division
Numbered Components

First Wave Divisions

Division Number	Infantry Regiment Numbers	Artillery Regiment & Battalion Numbers	Recon Battalion Number	Antitank Battalion Number	Engineer Battalion Number	Ersatz Battalion Number	Signal Battalion Number	Divisional Services Number
1	1,22,43	1/ I-IV	1	1	1	1	1	1
3	8,29,50	3/ I-III,I/39	3	3	3	3	3	3
4	10,52,103	4/ I-IV	4	4	4	4	4	4
7	19,61,62	7/ I-IV	7	7	7	7	7	7
8	28,38,84	8/ I-III,I/44	8	8	8	8	8	8
10	20,41,85	10/ I-III,I/46	10	10	10	10	10	10
11	2,23,44	11/ I-III,I/47	11	11	11	11	11	11
12	27,48,89	12/ I-III,I/48	12	12	12	12	12	12
14	11,53,101	74/ I-III,I/50	14	14	14	14	14	14
17	21,55,95	17/ I-III,I/53	17	17	17	17	17	17
18	30,51,54	18/ I-III,I/54	18	18	18	18	18	18
19	59,73,74	19/ I-III,I/55	19	19	19	19	19	19
21	3,24,45	21/ I-III,I/57	21	21	21	21	21	21
23	9,67,68	29/ I-III,I/59	23	23	23	23	23	23
24	31,32,102	24/ I-III,I/60	24	24	24	24	24	24
27	40,63,91	27/ I-III,I/63	27	27	27	27	27	27
28	7,49,83	28/ I-III,I/64	28	28	28	28	28	28
30	6,26,46	30/ I-III,II/60	30	30	30	30	30	30
31	12,17,82	31/ I-III,I/67	31	31	31	31	31	31
32	4,94,96	32/ I-III,I/68	32	32	32	32	32	32
44	131,132,134	96/ I-III,I/97	44	44	80	44	64	44
45	130,133,135	98/ I-II,I/99	45	45	81	45	65	45
46	42,72,97	115/ I-III/114,I/115	46	52	88	46	46	46

Second Wave Divisions

Division Number	Infantry Regiment Numbers	Artillery Regiment & Battalion Numbers	Recon Battalion Number	Antitank Battalion Number	Engineer Battalion Number	Ersatz Battalion Number	Signal Battalion Number	Divisional Services Number
56	171,192,234	156/ I-IV	156	156	156	-	156	156
57	179,199,217	157/ I-IV	157	157	157	-	157	157
61	151,162,176	161/ I-IV	161	161	161	-	161	161
62	164,183,190	162/ I-IV	162	162	162	-	162	162
68	169,188,196	168/ I-IV	168	168	168	-	168	168
73	170,186,213	173/ I-IV	173	173	173	-	173	173

Third Wave Divisions

Division Number	Infantry Regiment Numbers	Artillery Regiment & Battalion Numbers	Recon Battalion Number	Antitank Battalion Number	Engineer Battalion Number	Ersatz Battalion Number	Signal Battalion Number	Divisional Services Number
206	301,312,413	206/ I-IV	206	206	206	-	206	206
207	322,368,374	207/ I-IV	207	207	207	-	207	207
208	307,337,338	208/ I-IV	208	208	208	-	208	208
213	318,354,406	213/ I-IV	213	213	213	-	213	213
217	311,346,389	217/ I-IV	217	217	217	-	217	217
218	323,386,397	218/ I-IV	218	218	218	-	218	218
221	350,360,375	221/ I-IV	221	221	221	-	221	221
228	325,356,400	228/ I-IV	228	228	228	-	228	228
239	327,372,444	239/ I-IV	239	239	239	-	239	239

Fourth Wave Divisions

Division Number	Infantry Regiment Numbers	Artillery Regiment & Battalion Numbers	Recon Battalion Number	Antitank Battalion Number	Engineer Battalion Number	Ersatz Battalion Number	Signal Battalion Number	Divisional Services Number
257	457,466,477	257/ I-IV	257	257	257	-	257	257
258	458,478,479	258/ I-IV	258	258	258	-	258	258

Armored Fighting Vehicle Breakdowns

Table No. 2

Units	Pz I	Pz II	Pz III	Pz IV	Pz 35(t)/Pz 38(t)	Panzer Befehl X	Sdkfz 13	Sdkfz 221	Sdkfz 222, 223	Sdkfz 231, 232, 263	Sdkfz Befehl X	OA vz30	Tvz 35	Schupo-Sonderwagen 21	ADGZ
1st & 2nd Weapon Divisions	•	•	•	•	•	•	3	•	•	•	•	•	•	•	•
1st Panzer Div.	93	122	26	56	•	12	•	24	8/12	6/6/12	20	•	•	•	•
2nd Panzer Div.	124	155	6	17	•	20	•	24	8/12	6/6/12	20	•	•	•	•
3rd Panzer Div.	122	176	43	32	•	8	•	24	8/12	6/6/12	20	•	•	•	•
4th Panzer Div.	183	130	12	12	•	16	•	24	8/12	6/6/12	20	•	•	•	•
5th Panzer Div.	152	144	3	14	•	22	•	24	8/12	6/6/6	20	•	•	•	•
10th Panzer Div.	57	74	3	7	•	9	•	24	8/8	6/6/6	12	•	•	•	•
Kempf Panzer Div.	61	81	3	9	•	8	•	8	8/-	-/-/1	•	•	•	•	•
1st Light Div.	•	•	•	•	•	10	•	20	8/-	6/6/6	4	•	•	•	•
2nd Light Div.	41	65	•	41	•	2	•	24	8/12	12/12/6	4	•	•	•	•
3rd Light Div.	•	42	•	112	55	2	•	40	16/16	16/16/6	20	•	•	•	•
4th Light Div.	34	23	•	•	•	5	•	40	16/16	16/16/6	20	•	•	•	•
2nd Motorized Div.	•	•	•	•	•	•	•	10	4/4	3/3/2	4	•	•	•	•
13th Motorized Div.	•	•	•	•	•	•	•	10	4/4	3/3/2	4	•	•	•	•
20th Motorized Div.	•	•	•	•	•	•	•	10	4/4	3/3/2	4	•	•	•	•
29th Motorized Div.	•	•	•	•	•	•	•	10	4/4	3/3/2	4	•	•	•	•
SS Motorized Reg.	•	•	•	•	•	•	•	4	•	•	•	•	•	•	•
1st Cavalry Brig.	•	•	•	•	•	•	•	4	4/-	-/-/-	2	•	•	•	•
Lehr Recon Bn.	•	•	•	•	•	•	•	4	2/-	4/-	•	•	•	•	•
1st Aufkl. Bn.	•	•	•	•	•	•	•	24	4/-	6/6/12	1	•	•	•	•
I/10th Panzer Bn	28	34	3	4	•	5	•	•	•	•	20	•	•	•	•
I/23 Panzer Bn	39	29	•	3	•	•	•	•	•	•	•	•	•	•	•
(SR) 2nd Division	•	•	•	•	•	•	•	•	•	•	•	7	3	•	•
Eberhardt Brigade	•	•	•	•	•	•	•	•	•	•	•	•	•	2	2

X These are command or signal vehicles but are not armed.

Note: Model versions available for each of: Panzer I- a, b, ; Panzer II- a,b,c & d; Panzer III- a,b,c,d,e,f; Panzer IV- a,b,c & d.

Chapter 2

Organization of Combat Units

For the invasion of Poland, the German Army had available for offensive purposes forty infantry divisions, three mountain divisions, seven armored divisions, four motorized infantry divisions, four light divisions, one cavalry brigade, two SS motorized infantry regiments and one hundred and three non-divisional combat battalions. Also available for defense and rear area security were the border guard regiments, one police brigade and numerous landwehr and landesschützen battalions.

Infantry Divisions

The infantry (*infanterie*) divisions were divided by classes of what were called waves. The first wave of infantry divisions were existing active peacetime divisions. These divisions were part of the permanent army that grew from the one that was allowed by the Versailles Treaty then greatly expanded after the Nazis came to power. The army grew from seven divisions after World War One to thirty-five divisions by August 1939. Twenty-three of these divisions were used in Poland. The first wave infantry divisions (see chart numbers 1 and 1A) were the best trained and had the latest weapons and equipment. The personnel were, for the most part, made up of long term professionals though some reservists had to be used to bring some of the divisions up to full strength. Each division was organized with three infantry regiments (each with three infantry battalions), one artillery regiment (with four artillery battalions), one reconnaissance battalion, one motorized anti-tank battalion, one engineer battalion, one ersatz infantry battalion, one signals battalion, and divisional service units which consisted of one supply battalion, two food service companies, one medical company, one veterinary unit, one police unit and one postal unit.

The second wave infantry divisions (see chart numbers 1 and 1A) personnel consisted of first class reservist. Their weapons and equipment were generally the same as first wave units except they had no mortars or anti-aircraft guns. Organizationally they were the same as the first wave divisions except they lacked the ersatz infantry battalion.

The third wave infantry divisions (see chart number 1) personnel were made up of landwehr, class two reservists and some class one reservists. The weapons and equipment were all of World War One and 1920's vintage. These units also lacked the mortars, anti-aircraft guns and armored cars. Organizationally the third wave divisions were the same as the second wave divisions.

German
Infantry Divisions
Organization:

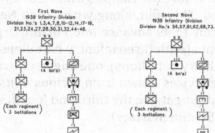

First Wave
1939 Infantry Division
Division No.'s 1,3,4,7,8,10-12,14,17-19,
21,23,24,27,28,30,31,32,44-46.

(4 bn's)

(Each regiment
3 battalions)

DS

Note: For Infantry Division numbered
components see Table No. 1

Second Wave
1939 Infantry Division
Division No.'s 56,57,61,62,68,73.

(4 bn's)

(Each regiment
3 battalions)

DS

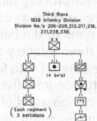

Third Wave
1939 Infantry Division
Division No.'s 206-208,213,217,218,
221,228,239.

(4 bn's)

(Each regiment
3 battalions)

DS

See Chart #1A for the
Men and Equipment of the
1st, 2nd, & 3rd Wave Infantry Divisions

Men and Equipment of the
1st, 2nd, & 3rd Wave Infantry Divisions

Men and Equipment:

	Division Number	Men	Rifles	Machine Pistols	Lt MG's	Hvy MG's	50 mm Mortars	81 mm Mortars	37 mm AT Guns	20 mm AA Guns	75 mm Art.	105 mm Art.	150 mm Art.	Horses	Horsedrawn Vehicles	Motor Vehicles	Mcy.'s	AFV's +
1st Wave Infantry Division	3,7,8,12,14, 17-19,23,24, 28,30-32.	17,734	12,609	3	378	138	93	54	75	12	26g	36h	12h	4,842	919	1,009	527	3
"	1	19,535	14,235	3	378	138	93	54	75	16	26g	36h	12h	6,884	1,668	808	498	3
"	4	17,993	12,883	3	378	138	93	54	75	16	26g	36h	12h	4,842	919	1,059	527	3
"	10 & 27	17,426	12,621	3	378	138	93	54	75	12	26g	36h	12h	4,842	919	1,009	527	3
"	44	17,409	12,421	-	370	138	93	54	75	-	26g	24h	12h	4,822	1,095	939	507	3
"	45	16,819	11,919	-	364	138	93	54	75	-	26g	24h	12h	4,822	1,095	807	481	3
"	46	17,169	12,130	3	372	138	93	54	75	12	26g	36h	12h	4,773	910	908	508	3
"	11 & 21	17,875	12,770	3	378	138	93	54	75	12	26g	36h	12h	5,226	1,134	789	593	3
2nd Wave Infantry Division	56,57,62, 68,71,73.	15,273	10,828	3	345	114	3	-	75	-	26g	36h	12h	4,854	823	902	497	3
"	61	16,940	12,311	3	345	114	-	-	75	12	26g	36h	12h	6,934	1,557	693	467	3
3rd Wave Infantry Division	207 & 221	17,911	12,979	-	559	150	-	-	75	-	26g	36h	12h	6,053	1,529	578	415	-
"	208,213, 218,239.	17,901	12,668	-	559	150	-	-	75	-	26g	36h	12h	6,033	1,529	578	415	-
"	206,217, 228.	18,645	13,359	-	559	150	-	-	75	-	26g	36h	12h	6,927	1,746	509	407	-

+See Table No. 2 for
AFV Breakdowns

The fourth wave infantry divisions (see chart number 2) were in all aspects identical to the third wave divisions for personnel, equipment and organization.

The 50th Infantry Division (see chart number 2) is unique in that it was an ad hoc unit organized just before the campaign started. It was not part of the wave system as organized. This unit, along with Group Netze, was to guard the flank of the Fourth Army in its advance into Poland. Organizationally it had three infantry regiments (with three infantry battalions each), one artillery regiment (with four artillery battalions), one engineer battalion, one signals battalion and divisional services drawn from various units. Its equipment was composed of older equipment like the third and fourth wave infantry divisions (except it did have 50 mm mortars).

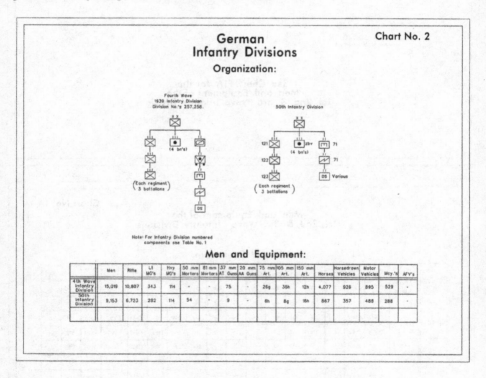

German
Infantry Divisions
Organization:

Chart No. 2

Men and Equipment:

	Men	Rifle	Lt MG's	Hvy MG's	50 mm Mortars	81 mm Mortars	37 mm AT Guns	20 mm AA Guns	75 mm Art.	105 mm Art.	150 mm Art.	Horses	Horsedrawn Vehicles	Motor Vehicles	Mcy.'s	AFV's
4th Wave Infantry Division	15,019	10,807	343	114	-	-	75	-	26g	36h	12h	4,077	926	895	529	-
50th Infantry Division	9,153	6,723	282	114	54	-	9	-	6h	8g	16h	867	357	488	288	-

Mountain Divisions

The mountain (*gebirg*) divisions (see chart number 3) were all composed of professional soldiers with modern equipment and because of their additional training for fighting in mountainous and rough terrain they were considered to be of a higher quality than the first wave infantry divisions. The 1st Mountain Division personnel consisted of German citizens (mostly Bavarian) while the 2nd and 3rd Mountain Divisions were formed from the former Austrian Army mountain troops after the Austrian Anschluss of March 1938.

This difference is reflected in the organization of these units. The 1st Mountain Division had three mountain infantry regiments (with three mountain infantry battalions for each regiment), one mountain artillery regiment (with four mountain artillery battalions), one reconnaissance battalion, one ersatz mountain infantry battalion, one motorized anti-tank battalion, one engineer battalion, one signals battalion and the same divisional services of a first wave infantry division. The 2nd and 3rd Mountain Divisions were organized the same except there were only two mountain infantry regiments (with three mountain infantry battalions each) and the mountain artillery regiment only had three mountain artillery battalions.

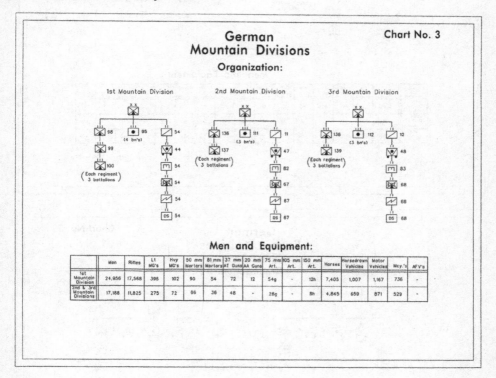

German Mountain Divisions

Chart No. 3

Organization:

Men and Equipment:

	Men	Rifles	Lt MG's	Hvy MG's	50 mm Mortars	81 mm Mortars	37 mm AT Guns	20 mm AA Guns	75 mm Art.	105 mm Art.	150 mm Art.	Horses	Horsedrawn Vehicles	Motor Vehicles	Mcy.'s	AFV's
1st Mountain Division	24,956	17,568	396	102	90	54	72	12	54g	-	12h	7,405	1,007	1,167	736	-
2nd & 3rd Mountain Divisions	17,188	11,825	275	72	66	36	48	-	28g	-	8h	4,845	659	871	529	-

Motorized Divisions

What were to become the major offensive weapon for the German Army, the armored (*panzer*) divisions, were not all organized uniformly. Each of the first five pre-war panzer divisions (see chart numbers 4 and 5) consisted of one panzer brigade (with two panzer regiments), one motorized infantry regiment (with two battalions of motorized infantry), one motorized artillery regiment (with two battalions of motorized artillery), one armored reconnaissance battalion, one motorized anti-tank battalion, one motorized engineer battalion, one motorized signals battalion and the motorized divisional services (same as an infantry dvision). It should be noted that some panzer

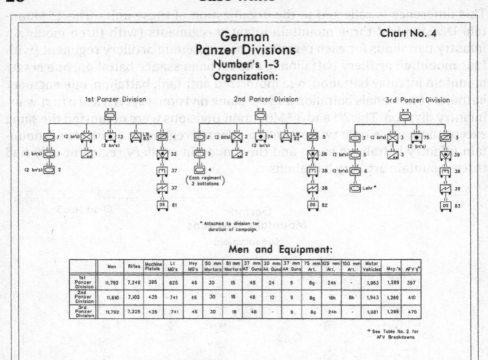

German
Panzer Divisions
Number's 1–3
Organization:
Chart No. 4

Men and Equipment:

	Men	Rifles	Machine Pistols	Lt MG's	Hvy MG's	50 mm Mortars	81 mm Mortars	37 mm AT Guns	20 mm AA Guns	37 mm AA Guns	75 mm Art.	105 mm Art.	150 mm Art.	Motor Vehicles	Mcy.'s	AFV's+
1st Panzer Division	11,792	7,249	395	825	46	30	18	48	24	9	8g	24h	-	1,963	1,289	397
2nd Panzer Division	11,610	7,102	435	741	46	30	18	48	12	9	8g	16h	8h	1,943	1,269	410
3rd Panzer Division	11,792	7,225	435	741	46	30	18	48	-	9	8g	24h	-	1,981	1,286	470

+ See Table No. 2 for AFV Breakdowns

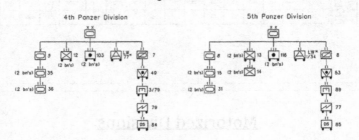

German
Panzer Divisions
Number's 4 & 5
Organization:
Chart No. 5

Men and Equipment:

	Men	Rifles	Machine Pistols	Lt MG's	Hvy MG's	50 mm Mortars	81 mm Mortars	37 mm AT Guns	20 mm AA Guns	37 mm AA Guns	88 mm AA Guns	75 mm Art.	105 mm Art.	150 mm Art.	Motor Vehicles	Mcy.'s	AFV's+
4th Panzer Division	10,286	6,161	433	740	28	21	12	30	24	18	-	10g	24h	-	1,786	915	429
5th Panzer Division	12,779	7,806	439	870	52	39	24	48	24	-	12	20g	24h	-	2,124	1,380	423

+ See Table No. 2 for AFV Breakdowns

divisions had an additional Luftwaffe light anti-aircraft battalion attached for the duration of the campaign and that the 5th Panzer Division had two motorized infantry regiments instead of one. A motorcycle battalion was attached to the motorized infantry regiments for the 1st, 2nd and 3rd Panzer Divisions. The other two panzer divisions, the 10th and Kempf (see chart number 6), were ad hoc formations using various units from other motorized divisions and other independent motorized formations. The 10th Panzer Division had one panzer regiment (with two panzer battalions), one motorized infantry regiment (with three motorized infantry battalions), one motorized artillery regiment (with two motorized artillery battalions), one armored reconnaissance battalion, one motorized anti-tank battalion, one motorized engineer company, one motorized signals battalion and motorized divisional services. Panzer Division Kempf had one panzer regiment (with two panzer battalions), one SS motorized infantry regiment (with three motorized infantry battalions), one SS motorized artillery regiment (with two motorized artillery battalions), one SS armored reconnaissance battalion, one motorized anti-tank battalion, one SS motorized signals battalion and some miscellaneous divisional service units. All the panzer divisions had professional, well-trained soldiers who received the best equipment available.

The light (leichte) divisions (see chart number 7) were all pre-war units formed to placate the strong cavalry interest that still existed in the German army in the 1930's. These were mechanized cavalry divisions that were to be used in the same role as horsed cavalry. Organizationally the 1st and 3rd Light Divisions had a similar structure, whereas the 2nd and 4th Light Divisions had a slightly different structure. The 1st Light Division had one panzer regiment (with two panzer battalions), plus one additional panzer battalion, one motorized infantry regiment (with three motorized infantry battalions), plus one motorcycle battalion, an attached Luftwaffe motorized anti-aircraft battalion, one motorized artillery regiment (with two motorized artillery battalions), one motorized anti-tank battalion, one armored reconnaissance battalion, one motorized engineer battalion, one motorized signals battalion and divisional services (with one supply battalion, one food service company, two medical companies, one police company and one field postal unit). The 3rd Light Division was organized the same as the 1st Light Division except it only had one panzer battalion. The 2nd and 4th Light Divisions were organized with one panzer battalion, two motorized infantry regiments (each with two motorized infantry battalions), one motorized artillery regiment (with two motorized artillery battalions), one armored reconnaissance regiment (with two armored reconnaissance battalions), one motorized anti-tank battalion, one motorized engineer battalion, one motorized signals battalion and the same motorized divisional services as the 1st and 3rd Light Divisions. The 4th Light Division also had one Luftwaffe motorized anti-aircraft battalion attached for the duration of the campaign. And, as with the panzer divisions, all the per-

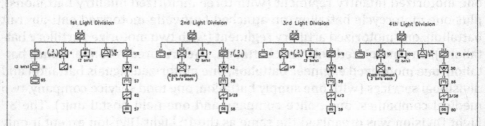

German Panzer Divisions — Chart No. 6
Number's 10 & Kempf
Organization:

10th Panzer Division / **Panzer Division Kempf**

Men and Equipment:

	Men	Rifles	Machine Pistols	Lt MG's	Hvy MG's	50 mm Mortars	81 mm Mortars	37 mm AT Guns	20 mm AA Guns	37 mm AA Guns	88 mm AA Guns	75 mm Art.	105 mm Art.	150 mm Art.	Motor Vehicles	Mcy.'s	AFV's[+]
10th Panzer Division	10,289	6,601	439	185	68	39	18	45	12	9	6	10g	16h	8h	1,707	1,121	216
Panzer Division Kempf	9,236	6,299	431	142	41	39	12	52	-	4	-	24g	36h	-	1,187	760	181

[+] See Table No. 2 for AFV Breakdowns

German Light Divisions — Chart No. 7
Organization:

1st Light Division / **2nd Light Division** / **3rd Light Division** / **4th Light Division**

* Attached to division for duration of campaign.

Men and Equipment:

	Men	Rifles	Machine Pistols	Lt MG's	Hvy MG's	50 mm Mortars	81 mm Mortars	37 mm AT Guns	20 mm AA Guns	37 mm AA Guns	75 mm Art.	105 mm Art.	150 mm Art.	Motor Vehicles	Mcy.'s	AFV's[+]
1st Light Division	9,935	6,799	160	465	60	39	24	51	24	9	10g	24h	-	1,819	974	314
2nd Light Division	11,512	7,856	219	575	62	45	30	51	12	-	20g	24h	-	2,048	1,130	207
3rd Light Division	10,772	7,300	223	533	62	42	24	54	12	-	12g	24h	-	1,963	1,098	168
4th Light Division	11,307	7,876	192	550	62	45	30	51	20	9	20g	24h	-	2,013	1,762	184

[+] See Table No. 2 for AFV Breakdowns

sonnel were well-trained professionals with the latest equipment.

The motorized infantry (motorisiert infanterie) divisions (see chart number 8) were all pre-war formations formed for the purpose of giving the panzer divisions additional infantry support when needed. These divisions were made up of professional troops and were well equipped. Each of the four motorized divisions were organized identically as follows: three motorized infantry regiments (with three motorized infantry battalions each), one motorized artillery regiment (with four motorized artillery battalions), one armored reconnaissance battalion, one motorized anti-tank battalion, one motorized engineer battalion, one motorized signals battalion and motorized divisional services (which consisted of the same units a panzer division had). One exception was the 29th Motorized Division, which had one motorized infantry regiment and one motorized artillery battalion detached to the 10th Panzer Division for the duration of the campaign. Each of the motorized divisions had one Luftwaffe motorized anti-aircraft battery attached for the duration of the campaign.

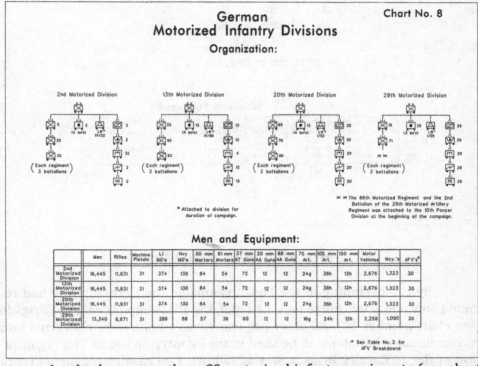

German Motorized Infantry Divisions

Chart No. 8

Organization:

2nd Motorized Division   13th Motorized Division   20th Motorized Division   29th Motorized Division

(Each regiment 3 battalions)

* Attached to division for duration of campaign.

⋈ ⋈ The 86th Motorized Regiment and the 2nd Battalion of the 29th Motorized Artillery Regiment was attached to the 10th Panzer Division at the beginning of the campaign.

Men and Equipment:

	Men	Rifles	Machine Pistols	LI MG's	Hvy MG's	50 mm Mortars	81 mm Mortars	37 mm AT Guns	20 mm AA Guns	88 mm AA Guns	75 mm Art.	105 mm Art.	150 mm Art.	Motor Vehicles	Mcy.'s	AFV's+
2nd Motorized Division	16,445	11,931	31	374	130	84	54	72	12	12	24g	36h	12h	2,676	1,323	30
13th Motorized Division	16,445	11,931	31	374	130	84	54	72	12	12	24g	36h	12h	2,676	1,323	30
20th Motorized Division	16,445	11,931	31	374	130	84	54	72	12	12	24g	36h	12h	2,676	1,323	30
29th Motorized Division	13,340	9,671	31	286	88	57	36	60	12	12	16g	24h	12h	2,258	1,090	30

+ See Table No. 2 for AFV Breakdowns

Lastly, there were three SS motorized infantry regiments (see chart number 9) involved in the campaign. Only two acted independently, the Leibstandarte Adolf Hitler and the Germania. The other, the Deutschland, was attached to Panzer Division Kempf to give the division an infantry component. The Deutschland and the Germania were each organized as follows: three motorized infantry battalions, one motorized artillery company, one armored reconnaissance company, one motorized anti-tank company and one motorcycle company. The Leibstandarte Adolf Hitler regiment was organized the same as the Germania and Deutschland except that it had an additional motorized engineer platoon attached. As to the personnel and equipment the SS regiments received first-rate equipment and top recruits. Only their training was considered inferior to army standards and were according to reports made by the army after the campaign were the reasons for their poor performance (see Appendix 2 for the full report).

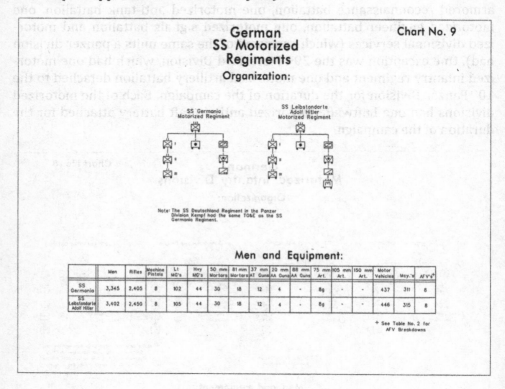

German
SS Motorized Regiments

Chart No. 9

Organization:

SS Germania
Motorized Regiment

SS Leibstandarte
Adolf Hitler
Motorized Regiment

Note: The SS Deutschland Regiment in the Panzer
Division Kempf had the same TO&E as the SS
Germania Regiment.

Men and Equipment:

	Men	Rifles	Machine Pistols	Lt MG's	Hvy MG's	50 mm Mortars	81 mm Mortars	37 mm AT Guns	20 mm AA Guns	88 mm AA Guns	75 mm Art.	105 mm Art.	150 mm Art.	Motor Vehicles	Mcy.'s	AFV's+
SS Germania	3,345	2,405	8	102	44	30	18	12	4	-	8g	-	-	437	311	8
SS Leibstandarte Adolf Hitler	3,402	2,450	8	105	44	30	18	12	4	-	8g	-	-	446	315	8

+ See Table No. 2 for
AFV Breakdowns

Miscellaneous Brigades

By the beginning of the Polish campaign the German army had retained only one active horse mounted unit, the 1st Cavalry (*kavallerie*) Brigade (see chart number 10). All other pre-war cavalry units were converted into reconnaissance battalions to be used in the infantry divisions. The organization of the 1st Cavalry Brigade was as follows: two cavalry regiments (with four cavalry troops each), one horse artillery battalion (with three horse artillery batteries), one motorized anti-tank company, one motorized machinegun company, one mounted engineer company, one signals company, one supply company, and an administrative service unit (with one motorized medical company, one ambulance platoon and one veterinary company). The cavalry troops were well trained and received first-rate equipment.

The Netze Brigade (see chart number 10) was formed from two border guard regiments and other army units for the purpose of providing the III Army Corps with additional infantry support. The brigade consisted of two border guard regiments (with three border guard battalions and one engineer battalion), one motorized artillery battalion, one motorized machinegun battalion and one motorized engineer battalion.

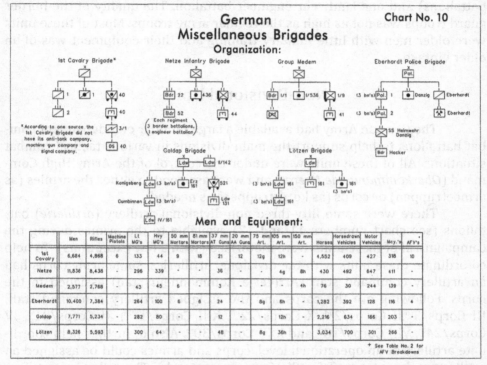

The Eberhardt Police Brigade (see chart number 10) consisted of units from the Danzig police force and one local SS infantry unit. The mission of the brigade was to help subdue local Polish forces in and around the city of Danzig. It was organized as follows: two police regiments (with three police battalions each), one SS infantry battalion, one battalion of border guard troops, one ad hoc artillery battalion, one reconnaissance battalion and one ad hoc engineer battalion. All of these units were of variable quality and were mostly armed with older equipment.

Group Medem (see chart number 10) was a special unit formed for the specific mission of proceeding from its base at Marienburg, East Prussia at the beginning of the campaign to Tczew (Dirschau in German) in Poland and seize the bridge over the Vistula to facilitate the eastward advance of the forces of the 4th Army. The brigade was organized with one battalion of border guard troops, one ersatz infantry battalion, one battery of artillery, one motorized machinegun company and one motorized engineer battalion.

The Goldap and Lötzen Brigades (see chart number 10) were formed from existing landwehr regiments in eastern East Prussia for the purpose of adding additional flank protection for the 3rd Army for its thrust into Poland. The Goldap Brigade was organized with two landwehr regiments (three battalions each), one ersatz landwehr artillery battalion and one landwehr engineer battalion. The Lötzen Brigade consisted of two landwehr regiments (three battalions each), one landwehr artillery regiment (with three artillery battalions) and one landwehr engineer battalion. The quality of the border guard troops was not as high as the regular army troops. Most of these units were older men with little military training and their equipment was of an older vintage.

Non-Divisional Units

The German Army had available a large number of independent combat battalions to help support the main divisions in various tactical combat situations. All of these units were under the control of the Army High Command (*Oberkommando de Heeres*) and were assigned to either the armies (as armeetruppen) or corps (as korpstruppen) as needed.

There were some fifty-three non-divisional artillery (*artillerie*) battalions (see chart numbers 11 and 12) available to the armies during the campaign. All of these units were motorized (with a few exceptions). To help co-ordinate these units with the divisional artilleries, some army corps had an artillery command staff (Artillerie Kommandeur stab) assigned to the corps. Following are the corps and the assigned artillery command staff; III Corps/3rd, II Corps/2nd, X Corps/22nd, XIII Corps/17th, XI Corps/31st, IV Corps/24th, VIII Corps/18th and XXII Corps/30th. Also to further help coordinate artillery at an operational level, corps and armies could be assigned an artillery regimental staff (artillerie regiments stab). The following artillery regimental staffs were available: the 49th, 50th, 80th, 109th, 110th, 501st, 511th, 603rd, 604th, 609th, 610th, 614th, 617th, 623rd and 627th. Some of these artillery staffs were created to help coordinate the large amount of artillery used at the siege of Warsaw, particularly the 50th and 80th artillery regimental staffs. Organizationally the mixed heavy motorized artillery battalions had each three artillery batteries. The super heavy and heavy motorized artillery battalions also had each three artillery batteries. For manpower and equipment, the artillery battalions had well trained personnel and their artillery was of high quality. Included with the artillery units were two smoke projector (*nebelwerfer*) battalions (see chart number 12). At this time, they were equipped with 105 mm mortar units with the prime purpose of laying down smoke, but could fire a high explosive round. It was not until 1941 that the nebelwerfer units were converted to rocket firing units. They were organized with three mortar batteries each. Quality wise they were the same as the artillery units.

German
Non–Divisional Units:
Artillery
(Part One)
Organization:

Mixed Heavy Motorized Artillery Battalions	Heavy Artillery Battalion	Heavy Artillery Battalion	Heavy Artillery Battalion	Heavy Artillery Battalion	Super Heavy Artillery Battalion
•II/37,II/38,II/39,II/40,II/43,II/44, II/46,II/47,II/48,II/49,II/50,II/53, II/54,II/55,II/56,II/57,II/58, II/59,II/60,II/63,II/64,II/66,II/67, II/68,II/93,I/109,II/109,III/109, II/115,101,102,103,422,436,445,506, 601,602,605,611,617,628,629, 634 & 639.	•526	•607	•631	•624,641	•I/84

Men and Equipment:

	Men	Rifles	Light MG,s	105 mm Mortar	105 mm Gun	150 mm Gun	150 mm How.	210 mm Gun	210 mm How.	240 mm Gun	305 mm How..	Motor Vehicles	Mcy.'s	Horses
II/37,etc Artillery Battalions	742	617	6	-	4	-	8	-	-	-	-	166	62	-
526th Artillery Battalion	716	557	6	-	-	3	8	-	-	-	-	134	50	-
607th Artillery Battalion	738	621	6	-	-	3	-	-	6	-	-	155	58	-
631st Artillery Battalion	714	557	6	-	4	-	-	-	6	-	-	102	44	-
624th,641st Artillery Battalions	594	475	6	-	4	-	-	-	-	-	4	120	33	-
I/84th Artillery Battalion	679	559	6	-	-	-	-	-	-	6	-	135	47	-

German
Non–Divisional Units:
Artillery
(Part Two)
Organization:

Nebelwerfer Battalion	Heavy Artillery Battalion	Heavy Artillery Battery	Heavy Artillery Battalion	Heavy Artillery Battalion
•1,2	•I/46,I/60	•Beck	•511	•536

Men and Equipment:

	Men	Rifles	Light MG,s	105 mm Mortar	105 mm Gun	150 mm Gun	150 mm How.	210 mm Gun	210 mm How.	240 mm Gun	305 mm How.	Motor Vehicles	Mcy.'s	Horses
1st & 2nd Nebelwerfer Battalions	764	681	6	24	-	-	-	-	-	-	-	204	59	-
I/46th,etc Artillery Battalion	718	634	6	-	-	12	-	-	-	-	-	39	14	552
Beck Artillery Battery	98	80	-	-	-	-	-	-	-	2	-	30	12	-
511th Artillery Battalion	389	312	6	-	-	8	-	-	-	-	-	73	27	-
536th Artillery Battalion	521	432	4	-	-	-	8	-	-	-	-	97	36	-

The motorized anti-tank (panzerabwehr) battalions (see chart number 13) were formed to give additional anti-tank support where a strong enemy armored presence would threaten friendly non-armored units. Each battalion consisted of three motorized anti-tank companies. It should be noted that because of Poland's weak armored strength, the independent anti-tank battalions were used to supplement combat units that needed additional firepower. The anti-tank units were well trained and had first-rate equipment.

The motorized machinegun (machinengewehr) battalions (see chart number 13) were to be used to supplement the firepower of the infantry divisions where needed at the frontline. Though these unit's origins were of a defensive nature stemming from the First World War, they were used more aggressively by the Germans. They were organized with three motorized machinegun companies and one motorized anti-tank company. These units were well equipped and their personnel were well trained.

The Luftwaffe motorized anti-aircraft (flak) battalions (see chart number 13) were units that accompanied the ground units to give cover against enemy aircraft. These units were technically under the control of the Luftwaffe, usually through the Luftwaffe anti-aircraft regimental staffs. Since the Polish Air Force did not present as much of a threat during the campaign, many of the anti-aircraft battalions were used by the army to supplement the firepower of their ground units. Each motorized antiaircraft battalion consisted of two mixed motorized anti-aircraft batteries, one light motorized anti-aircraft battery, one heavy searchlight unit and one motorized balloon barrage unit. The Luftwaffe (mostly because of Goerings influence) had the pick of trained personnel and equipment.

The motorized combat engineer (pionier) battalions (see chart number 13) were used to aid the divisions in overcoming more potent engineering obstacles (such as fortified positions, heavily defended river crossings, etc) that the divisional engineers may need in assistance. The motorized engineer battalion consisted of three motorized engineer companies and one motorized bridging column. Of special note was that there was one independent SS motorized engineer battalion. This unit does not appear to have been equipped any differently (or better) than its army counterparts. The engineers appear to have been well trained and supplied with the latest equipment.

There were two independent armored reconnaissance (aufklärung) battalions (see chart number 13) used during the campaign. The 1st Armored Reconnaissance Battalion consisted of two armored car platoons, one motorized heavy weapons company, one motorcycle company and one motorized supply column. The Lehr Armored Reconnaissance Battalion consisted of one armored reconnaissance company, one motorized infantry company, two motorcycle companies, one motorized heavy weapons company and one motorized anti-tank company. Both units were well equipped and had first-rate personnel.

German Non–Divisional Units: Anti–Tank, Machine Gun, Anti–Aircraft, Engineer, Recon and Panzer. Chart No. 13

Organization:

Anti–Tank Battalions
☒
*521,560,561, 563,605.

Machinegun Battalions
☒
*6,7,8,9 & 15

Anti–Aircraft Battalions(Luftwaffe)
△
*I/3,I/7,I/11,II/11,III/11, II/22,I/23,II/23,I/33,I/36,II/38 I/43,I/52,I/61,I/411,II/411,I/711 I/Lehr & II/Lehr.

Light Anti–Aircraft Battalions(Luftwaffe)
△
*76,77,83, 92 & 94.

Engineer Battalions
⊡
*42,43,44,47,48,50,51,60, 62,70,85 & SS Dresden. 827,830.

Reconaissance Battalions
◹
*1 Auf.,Lehr

Panzer Battalions
◹
*I/10 & I/23

Men and Equipment:

	Men	Rifles	Machine Pistols	Light MG.s	Heavy MG's	50 mm Mortars	81 mm Mortars	37 mm AT Guns	20 mm AA Guns	37 mm AA Guns	88 mm AA Guns	75 mm Art.	Motor Vehicles	Mcy.'s	AFV's+
Anti-Tank Battalions	555	359	-	18	-	-	-	36	-	-	-	-	135	63	-
Machinegun Battalions	995	848	-	7	51	-	-	12	-	-	-	-	181	187	-
Anti-Aircraft Battalions	1068	834	90	-	-	-	-	-	24	-	12	-	280	32	-
Light Anti-Aircraft Battalions	800	571	61	-	-	-	-	-	24	9	-	-	220	25	-
Engineer Battalions	831	689	-	27	-	-	-	-	-	-	-	-	156	58	-
Lehr Recon Battalion	877	496	72	54	4	9	6	15	-	-	-	2g	68	67	7
1st Auf. Recon Battalion	1,790	1,012	146	18	2	3	-	3	20	-	-	2g	132	125	68
I/10th Panzer Battalion	230	74	30	-	8	-	-	-	-	-	-	-	18	24	74
I/23rd Panzer Battalion	427	138	56	-	8	-	-	-	-	-	-	-	18	24	76

+See Table No. 2 for AFV Breakdowns

The German Army had three independent panzer battalions (see chart number 13) to serve during the campaign. The 1st Battalion of the 25th Panzer Regiment was attached to the 2nd Light Division during the campaign, while the 1st Battalion of the 10th Panzer Regiment and the 1st Battalion of the 23rd Panzer Regiment remained under OKH control. Each battalion consisted of three light tank companies, one light tank platoon and one armored signals platoon. All three battalions, like the larger panzer divisions were staffed with well trained soldiers and had the best equipment available.

Although not considered combat troops, the construction troop (bau-truppen) battalions (see chart number 14) were often used in conjunction with the combat engineers in their tasks. Their main function was to repair bridges and roads, to repair or construct fortified positions behind the front lines. The rank and file were made up of males aged 18 and some older men from the Reich Labor Services. Each battalion was composed of six labor companies. All battalions were controlled either by a regimental or brigade staff. Either of these command staffs could control from one to a dozen construction battalions at a time.

The border guard (*grenzwacht*) regiments (see chart number 14) were units that were responsible during peacetime for maintaining the security of the Reich's international borders. Since these units were already in a semi-militarized state they could be used as defensive forces in times of war and help secure the rear areas after the main army units had moved through and in some cases used to help give manpower support to the armies (Group Netze under the 4th Army being a good example). Normally all border guard regiments were under control of a regional border guard command (equivalent to a corps sized headquarters). Organizationally each regiment would control three border guard battalions, one company of engineers (specifically called 'sperrier pionier' or in English 'blockade engineers'), one company of anti-tank guns and one motorized transport echelon. The quality of these units were low value and their equipment was all second hand issue.

    The regional defense (*landesschützen*) battalions (see chart number 14) were forces whose main purpose, as the name implies, a regional defense in times of war. As the main German armies moved into Poland many of these units were used to help secure the lines of communications and perform rear area security (see Posen Military District as an example). These units were controlled by a regimental headquarters (which would control three to five battalions) under the command of a divisional headquarters. Organizationally each battalion had four companies of landesschützen infantry. These units were of a slightly higher quality than the border guard regiments and their equipment also consisted of second hand material.

    The army reserve (*landwehr*) battalions (see chart number 14) functioned as army reserve units for the army. Made up of retired military reservists aged 35 to 45, this is where the third and fourth wave infantry divisions

---

German   Chart No. 14

Non–Divisional Units:
Construction Engineer, Border Guard,
Landesschutzen, Landwehr
and Garrison Security.

Organization:

Construction Engineer Battalions	Border guard Regiments	Landesschutzen Regiments	Landwehr Regiment	Garrison Security Regiments
⊠	Bdr	Lds	Ldw	Sec
*7-27, 29-37, 94-133,301-335, 602 and 504.	*1,21,31,41,51,66,78, 98,96,109,116.	*2/X,3/V,3/X,3/XI,2/III,Dohna, 3/III,2/XVIII,3/XVII,4/XI	• 183	• 128,138,148.

Men and Equipment:

	Men	Rifles	Light MG,s	Heavy MG's	50 mm Mortars	37 mm AT Guns	75 mm Art.	Horses	Horse Drawn Vehicles	Motor Vehicles	Mcy.'s
Construction Engineer Battalions	1,285	383	•	•	•	•	•	40	18	13	7
Border Regiments	1,752	1,185	144	•	•	8	•	144	108	28	83
Landes-schutzen Battalions	1,416	992	12	•	•	•	•	72	24	•	4
Landwehr Regiment	3,537	2,489	157	48	•	12	8	775	256	39	66
Garrison Security Regiments	1,600	1,120	-	324	•	•	•	174	81	•	•

filled out the additional manpower that was needed to bring them to full strength at the beginning of the campaign. Only one landwehr regiment participated as a unit during the campaign, the 183rd Landwehr Regiment (see chart number 14). This unit consisted of two landwehr infantry battalions, one motorized anti-tank company, one engineer platoon, one motorized signals company and one supply column. These units were only of a slightly lower quality than their army counterparts and their weaponry was comparable to those of the army.

Lastly the garrison security (*sicherheitbesatzungen*) regiments (see chart number 14) were local area defense units tied to a specific city or town (in this case the 128th to Breslau, the 138th to Glogau and the 148th to Freystadt). These units were heavily armed with machineguns and had very limited mobility. Still, they were used as rear area security units to aid the border guard and regional defense regiments in their duties. The 138th garrison security regiment had three battalions whereas the 128th and the 148th only had two battalions each. The quality of these units were comparable to that of the regional defense units.

The German army also had at its disposal three infantry divisions from the newly formed state of Slovakia. The new Slovak nations army was deemed useful to cover the right flank of Army Group South for its planned advance into Poland. All three divisions (see chart number 15) were pieced together from recently reformed units of the Czechoslovakian army and therefore did not have a set divisional organization. The 1st Infantry Division had two infantry regiments (with three infantry battalions each), two artillery regiments (one with four artillery battalions and the other with two artillery battalions), one cavalry reconnaissance battalion, one anti-aircraft regiment (with two anti-aircraft battalions), one engineer battalion, one signals battalion and one divisional services unit. The 2nd Infantry Division was composed of one infantry regiment (with three infantry battalions), three independent infantry battalions, one bicycle battalion, one ersatz infantry battalion, two artillery regiments (with four artillery battalions each), one cavalry reconnaissance battalion, one engineer battalion, one signals battalion and one divisional services unit. The 3rd Infantry Division had two infantry regiments (with three infantry battalions each), two artillery regiments (one regiment with three artillery battalions and the other with four artillery battalions), one cavalry reconnaissance battalion, one company of engineers, one signals battalion and one divisional services unit. Not shown on the tables of organization charts is an ad hoc Slovak formation created in the early part of the campaign to give the Slovaks a more mobile unit available to strike deeper into Poland. This unit, named Mobile Group Kalineciak, was formed from taking mobile units from the existing infantry divisions and independent armored formations. It consisted of one cavalry squadron, one bicycle company, two armored companies, one armored car company and one anti-tank company. The quality of the equipment available to the Slovak army was variable, ranging from the modern (they had the Czech T-35 tanks available) to vintage World War One and 1920's equipment. The manpower quality was of uneven quality.

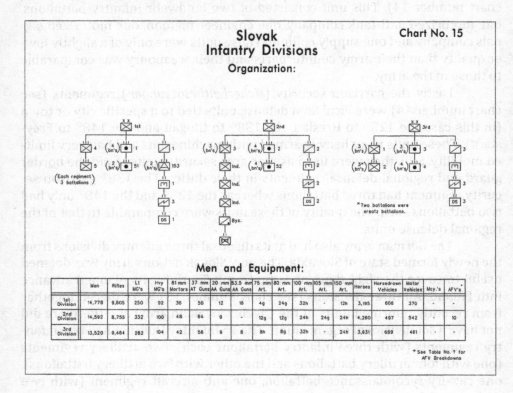

Slovak Infantry Divisions

Chart No. 15

Organization:

Men and Equipment:

	Men	Rifles	Lt MG's	Hvy MG's	81 mm Mortars	37 mm AT Guns	20 mm AA Guns	83.5 mm AA Guns	75 mm Art.	80 mm Art.	100 mm Art.	105 mm Art.	150 mm Art.	Horses	Horsedrawn Vehicles	Motor Vehicles	Mcy.'s	AFV's
1st Division	14,778	9,605	250	92	36	50	12	16	4g	24g	32h	-	12h	3,195	606	370	-	-
2nd Division	14,592	8,755	332	100	48	64	9	-	12g	12g	24h	24g	24h	4,260	497	542	-	10
3rd Division	13,520	9,464	282	104	42	56	9	8	8h	8g	32h	-	24h	3,631	689	481	-	-

+ See Table No. 9 for AFV Breakdowns

Chapter 3

Combat Operations – 1– 5 September
The Breakthrough

Army Group North – 1 September

After receiving a teletype message from the operations department of OKH on the evening of 31 August, saying that there had been border incursions by the Polish Army, orders to begin offensive hostilities against Poland were to begin at 4:45 AM that morning of 1 September. Movement began according to plan in somewhat foggy weather conditions. The XIX Army Corps, the 4th Army's spearhead force through the Polish Corridor, moved across the international border seeing little of an enemy presence. It wasn't long however, before the 3rd Panzer Division had run into some Polish anti-tank positions at Tryziany. This opposition was quickly dealt with and the advance elements of the 3rd Panzer had reached the town of Kamnitz around noon, where the division ran into more anti-tank guns bringing the advance to a halt. The 6th panzer Regiment quickly deployed its forces and in short order had overcome this defensive position. By the afternoon the 3rd Panzer Division was approaching its first major obstacle, the Brda River. Probing by the 3rd Reconnaissance Battalion had found the crossing at Sokale Kuznia was only lightly held. This was quickly exploited by the 5th Panzer Regiment by making a forced crossing here around 4:00 PM. By 7:00 PM elements of the 3rd Reconnaissance and Panzer Lehr Battalions had reached the town of Swiekatowo, only some 19 kilometers from the Vistula River. Ordered by the corps commander, General Guderian, the 3rd Reconnaissance Battalion proceeded by night march to the town of Swiecie on the Vistula River. By this action, in only one day the 3rd Panzer Division had crossed the entire corridor cutting off the southerly escape routes for the Polish forces still to the north in the corridor. By the next day, with the cooperation of the XXI Army Corps pushing south towards Grudziadz, the XIX Army Corps would completely seal off the corridor.

The XIX Corps two other divisions got off to a slower start. The 2nd Motorized Division ran into well-sited Polish bunkers in the area of Obkaz – Drozdzienicz around 11:30 AM. It was not until after 5:00 PM this line was broken through, but shortly afterwards the division ran

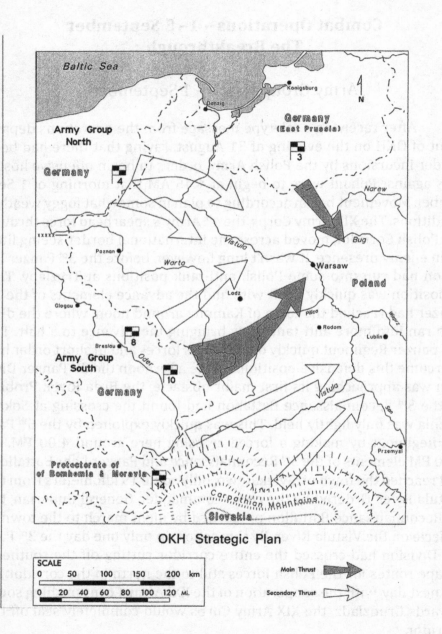

OKH Strategic Plan

into another fortified line just a few miles east of the Obrowo – Pamietowo axis. The 2nd Motorized Division remained there the rest of the day. The 20th Motorized Division bypassed the city of Chojnice to the north and south not wanting to get entangled in any urban fighting. It was left to Armored Train Number 3 to try and seize the city by a coup de main (see below). By noon most of the 20th Motorized forces had moved directly north and south of Chojnice without encountering any significant Polish forces. But, because of the disaster that befell Armored Train Number 3's attempt to take the city, the 20th had to halt its forward progress and assist in taking the city instead. The Germans certainly felt that the Poles would not try and defend Chojnice because of its location, being that it was only a few miles from the German – Polish border. The Germans thought that they could take Chojnice by surprise with an armored train at dawn. In the early hours of 1 September, Armored Train Number 3 moved out of its base at Jastrow and arrived just outside of Chojnice around 4:15 AM. The armored trains two armored cars (Sd. Kfz 231's) unloaded and preceded to the train station in the city radioing back that all seemed to be clear. The armored train pulled into the railway station, its infantry contingent occupying the station. By this time though, the Polish forces became aware of what was happening and opened fire on both the train and the troops holding the railway station. With parts of the train sustaining heavy damage and the Germans in the station were coming under increasingly heavy fire, the armored train commander decided to evacuate the infantry from the station and to pull back the train out of range of the Polish guns. Some of the train's component cars were so heavily damaged while pulling out of station that they had to be uncoupled and left behind. After calling for assistance from the 20th Motorized Division, the III/ 90th Infantry Regiment arrived around 10:00 AM to lend assistance. The battalion launched an attack into the city, rapidly overcoming any resistance put up by the Poles and by 2:30 PM the battalion had secured the city.[1]

The XXI Army Corps initial objective was the capture of the city of Grudziadz with its bridge over the Vistula River. This was deemed important as it would deny the Polish forces in the corridor an escape route and conversely to keep any Polish reinforcements from reaching the corridor from the east. In the morning the corps two divisions, the 21st and 208th, had advanced against very little resistance from the Poles. But by late afternoon, the divisions were running into stiffer resistance as they approached the Ossa River. The 21st Infantry Divi-

---

[1]National Archives: T314/611/000607-611; Records of the XIX Army Corps.

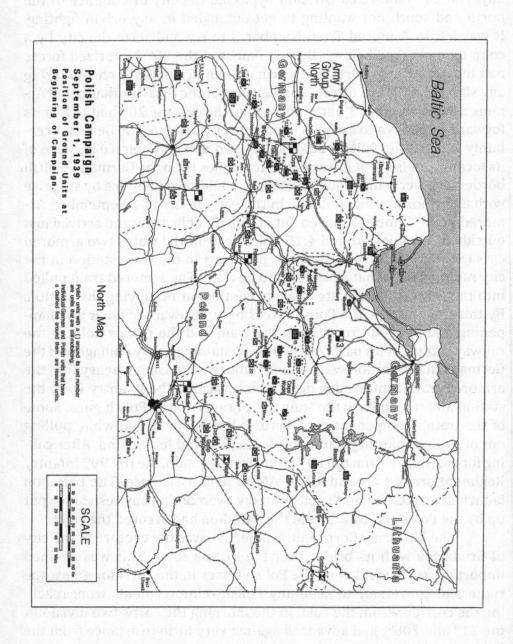

Polish Campaign
September 1, 1939
Position of Ground Units at
Beginning of Campaign.

North Map

Polish units with a () around its unit number
are units that are still mobilizing.
Individual German and Polish units that have
a slashed line around them are reserve units.

SCALE
0 10 20 30 40 50 60 70 80 90 100
0   10   20   30   40   50 Mles

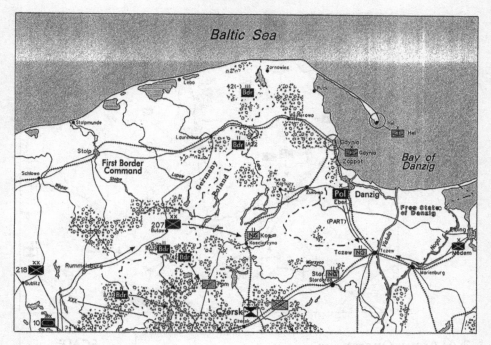

Offensive of the First Borderguard Command

Operations from
September 1–2, 1939

German Movement ⟶
Polish Movement – – →

SCALE

0   5   10   15   20 km

0   5   10   15   20 MI.

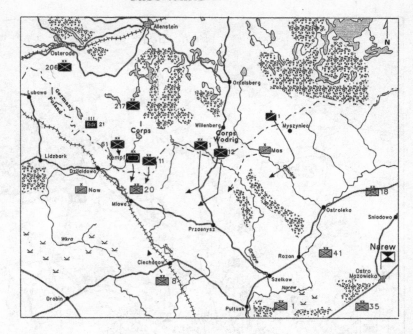

3rd Army Operations
First Corps and Corps Wodrig
September 1–2, 1939

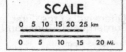

German Movement ——→
Polish Movement ----→

SCALE

0 5 10 15 20 25 km

0 5 10 15 20 Mi.

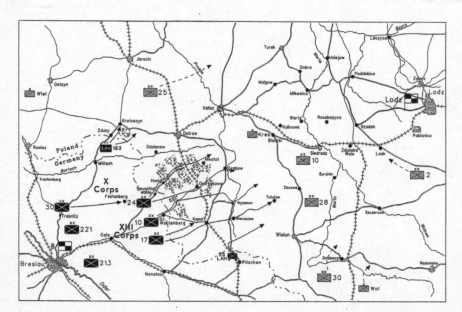

8th Army Operations
September 1–2, 1939

German Movement ——→
Polish Movement ----→

SCALE

0 5 10 15 20 km

0 5 10 15 Mi.

sion's right flank regiment, the 45th Infantry, had been moving parallel to the Vistula River's east bank when it ran into strong Polish positions at Stanislawo. As the regiment began to engage the Poles, it also was coming under the fire of the Polish heavy artillery in Grudziadz. The rest of the division was being held up in front of Roggenhausen by effective Polish battery fire from beyond the Ossa River. Late in the afternoon the 24th Infantry Regiment was able to storm Roggenhausen and thus gained a bridgehead across the Ossa River, which was quickly exploited. The 24th Regiment pushed south to Dombrowka and Sellno, thus outflanking the Poles position on the Ossa and allowed the rest of the 21st Division to move forward. On the XXI Corps left flank, the 228th Infantry Division had only advanced a few miles inside the border against very light resistance. Maneuvering between the two divisions the I/10th Panzer Regiment had driven some 4 kilometers near Szczepanken before being stopped by Polish entrenchments supported by effective artillery fire and anti-tank guns. Without any infantry support the panzer battalion could not budge the Poles out of their positions. The corps command decided to shift the I/10th Panzer to a more effective use in aiding the 21st Infantry Division's breakthrough. The panzer battalion was moved to support the 21st Division's left flank and to drive south through the Orle Forest. By evening the panzer battalion had not only moved through the forest, but had outflanked the Poles at the Szczepanken position and had attacked and destroyed a Polish command post at Slupp.[2]

The 3rd Army ran into slightly tougher resistance in the border region on its front. The planned surprise seizure of the Dirschau (Tzcew) bridge did not succeed, but another try was planned for the next day. In Danzig, the surprise attack to seize the Westerplatte fort by a naval landing force also failed. Unbeknownst to the attacking force, the Poles had greatly strengthened the Westerplatte fortress. After the old battleship Schleswig-Holstein had opened fire on the garrison, the marine commando group designated to take the fortress were initially repulsed by heavy Polish fire. The marine commandos tried three more attacks during the day, but even with the assitance of Stuka attacks, they all faltered under the withering fire of the Poles. The assault forces would regroup and try another approach tomorrow. Air activity by the Poles was slight and the Luftwaffe reported very little anti-aircraft fire from enemy ground units. At 11:00 AM the army requested more Stuka attacks at the railroad bridge at Dirschau.

---

[2]National Archives: T314/660/000111-113; Records of the XXI Army Corps.

Army Group South

Polish Campaign
September 1, 1939
Position of Ground Units at
Beginning of Campaign.

Germany

Slovakia

South Map

Hungary

SCALE

0 10 20 30 40 50 60 70 80 90 100 Km
0 10 20 30 40 50 Miles

The general impression of Army Group North headquarters at noon was that tactical and operational surprise had been achieved, even though there were isolated areas of strong resistance. It was not clear whether the 4th Army had encountered the Polish mainline of resistance and also if the Poles were going to defend in front of or behind the Brda River. The 3rd Army was encountering more resistance at Grudziadz and Mlawa and was requesting Luftwaffe air strikes against these targets. Group Brandt had reported of no Polish incursions in the eastern section of East Prussia. The I Army Corps had encountered stiff resistance on the Polish fortified line in front of Mława. The 11th Infantry Divisions attack north of Mława had bogged down in front of the well-prepared Polish bunkers. Even with the assistance of armor from the Panzer Division Kempf, the well-placed positions caught the tanks in a crossfire. After losing several tanks the rest had to beat a hasty retreat. The 11th Infantry Division was directed to launch another assault the next day to try and affect a breakthrough.[3]

Of note by the advancing armies was that in the press of the advance traffic control was poor and priority was given to the major combat elements: the motorized forces and the artillery.

Army Group South – 1 September

Orders issued on 31 August, 4:00 PM, directed Army Group South to begin offensive operations at 4:45 AM on 1 September. Evening messages were sent out to all commands to proceed with the offense according to previously worked out plans. When operations began in the morning, there were no reports of any serious enemy resistance. The Polish border guard units were quickly brushed aside. There were few problems reported for traffic control in the marching columns. The Luftwaffe reported successful attacks on Polish airfields and other military targets despite the fog in some areas.

An early morning telephone call from General Stülpnagel, chief of army operations, passed on an order for the 57th Infantry Division to be brought up from reserve and moved to a supporting position behind the 1st Mountain Division. Orders were also issued to strengthen the 13th Border Command against any enemy threats directed against Glogau. To this end, one regiment of the 252nd Infantry Division was to be detached and placed under the command of the 13th Border Command.

---

[3]National Archives: T314/34/000406; Records of the I Army Corps.

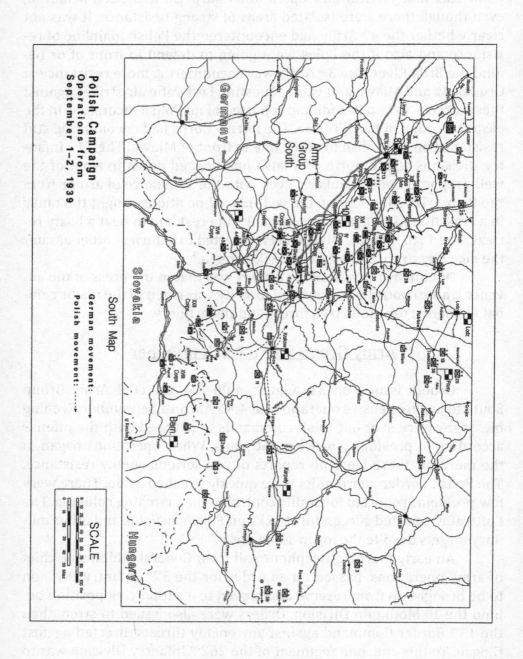

Polish Campaign
Operations from
September 1–2, 1939

South Map

German movement: ➝
Polish movement: ⇢

SCALE

0 10 20 30 40 50 Miles
0 10 20 30 40 50 60 70 80 90 100 km

The military response of the Poles on the morning of 1 September was generally weak. Only Polish border guard units, not elements of the regular army, had been encountered at this stage of the invasion. The initial artillery strikes had provoked little counter battery response from the Poles, indicating that their regular forces were not close to the border. In the afternoon, a message from the 10th Army indicated that a reinforced Polish cavalry unit had passed through a forest west of Landsberg behind the 1st Light Division as it was moving into Poland, but this was never substantiated. By late afternoon, progress had been delayed more by terrain and demolished bridges than by enemy resistance. Still, all the armies were making good progress by late afternoon. In the first day they had averaged a penetration of 25 kilometers. By late evening in the 14th Army sector, the Slovak troops allied with the Germans were reported to have reached as far as the Javorina region. The 3rd Mountain, 4th Light and 2nd Panzer Divisions of the XVIII Army Corps advanced out of the northwest region of the high Tatra Mountains, throwing back the Polish borderguard command units in constant fighting. By nightfall, the 3rd Mountain Division had reached the area southwest of Nowy Targ and the 4th Light and 2nd Panzer Divisions had reached the Rabawya - Spytkowice area.[4] The 5th Panzer Division (VIII Corps), after struggling through the numerous enemy erected barriers, made passage to the town of Rybnik. The road ahead was still strewn with such barriers, so the 8th Panzer Brigade commander (Colonel Harde) sought a path through the forest northeast of the town as it seemed passable to motor vehicles. By evening, the division found itself approaching the town of Pszczyna and the division seemed to have bypassed most of the road obstacles. The 28th Infantry Division itself had virtually no contact with the enemy as it advanced into Poland in the morning and afternoon hours. However, by 5:00 PM the division encountered a forward bunker position held by units of the Polish 55th Infantry Division. The division sought to break through this position before dark, but its efforts fell short. The 8th Infantry Division made early contact with enemy forces, with the Poles fighting a continual battle of retreat along the Gotsyn-Laziska road. By evening, the division was heavily engaged with the Polish forces holding out at Laziska, which entailed using some of the corps heavy artillery to blast the enemy out of the town.[5] The 7th Infantry Division of the XVII Army Corps had moved to a line slightly north of Kasperky and Jablonkow.

[4]National Archives: T314/665/000010; Records of the XXII Army Corps.
[5]National Archives: T314/367/000222; Records of the VIII Army Corps.

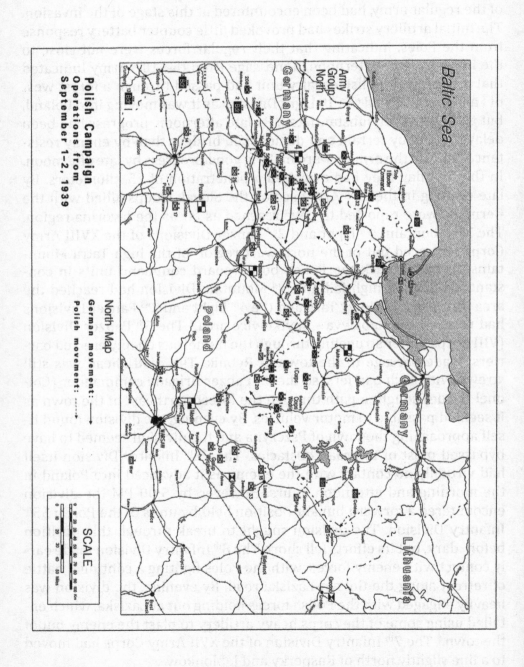

Polish Campaign
Operations from
September 1-2, 1939

North Map

German movement: ──▶
Polish movement: ----▶

Army
Group
North

Germany

Germany

Poland

Baltic Sea

Lithuania

WARSAW

KÖNIGSBERG

SCALE

0 10 20 30 40 50 60 70 80 90 100 Km

0 10 20 30 40 50 60 Miles

The army group reserve divisions had reached the following locations: the 27th Infantry Division at Peis Kretscham, the 68th Infantry Division at Gross Strehlitz, the 62nd Infantry Division east of Oppeln and the 221st Infantry Division north of Breslau. The 57th Infantry Division was brought up by rail to Poprad and positioned behind the 1st Mountain Division.

During the first day's fighting against Army Group South, the Poles had given way and rapidly retreated before the 8th and 10th Armies. On the 8th Army's front, the mornings advance across the border proceeded at the expected pace. The army's units were held up more by the difficult terrain and destroyed bridges than by enemy resistance. Only some Polish border guard units and forward units of the Polish 10th and 25th Infantry Divisions were encountered. The SS Leibstandarte Adolf Hitler motorized Regiment ran into the most resistance at the village of Boleslawiec and by evening, the Poles had stopped the regiment with its stout defense at the village. The 17th Infantry Division was involved in some heavy fighting in crossing the Prosna River at Wieruzow and the 24th Infantry Division was fighting its way through a forest trying to secure the town of Mikstat. The advance of the183rd Landwehr Infantry Regiment was held up in front of Krotoszyn and there were Polish stragglers still holding onto Zduny in its rear.[6] The 10th Army's march into Poland found little resistance except from some battles with Polish border guard units and national guard battalions. Like the 8th Army, the advances of the 10th Army's forces were slowed more by destroyed bridges and difficult terrain. All of the 10th Army's motorized forces were making rapid progress and the Poles were hastily retreating toward the Warta River line. By nightfall, the majority of the army's forces were approaching the Warta River where resistance was expected to be much tougher. The army group perceived that the Poles were attempting to build a defensive line behind the Warta River, however the reinforcements for this newly forming line arrived in penny-packets. Despite this, it was felt that it would require serious and hard fighting to break the line on the Warta. To this respect, the army group would bring up the 27th Infantry Division as well as VII Army Corps and its supporting *korpstruppen* as reinforcements.

Army groups intentions for 2 September envisioned the 14th Army pushing the XVIII Army Corps to fight its way through and breakout of the Carpathian Mountain passes and the XVII and VIII Army Corps to advance on both sides of the Vistula River. The 10th Army was to push

---

[6]National Archives: T312/37/7545197; Records of the 8th Army.

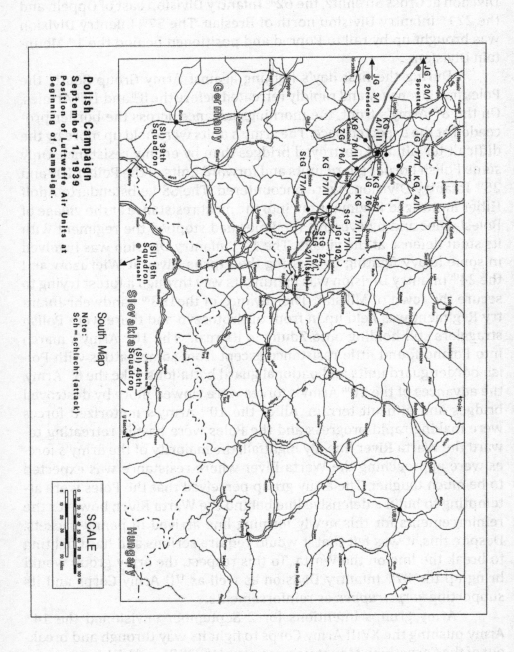

Polish Campaign
September 1, 1939
Position of Luftwaffe Air Units at
Beginning of Campaign.

South Map

Note:
Sch = schlacht (attack)

SCALE

over the Warta River line and establish a bridgehead. The 8th Army was to attack over the Prosna River with its main focus being the capture of Sieradz. Units to be kept in army group reserve were the 62nd Infantry Division, the 610th, 614th and 617th motorized Artillery Regimental Staffs, the 617th motorized Engineer Regimental Staff, the 605th, 629th and 634th motorized heavy Artillery Battalions and the 545th Anti-tank Battalion.

Army Group North – 2 September

At dawn of 2 September, the 4th Army reported that the II Army Corps had reached the area just west of the chain of lakes near Koronowo and the 3rd Panzer Division had arrived in the area west of Swiecie on the Vistula River. And even though the 3rd Panzer Division had sliced a path across the Polish Corridor from Pomerania to East Prussia, it was just a small and tenuous one and that substantial groups of Polish forces could easily slip out to the east and south. The units that would help seal this, the motorized divisions of XIX Army Corps, had been held up by Polish resistance on their on fronts. To aid the 3rd Panzer Division, the 23rd Infantry Division was rapidly brought up from its reserve position and was to close up behind the 3rd Panzer Division to consolidate its positions. By 10:00 AM the 23rd's forward regiment, the 9th Infantry, had reached Bagieniea (about halfway across the corridor) without encountering any significant Polish forces. However, when the 9th Infantry began crossing the Brda River at Sokole Kuznica in the afternoon, the regiment came under violent attacks from the north by Polish units trying to breakthrough to the south. The 9th Regiment was ordered by the XIX Corps headquarters to hold its position till the next day when her sister regiment, the 67th, could arrive to relief it.

Meanwhile, the 3rd Panzer Division continued its move forward to consolidate its gains on the west bank of the Vistula River and to seize a river crossing if possible. With the mass of the division centered around the town of Swiekatowo (some 36 kilometers west of Swiecie), the 3rd Panzer moved east in two battle groups; *Kampfgruppe* Kleeman (made up of the divisions II/3 Rifle Regiment, the II/68 and II/75 Artillery Regiments, the motorcycle, anti-tank and parts of the reconnaissance battalions) would take the left flank, while *Kampfgruppe* Angern (made up of the I/3 Rifle Regiment, the 48th Artillery Battalion, the I/75 Artillery Regiment and the 43rd Engineer Battalion) would assume the divisions right flank. Since elements of *Kampfgruppe* Kleeman were still over the Warta river, line and establish a bridgehead. The 8th Army was to attack over the Prosna River with its main focus being the capture of Sieradz. Units to be kept in army group reserve were the 62nd Infantry Division, the 610th, 613th and 617th motorized Artillery Regimental Staffs, the 11th motorized Engineer... in general, apart the motorized... and the 653rd motorized Heavy Artillery Battalion, and the 648th Anti-tank battalion.

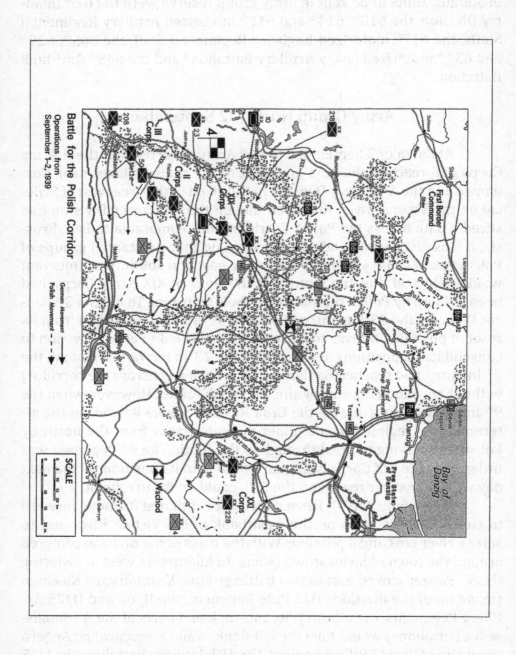

Battle for the Polish Corridor
Operations from
September 1–2, 1939

German Movement →
Polish Movement ⇢

SCALE

crossing the Brda River in the morning hours, *Kampfgruppe* Angern led the drive eastward. Angerns group ran into several Polish units moving across its front attempting to move south. This slowed Angerns progress, with the group only covering about 10 kilometers by evening. Kleemans goup also ran into the same stiff resistance after moving forward on the left flank, making little progress.

The XIX Army Corps two motorized divisions were themselves meeting variable resistance as they moved forward. The 20th Motorized Division was hung up all day on fighting its way through the Polish positions northwest of Chojnice. Combined with the heavy forest and the extensive bunker system in that area, the 20th Division was having a difficult time driving the Poles back. The 4th Army was considering moving the 20th further south to aid the rest of the XIX Corps larger breakthrough further south. The 2nd Motorized Division, wanting to make a rapid breakthrough against the Poles they were facing, were reinforced by the corps with an additional heavy artillery battalion, one mortar battalion and additional artillery from the 23rd Infantry Division. With this additional firepower, the division easily broke through in the morning hours. By the afternoon, the division's forward elements had reached the Brda River just south of Tuchola and was preparing to cross the river by early evening. The 2nd Motorized Division's reconnaissance battalion had already forded the Brda earlier and by late evening had cut the main road between Tuchola and Swiecie.[7]

The border command units assigned to Army Group North reported no resistance by the Poles as they'd advanced the previous day. General Stülpnagel directed Army Group North to apply some pressure in the Poznan province if possible. Stülpnagel also ordered Army Group North to regroup its motorized forces after reaching the Vistula River where they would be prepared for transport to eastern East Prussia as soon as possible. General Brauchitsch, commander in chief of the army, and General Halder, chief of the general staff, agreed on this course of action. Plans were to be made, selecting the best routes to be taken for transport to the assembly areas and identifying which bridges over the Vistula River were still usable (the bridges at Marienwerder and Gniew were chosen).

That morning the bridges at Dirschau were finally taken, but not before the Poles had destroyed some of the spans across the river. Air reconnaissance was still being hindered in the morning by fog, but it cleared by mid-day.

---

[7]National Archives: T314/611/000613-623; Records of the XIX Army Corps.

Because of its propaganda value, General Stülpnagel had placed at the highest order of priority the capture of the Westerplatte fortress. General Bock said it is not possible for now because of a lack of suitable troops and weapons needed to supplement the attacking forces. Bock also added that he felt that further preparations were needed before the attack would be successful. General Eberhardt, the commander of the forces facing the Westerplatte agreed. Eberhardt stated that he required additional assault engineer troops before he could take this fortified position. The naval artillery directed against the Westerplatte seemed to have ceased being effective, but the Luftwaffe would continue its attacks against the Polish fortifications with the limited forces available.

The XXI Army Corps was still pushing slowly south against determined Polish resistance. The 21st Infantry Division was encountering well-placed machine gun nests that made good use of the many small lakes in the area that funneled the attacks into constricted fronts. With the attack stalled, the corps inserted the I/10 Panzer Regiment to assist the 21st and asked the Luftwaffe's Kampfgeschwader 3 to bomb the area of Grabowitz and Nitzwalde where there appeared to the largest concentration of Polish positions. The aerial bombardment seemed to have had the desired effect. After the air attack, the division rapidly moved forward at 4:00 PM and by the fall of darkness the division had reached the Grabowitz – Klein – Ellerwitz line. The 228th Infantry Division found that the Poles had abandoned their positions to their front and had retreated to the Ossa River. Moving up to the river, the division found several crossing points lightly guarded. These were quickly brushed aside and the 228th began crossing the Ossa River in earnest, making only contact with Polish rearguard units.[8]

The I Army Corps was still hung up in front of the Mława fortified position. The 11th Infantry Division continued its attacks on the bunkers in front of Mława, but they were all repulsed. The 61st Infantry Division had been ordered up to outflank the Mława position if necessary and air support had been requested by the corps for the next days attack. Since so many tanks were lost trying to take this position on the previous day, Panzer Division Kempf was to be reassigned to Corps Wodrig so that it might support the operation of the 12th Infantry Division. The 206th Infantry Division was ordered to move up from the Osterode-Allenstein area.[9]

---

[8]National Archives; T314/660/000114-115: Records of the XXI Army Corps.
[9]National Archives; T314/34/000414-416: Records of the I Army Corps.

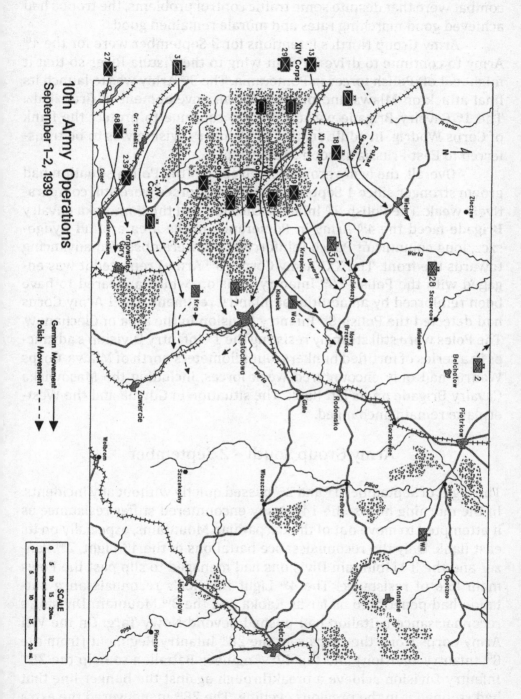

10th Army Operations
September 1-2, 1939

German Movement
Polish Movement

Impressions drawn by the general staff of the second day of combat were that despite some traffic control problems, the troops had achieved good marching rates and morale remained good.

Army Group North's intentions for 3 September were for the 4th Army to continue to drive its right wing to the Vistula River so that it might cut off Polish forces in Pomerania. The 3rd Army was to launch its final attack on Mława and prepare for an envelopment of Grudziadz. The 1st Cavalry Brigade was ordered to continue to protect the flank of Corps Wodrig. In addition, the 10th Panzer Division was to be transferred to East Prussia as soon as possible.

Overall, the army group perceived that the Polish situation had grown stronger since 1 September, but their forces were still comparatively weak. The Polish 9th Infantry Division and the Pomorska Cavalry Brigade faced the 4th Army in Pomerania. In the area around Bydgoszcz, long columns of Polish reinforcements were observed advancing towards the front. The XXI Army Corps (3rd Army) reported it was engaged with the Polish 16th Infantry Division, which appeared to have been reinforced by an additional infantry regiment. The I Army Corps had detected the Polish 8th Infantry Division in the area of Ciechanow. The Poles were still strongly resisting the 1st Infantry Division's advances in a series of fortified bunkers four kilometers north of Mlawa. Corps Wodrig had only encountered weak forces, including the Masowicka Cavalry Brigade on its left flank. The situation in Gdynia and the Westerplatte remain unchanged.

Army Group South – 2 September

The night of September 1st and 2nd passed quietly without any incidents. In the morning hours, the 14th Army encountered stiffer resistance as it attempted to move out of the Carpathian Mountains, especially on its east flank. Only the reconnaissance battalions of the 4th Light, 2nd Panzer and the 3rd Mountain Divisions had managed to slip past the Poles main line of resistance. The 4th Light Division's reconnaissance battalion had penetrated as far as Rabka and the 3rd Mountain Division's reconnaissance battalion had pushed beyond Nowy Targ. On the VIII Army Corps front, the corps sent the 28th Infantry Regiment (from the 8th Infantry Division) and the 47th Engineer Battalion to help the 28th Infantry Division achieve a breakthrough against the bunker line that had stopped it in the previous evening. The 28th maneuvered the extra infantry regiment around the bunker line north of Kobier to outflank

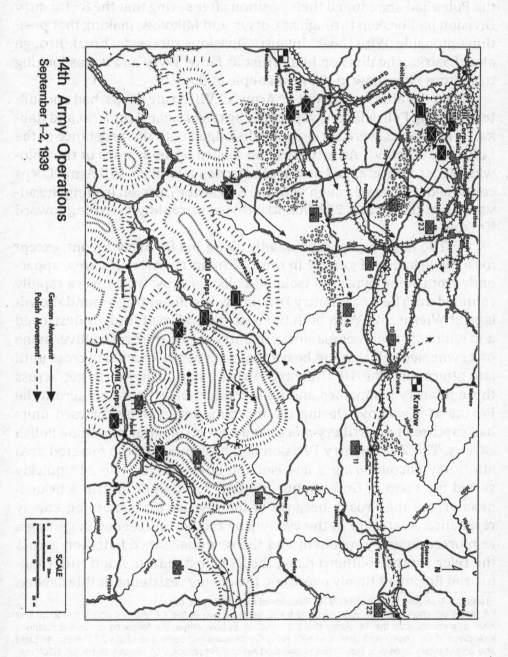

14th Army Operations
September 1-2, 1939

German Movement →
Polish Movement - - - ▷

SCALE

the position while the mass of the division would pin down the Poles with a frontal assault. By the time the division moved into the attack, the Poles had abandoned their position after seeing that the 8th Infantry Division had broken through at Gotsyn and Mikolow, making that position untenable. With the 8th Infantry Divisions successful breakthrough after Laziska, the division had thrust as far as Wyry and it was looking to capture Chrzanow in the next couple of days .[10]

In the afternoon, the 14th Army's XVIII Army Corps had encountered strong Polish forces, supported by tanks, near Neumarkt and Rabka.[11] These units were successfully dislodged with the assistance of the Luftwaffe. The XVII Army Corps had moved up both sides of the Milowka River to the area of between Skotschau and Biala. VIII Army Corps continued its breakthrough with the 5th Panzer Division leading the advance and the 8th and 28th Infantry Divisions rapidly marching toward Krakow.

The night had passed quietly along the 8th Army's front, except for a disturbance of gunfire in the 10th Infantry Division's area, apparently from some bypassed isolated Polish groups, which were rapidly rounded up. The 17th Infantry Division was still fighting around the village of Wieruszow. With both the road and railroad bridges destroyed and with only a few companies of infantry across the Prosna River, none of its wheeled vehicles and heavy weapons were expected to cross until late afternoon. The 10th Infantry Division had managed to get across three infantry companies and its reconnaissance battalion across the Prosna at Wyzanow. During the morning hours, these forward units had captured two artillery pieces and beat off an attack by some Polish cavalry. The 24th Infantry Division had broken out of the forested area after only encountering a few isolated enemy units. The 24th quickly seized the town of Grabow, but failed in its attempt to gain a bridgehead across the Prosna because of the heavier than expected enemy resistance. A later try in the evening by the 24th succeeded in getting a reinforced infantry regiment and the reconnaissance battalion across the river. On the southern flank, the SS Leibstandarte Adolf Hitler motorized Regiment finally overcame the enemy resistance at Bileslawiec,

[10]National Archives: T314/366/000998; Records of the VIII Army Corps.

[11]A major command change took place at 6 PM between two of the 14th Army's corps, the XVIII and XXII. In an order from the 14th Army dated 31 August to both corps, the following command changes took place at the designated time. The XXII Army Corps assumed command of the 2nd Panzer, 4th Light and 3rd Mountain Divisions, the III/109th motorized Artillery Regiment, 70th Signals Battalion, 620th motorized Engineer Regimental Staff, 634th Engineer Blocking Battalion and the 85th motorized Engineer Battalion. The XVIII Army Corps assumed command of the 1st and 2nd Mountain Divisions, the 445th motorized Artillery Battalion and the 422nd Signals Battalion. The corps service and supply units remained with their respective corps.

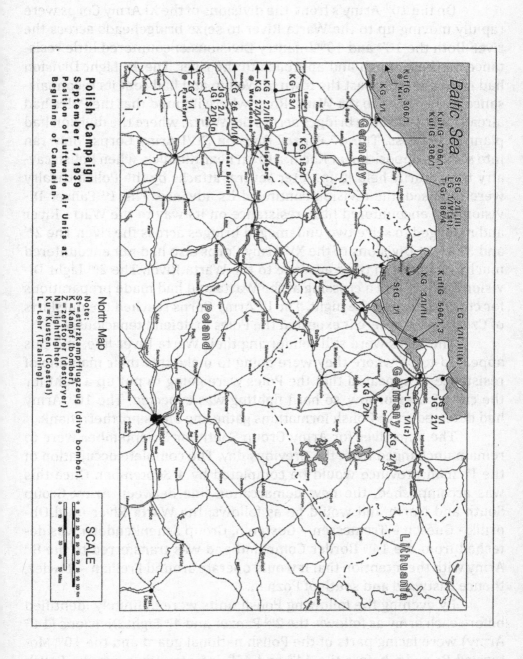

Baltic Sea

Germany

Poland

Germany

Lithuania

KuflG 706/1
KuflG 306/1

KuflG 306/1
@ Kiel

KG 1/1

StG 2/I, III,
LG 1/V(St)
T/Gr. 186/4

KuflG 506/1,3

KG 3/I/(H)

StG 1/1

LG 1/V(H)(K)

JG 1/1
JG 2/1

KG 2/1

LG 1/(z)

KG 2/1/H

KG 26, M/III
JG 26, M/III
JG 2/10(n)

KG 27/I/II
KG 27/I/II
@ Wernsdorf

KG 53/1

KG 152/1

KG 2/1
@ Kiel

@ ZG 1/1
Frankfurt

Polish Campaign
September 1, 1939
Position of Luftwaffe Air Units at
Beginning of Campaign.

North Map

Note:
St=sturzkampfflugzeug (dive bomber)
K=Kampf (bomber)
Z=zerstorer (destoryer)
N=nightfighter
Ku=Kusten (Coastal)
L=Lehr (Training)

SCALE
0 10 20 30 40 50 60 70 80 90 100 Km
0 10 20 30 40 50 Miles

then moving north to meet up with elements of the 17th Infantry Division.

On the 10th Army's front, the divisions of the XI Army Corps were rapidly moving up to the Warta River to seize bridgeheads across the river. Both the 18th and 19th Infantry Divisions encountered little resistance on their march and approach to the river. The 1st Light Division had moved rapidly past the town of Weilun and had sent its reconnaissance battalion on to the Warta River where it found that the Poles had already destroyed the bridges across the Warta, where the division had planned to cross. The 4th Panzer Division (XVI Army Corps) only ran into serious opposition at Kocin, a town near Klobuck, when Polish cavalry temporarily held it up. After several attacks by the Polish cavalry were repulsed, the division continued its advance. The 1st Panzer Division had encountered little resistance on its way to the Warta River and managed to seize two undamaged bridges across the river. The 2nd and 3rd Light Divisions of the XV Army Corps also had not encountered much resistance in their advance to the Warta River. The 2nd Light Division easily found a crossing at the Warta and had made preparations for crossing during the night. The IV Army Corps reached the outskirts of Czestochow, where it expected the Poles to defend tenaciously.

The Poles were still reinforcing their Warta River line, and this appeared to be where they were going to make this their mainline of resistance. It appeared that the Poles were going to put up a fight for the city of Czestochow, so hard fighting was expected. The 10th Army had detected fresh Polish formations gathering on its northern flank.

The objectives for Army Group South for 3 September were to remain unchanged from the previous day. The complete occupation of the Poznan province would be completed by 4 September. Once this was accomplished, the new demarcation line between Army Group South and North and would be as follows; the Warta River until Obornik - Gnesen – Tremessen – Gostynin. Group Schenkendorff was detached from the 14th Border Command and was transferred to the 8th Army with the intention that it would operate around Freihan – Rawiez, thence eastward and south of Poznan.

By evening the following Polish units were definitely identified before each army as follows: the 2nd Panzer and 4th Light Divisions (14th Army) were facing parts of the Polish national guard and the 10th Motorized Brigade; before the 44th and 45th Infantry Divisions the Polish 21st Infantry Division and before the 8th and 28th Infantry Divisions was the Polish 23rd Infantry Division. On the 10th Army's front the 4th Infantry Division was opposed by the Polish 7th Infantry Division; the 1st and 4th Panzer Divisions and 2nd Light Division were engaged with the Polish 30th Infantry Division; the Polish 13th Infantry Division and the Wolynska Cavalry Brigade opposed the XI Army Corps. Facing the 8th Army were the Polish 10th and 25th Infantry Divisions.

By late evening, the 7th Infantry Division (14th Army, XVII Army Corps) had broken through a bunker line in the Wegierska – Gorke region. The 5th Panzer Division (VIII Army Corps) had seized a bridgehead over the Vistula River at Grojec, 10 kilometers south of Oswiecim. The IV Army Corps was moving in on the city of Czestochow and the 18th Infantry Division (XI Corps) had gained a bridgehead over the Warta River at Dzialocayn.

Army Group North – 3 September

On the 4th Army's front, the 10th Panzer Division supported the infantry attacking the Polish units that were trying to escape across the Vistula River from Pomerania in the Tczew region. The II Army Corps had reached the area around Chelmo region without encountering much enemy resistance. The 32nd Infantry Division prepared for crossing the Vistula at Chelmo to gain a bridgehead on the east bank.

General Eberhardt, still confronting the problem of the fortress at Westerplatte, found the reduction of the fortress beyond the means of the resources he had at hand. He brought this to the attention of General Stülpnagel, who agreed and the planned assault for the day was cancelled.

The XXI Army Corps efforts to surround and capture Grudziadz were now picking up momentum. The bombers of *Kampfgeschwader 3* once again attacked Polish targets near the Pfaffen Berge to help the morning attack of the 21st Infantry Division. The division launched its attack at 10:00 AM and, with only small pockets of resistance in some towns and forests, the 21st made excellent progress. There was some concern about the 21st Division's left flank as there had been some reportedly enemy activity in that area. The 1st Reconnaissance Battalion was dispatched to investigate and found little presence of Polish forces and these seemed to be retreating. The 228th Infantry Division moved a battalion to link up with the 1st Reconnaissance Battalion to ensure the security of the division's flanks. The 21st Divisions attack continued in the afternoon with Polish resistance now rapidly collapsing, and by 4:00 PM, the I/3rd Infantry Regiment was in control of the heights

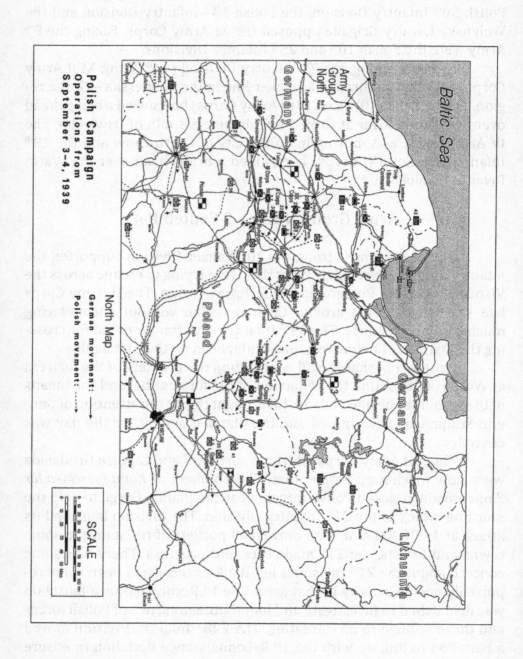

Polish Campaign
Operations from
September 3-4, 1939

North Map

German movement:
Polish movement:

SCALE
0 10 20 30 40 50 60 70 80 90 100 km
0 10 20 30 40 50 Miles

just east of the city. The 3rd Infantry Regiment continued to move south and west until it had reached the Vistula River, thereby completely surrounding the city. The 45th Infantry Regiment had started to make an incursion into the city from the north, but this attack quickly bogged down in house to house fighting. The XXI Corps called off any other attempts by the 21st Division to take Grudziadz. The corps wanted to bring up the necessary forces it felt that would be required to take the city, since it appeared the Poles were going to put up a fight for the city. The 228th Infantry Division continued its move south over the Ossa River, only running into a few Polish rearguard units. The only serious threat to the division was when the Poles launched an attack out of the Klein Lindenau – Richnowo area, but this was easily beaten back with the assistance of the 9th Machinegun Battalion.[12]

For the units of the XIX Army Corps, it was going to be a day for making the final push to the Vistula River to cut off and destroy the remaining Polish forces trapped in the Polish Corridor. The 3rd Panzer Division started the day battling Polish forces in the Przechowo – Plewno region, just some 5 kilometers west of Swiecie. By the afternoon, the divisions 5th Panzer Brigade (*Kampfgruppe Stumpf*) had taken the lead, engaging scattered Polish forces along the way. Instead of moving on Swiecie itself, the panzer brigade turned northeast to link up with units of the XXI Army Corps at Grudziadz. By evening, the 5th Panzer Brigade had secured the town of Gruppa, which was just opposite Grudziadz across the Vistula River and had established radio contact with the 21st Infantry Division. The 3rd Panzer Division's other units closely followed the 5th Panzer Brigades advance, seizing the town of Swiecie without resistance.

The 3rd Panzer Division was now facing serious depletion of its fuel and ammunition for most of its combat units after two days of constant fighting. The division requested more supplies from the corps, but was told by the corps headquarters that none could be brought forward till the next day. The supply problem arose from the rapid movement of the 23rd Infantry Division being brought forward. The 23rd Division used the same routes the XIX Corps supplies were being brought forward on and this caused the infantry division and the XIX Corps supply columns to become entangled, thus causing the delays. It would be another day before the 3rd Panzer's forces were fully re-supplied. Luckily for the 3rd Panzer, they were meeting little or no resistance from Polish forces for now.

---

[12]National Archives: T314/660/000116-118; Records of the XXI Army Corps.

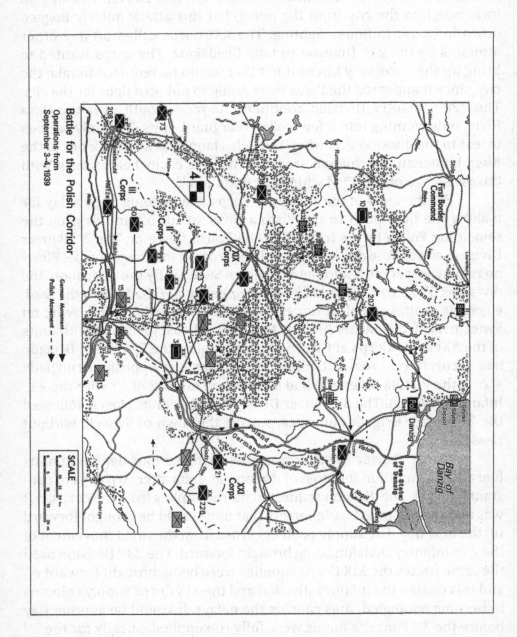

Battle for the Polish Corridor

Operations from
September 3–4, 1939

German Movement
Polish Movement ---

SCALE

When the majority of the 2nd Motorized Divisions units had completed their crossing of the Brda River in the morning, the division drove forward towards Grudziadz meeting only weak opposition from the Poles. By the afternoon, the division's spearhead had reached Dabrowka, only 10 kilometers from Swiecie with the rest of the division pulling up along the Czarna River between Grodeck and Dabrowka. There the 2nd Motorized halted momentarily to replenish its supply of fuel and ammunition and, like the 3rd Panzer Division, would have to wait until the next day before the supplies could be brought forward.

The 20th Motorized Division had shifted its axis of attack towards Tuchola and after capturing the city swiftly crossed the Brda River. On its approach to the Czarna River the division had encountered little resistance from the Poles. By evening the 20th's reconnaissance battalion had reached the town of Nowe on the Vistula River with the mass of the division still crossing the Czarna River between Grodeck and Osie.[13]

Generals Kluge and Bock met to discuss the future operations concerning the 4th Army's final clearing of the Polish corridor and its subsequent move to East Prussia. They agreed that the panzer and motorized infantry divisions needed to be moved as quickly as possible to begin operations from East Prussia.

The 4th Army's II and XIX Army Corps reached the west bank of the Vistula River and the III Army Corps reached the outskirts of the city of Bydgoszcz and made preparations to seize bridgeheads over the Netze River. Several small groups of Polish units were trying to breakout to the south from the corridor through the rear areas of the II and XIX Army Corps.

The 3rd Army reported that the Polish forces facing it had launched counterattacks along its entire front. There were still, apparently, pockets of resistance in Grudziadz and would have to be cleared out by the next day. The I Army Corps had become entangled in the Mlawa fortified line. To help break the deadlock, the corps would have available for the days attack one stuka, two bomber groups and one battalion of heavy artillery. The Luftwaffe pounded the fortified line for most of the morning and that when the infantry went in during the afternoon, the attacks still stalled after making little progress. More air attacks were made, but these seem to have made little impression. In order to break the deadlock, the 3rd Army ordered Corps Wodrig to move southwest of the Mlawa position to attack this position in the rear, even though this was contrary to the current plan of operations.[14]

[13]National Archives: T314/611/000618-628; Records of the XIX Army Corps
[14]National Archives: T312/31/7539371; Records of the 3rd Army.

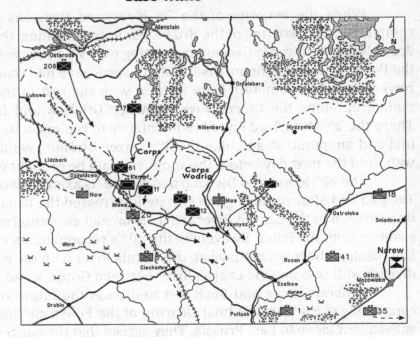

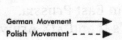

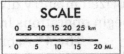

3rd Army Operations
First Corps and Corps Wodrig
September 3–4, 1939

German Movement ⟶
Polish Movement ⇢

SCALE
0 5 10 15 20 25 km
0   5   10   15   20 Mi.

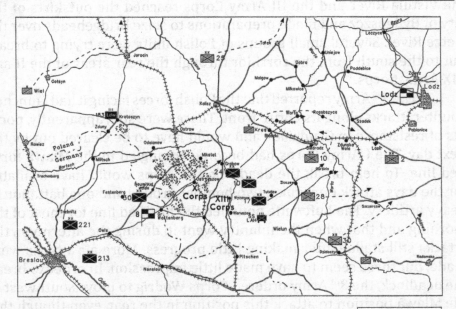

8th Army Operations
September 3–4, 1939

German Movement ⟶
Polish Movement ⇢

SCALE
0 5 10 15 20 km
0   5   10   15 Mi.

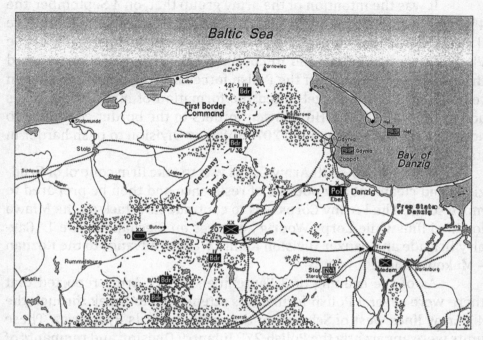

**Offensive of the First
Borderguard Command**

Operations from
September 3–4, 1939

German Movement ⟶
Polish Movement - - -⟶

SCALE

0   5   10   15   20 km

0   5   10   15   20 Mi.

It was the intention of the army group that, on 4 September, the 4th Army would clear the Danzig corridor of major enemy units. The II Army Corps was to establish bridgeheads on the east bank of the Vistula River at Chelmo and to continue offensive operations toward Briesen. In order to cut off the Polish forces moving out of the Poznan region, General Stülpnagel urged the formation of more bridgeheads across the Netze River. He also sent orders to the border command to act more aggressively and the 207th Infantry Division to push harder in its advance on Gdynia.

The 3rd Army's XXI Army Corps was to take firm control of Grudziadz and clean out any pockets of resistance and then be prepared to move south. The I Army Corps was to continue its attack on the Mława fortified line while Corps Wodrig advances on Ciechanow. The 1st Cavalry Brigade and Panzer Division Kempf were to advance to the Roznan – Makow region.

As of the evening of 3 September, the 4th Army reported that there were several Polish formations attempting to break through the 4th Army lines west of Schwetz to the south towards Bydgoszcz. These units were apparently the Polish 27th Infantry Division and remnants of the 9th and 15th Infantry Divisions. In the Gdynia area, the army group believed the Poles had massed one infantry division, one cavalry brigade and several national guard units. Two newly identified Polish infantry regiments appeared before the 3rd Army and, supported by a heavy artillery battalion and a machine gun battalion, they launched an unsuccessful attack on the left wing of the XXI Army Corps. The Poles continued to strongly resist the advance of the I Army Corps and Corps Wodrig, especially in the Mława sector.

In the southeast area of operations, two Polish cavalry regiments probed into this area and were repulsed. The situation in Gdynia and the Westerplatte were unchanged.

Army Group South – 3 September

During the morning of 3 September, the army group's troops continued their advance across the entire front from the high Tatra Mountains to Kalisch, advancing to the north and northeast. The 1st and 2nd Mountain Divisions of the XVIII Army Corps were slowly moving their way over the high Tatra Mountains. The leading group of the 2nd Mountain Division (one reinforced infantry battalion) had crossed the Dunajec River at Kroscienko and had encountered stiff resistance by the Poles trying

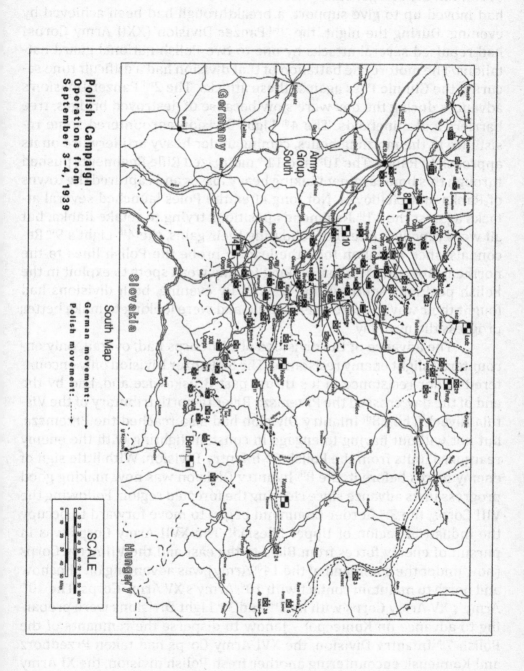

to contain the bridgehead. When the mass of the 2nd Mountain Division had moved up to give support, a breakthrough had been achieved by evening. During the night, the 2nd Panzer Division (XXII Army Corps) had repulsed several attacks by one to two Polish national guard battalions. The motorcycle battalion of that division had a difficult time securing the Glinnie Pass against these attacks. The 2nd Panzer Division's advances during the day were slow because of destroyed bridges, tree barriers and minefields. The 4th Light Division encountered some resistance in the morning hours, coming under heavy artillery fire on its approach to Rabka. The 10th and 11th motorized Rifle Regiments pushed through this bombardment taking heavy losses and captured the towns of Rabka and Chabovka. Not long after, the Poles launched several attacks against the 11th Regiment's positions trying to retake Rabka, but all were repelled. After consolidating their gains, the 4th Light's 9th Reconnaissance Battalion took the lead to probe the Polish lines to the northeast towards Mszana, looking for any weak spots to exploit in the Polish positions south of that town.[15] By evening, both divisions had fought their way to more open terrain and were looking to make better progress the next day.

The advance of the divisions of VIII Corps had, overall, only encountered slight enemy resistance. The 5th Panzer Division only encountered minor resistance in it's thrust past Broskowice and, had by the end of the day, crossed the Przemsza River (a north tributary of the Vistula River). The 28th Infantry Division had also reached the Przemsza, but not without having to engage in constant fighting with the enemy rearguard units from the Polish 6th Infantry Division. With little sign of enemy forces before it, the 8th Infantry Division was now making good progress in its advance since clearing the forested region. Following the VIII Corps, the 3rd Border Command began to move forward to occupy the industrial region of Upper Silesia.[16] The XVII Army Corps was in pursuit of enemy forces from Biala to the east and the VII Army Corps (now under the command of the 14th Army) was advancing on Miechow and north to maintain contact with 10th Army's XV Army Corps. The 10th Army's XV Army Corps with its 2nd and 3rd Light Divisions were preparing to advance on Koniecpol – Janow to disperse the remnants of the Polish 7th Infantry Division, the XVI Army Corps had taken Przedborz and Kamiensk encountering another fresh Polish division, the XI Army Corps had completed building a bridge across the Warta River at Dz-

[15]National Archives: T315/230/000175-176; Records of the 4th Light Division.
[16]National Archives: T314/366/001002; Records of the VIII Army Corps.

ialoszyn and would continue its advance to the Widowka River. Mean-while, the 1st Light Division (XIV Army Corps) had taken Osjakow after a sharp fight, and then advanced to seize a bridgehead across the War-ta River. The 13th Motorized Division had already formed a bridgehead across the Warta River at Restarzew and was thrusting its forward ele-ment (the 33rd Motorized Infantry Regiment) to try and seize a bridge at Szczercow. The 8th Army's XIII Army Corps had reached the Bedkow – Barczew – Kliszkow line against light resistance.

For operational purposes, Army Group South kept the 62nd In-fantry Division at Peiskretscham and the 213th Infantry Division at Schildberg. These two divisions formed its principal reserve.

The army group saw the heavy movement of troop trains in the Leczyce-Pabiance-Lodz area as an indication of a probable attack form-ing to strike the 10th Army. The Polish appeared to have brought two new infantry divisions and a new cavalry brigade into the area. No oth-er major changes were observed in the Polish forces facing the army group since the preceding day.

On the evening of 3 September, Army Group South sent a report to OKH written by the army group's chief of staff, General Erich von Manstein, summarizing the army group's appreciation on the present situation and on the course of future operations. Manstein stated that the results of the first three days of fighting had shown that the Poles had never intended to make the border their mainline of defense. The Poles intention seems to have been to fall back to the San – Vistula Riv-er line and to utilize those barriers as the main line of resistance. But because of the rapid advances of the 14th Army's offense on its eastern flank and the 10th Army's breakthroughs across its front, this would make this position a precarious one to hold. The Poles may make the decision to rapidly pull back all units behind the San – Vistula line and beyond to form another defensive line. Manstein urged that all mobile units of the 10th Army thrust forward to seize bridgeheads over the Vis-tula River (mostly south of Warsaw) and for the 14th Army to continue its eastern thrust to outflank the San River line. He then gave a more detailed breakdown on how this should be pursued.

Manstein recommended that OKH order the 14th Army to con-tinue its offensive down both sides of the Vistula River eastwards and to pin down the major Polish forces around Krakow and destroy them.[17] The VII Army Corps was to continue its advance and maintain the se-curity of the 10th and 14th Armies flanks. The 10th Army, to maintain its

---

[17]There is no evidence that OKH followed any of Manstein's recommendations.

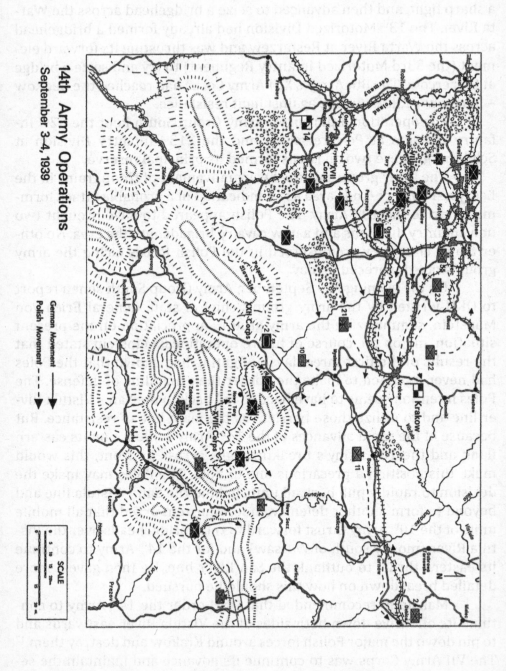

14th Army Operations
September 3-4, 1939

German Movement
Polish Movement

SCALE
0 5 10 15 20km
0 5 10 15 20 mi.

freedom of strategic movement, was to seize the important road and rail junction at Radom for its right flank anchor and advance the left flank north of the Pilica River to advance on Warsaw. The 10th Army should also look to seizing a bridgehead across the Vistula River around Pulawy – Deblin to secure future operations east of the Vistula River. The 8th Army was directed to secure its northern flank and to destroy the mass of Polish forces in and around Lodz. The Luftwaffe's 4th Air Fleet was to continue attacking any Polish forces that could be massing for a counterattack or pose any threats to the flank security of the armies. Finally, Manstein asked that the 14th Army be reinforced with additional forces to help carry out its eastern flanking movement to and beyond the San River.

Army Group North – 4 September

The Poles launched some violent attacks in the II Army Corps area of operations (the Danzig Corridor) during the night. There was some panic among the Germans, with some wild firing, but the officers rapidly brought the situation under control. During the day, the 3rd and 32nd Infantry Divisions reached the Vistula River with the 3rd Infantry Division placing some of its infantry units across the river at Topolno and the 32nd Infantry Division doing the same at Chelmo. The 3rd Infantry's initial ferrying operations were difficult, as the water was very shallow along the riverbanks. At first it was only possible to ferry the infantry across without vehicles. It was not until the late evening hours that it was finally possible to take across an artillery battery to the other shore. In the afternoon, elements of the Polish 35th Infantry Regiment, which had been reformed in some woods by their regimental commander, attacked parts of the rear service and supply units.[18]

Following the capture of Naklo, the III Army Corps began its advance to its next objective; to cross the Notec River and capture the city of Bydgoszcz. Leaving some of the units of the Netze Brigade in Naklo for lines of communication security, the 50th Infantry Division and the Netze Brigade advanced to Bydgoszcz. The corps encountered little resistance in crossing the Brda River and found that the Poles made little use of the extensive field positions the Poles had prepared before the war. Late in the afternoon the corps reached the northwest entrance to Bydgoszcz and, predictably, the enemy blew up the bridges across the Notec, making it necessary to force a crossing the next day. The Poles

---

[18]National Archives: T314/81/000215; Records of the II Army Corps.

were, more and more, launching desperate attacks to get out of the corridor and towards the south. All of these attacks were repulsed and the fate of these Polish formations in the pocket was sealed.[19]

Preparations were in progress for the 4th Army to move to East Prussia and begin an offensive east of Warsaw over the Narew River. The actual movement of forces had begun, with priority being given to infantry, which would be necessary to deal with the difficult terrain that existed in that region.

The 3rd Army was to continue its mission of tying down enemy units north and northeast of Warsaw. In the north part of the Polish corridor, the 1st Border Command (consisting of the 32nd and 42nd Borderguard Regiments), 207th Infantry Division and Group Eberhardt were assigned the task of clearing out of what remained of the Polish forces on the Baltic coast.

In the morning hours, the 3rd Infantry Division began its move to cross over to the east bank of the Vistula River by nightfall. The 3rd Panzer Division had consolidated its previous days gains during the night. In the morning Kleeman's battlegroup drove towards the north and northwest to clear out any of the remaining pockets of Poles left behind after the final thrust to the Vistula River. The rest of the panzer division was ordered to stand down to await its shipment to eastern East Prussia. Meanwhile the 2nd Motorized Division and units of the 23rd Infantry Division were destroying much of what was left of the Polish 9th Infantry Division in the forest northwest of Swiecie. At 10:00 AM, the 2nd Motorized pushed east, driving any remnants of the Polish division into the path of the 20th Motorized Division. By noon the 2nd Motorized Division turned northeast to completely cut off the remaining Poles in the Black Lakes region, meeting advanced elements of the 20th Motorized Division just outside of Nowe. Following closely behind, the 23rd Infantry Division battled with the remaining Polish forces that the motorized units had bypassed. Several times the Poles launched cavalry and infantry attacks against the 23rd Infantry and 2nd Motorized Divisions, but all of their attempts to breakthrough the German lines failed. The 20th Motorized Division helped complete the destruction of the Poles by holding its position along the Osie – Nowe line and not allowing any Poles to escape to the north. By evening, the corps had captured about 4,000 – 6,000 men and countless pieces of equipment from the 9th Polish Infantry Division.[20]

[19]National Archives: T312/37/7545306; Records of the 8th Army.
[20]National Archives: T314/611/000618-623; Records of the XIX Army Corps.

The II Army Corps units had begun their transition over the Vistula River in the following sequence; first the 3rd Infantry Division followed by the 208th and 32nd Infantry Divisions. The 218th Infantry Division was ordered to discontinue its movement towards Dirschau and to move directly east for a crossing of the Vistula at Chelmo. The 21st Infantry Division was to begin preparations for its transfer to East Prussia where it was to become part of the 4th Army. The movement of these units assigned to the 4th Army to East Prussia was delayed because of the slow development of the bridgehead over the Notec River at Nakel and Bydgoszcz. The III Army Corps did not have the adequate resources to gain a bridgehead at these locations.

The progress of the 3rd Army by the afternoon hours showed that most Polish forces were in retreat. The 21st Infantry Division renewed its effort to take Grudziadz, maneuvering its three regiments up to a line just outside the city. At 1:00 PM, the 45th Infantry Regiment drove forward into the city meeting only weak enemy resistance. By evening the 45th Infantry had cleared out any remnants of Polish forces in the city and had made contact with units of the 4th Army across the Vistula River. Unfortunately for the Germans, the Poles had enough time to damage the bridge across the Vistula enough to make it unusable to military traffic. It would take a couple of days work by the engineers to make the bridge traffic worthy again.[21]

Mlawa had finally fallen. During the night, the majority of the Polish 20th Infantry Division had retreated south, leaving only some rearguard units. Some of the captured Polish officers indicated from interrogation that the reason the position was abandoned was because they had detected Corps Wodrigs flanking maneuver to cut off the position. In order to save the majority of the division the order was given to retreat. The attack and capture of the Mlawa line by the I Army Corps had been prolonged by the resistance of the Polish forces and by the depth of the fortified bunker line. This held up the planned move of both I Army Corps and Corps Wodrig's eastward movement to cross the Narew River northeast of Warsaw by several days.[22]

In a surprise visit, the Führer arrived at 4th Army headquarters to tour the front. He wanted to see units crossing the Vistula River, so it was arranged for him to observe the 3rd Infantry Division at its crossing at the town of Topolno. The Führer said he was deeply impressed by the manner of the troops and praised the army for its accomplishments so far.

[21]National Archives: T314/660/000118; Records of the XXI Army Corps.
[22]National Archives: T312/31/7539371 & 7539280; Records of the I Army Corps.

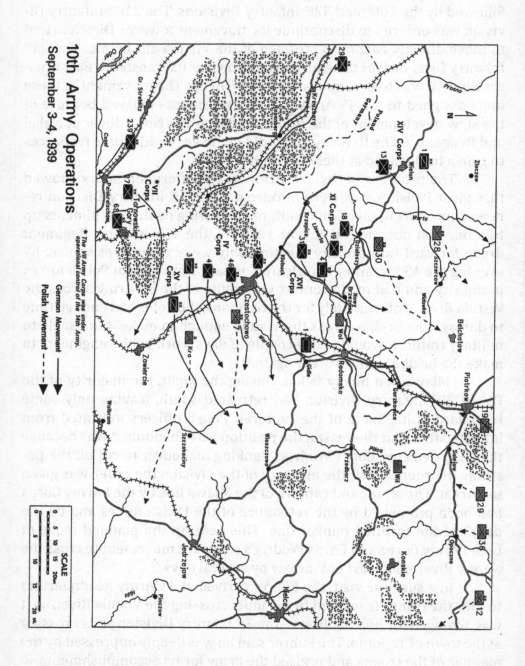

10th Army Operations
September 3-4, 1939

* The VII Army Corps was under operational control of the 14th Army.

German Movement →
Polish Movement ---→

SCALE

0 5 10 15 20km
0 5 10 15 20 mi.

The intentions for Army Group North for the next day were to transfer command of the First Borderguard Command from under the 4th Army to direct control under the army group. Further, continuation of moving II and III Army Corps units over the Vistula River and the transfer of the 2nd and 20th Motorized Divisions over the Vistula at Käsemark (near Marienwerder). The 228th Infantry Division was to mop up any Polish stragglers in the area of Grudziadz. The II Army Corps was to be transferred to under the command of the 3rd Army after completing it's crossing of the Vistula. The 21st Infantry Division would be entrained at Grudziadz to begin movement to East Prussia. The I Army Corps was to make its advance on Ciechanow and Corps Wodrig to march on Rozan with the 1st Cavalry Brigade guarding its flank.

Army Group South – 4 September

There were no significant events to report for the night of 3rd/4th September. In the early morning, 14th Army's XVII Army Corps had achieved a breakthrough at the bridgehead at Sola. This breakout permitted the 14th Army to advance its left flank to the Sucha – Wadowice – Chozanow line and with its right flank at the mountain passes into Poland proper. The VIII Army was closing in on its next objective, the city of Krakow. It was expected that the Poles would put up a fight for this important road and rail junction. During the night of 3rd/4th September, the 5th Panzer Division had been caught unawares by a couple of Polish infantry battalions that were trying to breakthrough the corps area back to their own friendly lines. The main effort by the Poles happened to go straight through where the divisional headquarters had encamped for the night. Luckily, the staff was able to fight off the enemy forces long enough so that other units could come to their aid. By morning the attack had been broken and some 1,000 prisoners were taken. The division did not meet much resistance for the rest of the day as it advanced eastward to the Oklesna-Nieporas region east of Oswiecim. The 28th Infantry Division, following on the 5th Panzer Divsions left flank, also found little or no resistance in its advance on Chrzanow. The 8th Infantry Division was meeting some resistance on its march to Jaworano, but not enough to slow it down to not keep pace with the other corps divisions.[23]

This day, the XV Army Corps (10th Army) found itself in a position to destroy the Polish 7th Infantry Division. In the morning the 2nd

---

[23]National Archives: T314/366/001004; Records of the VIII Army Corps.

Light Division, after fighting off an early Polish attack on its positions around Lelow, advanced under sporadic enemy artillery fire with the aim of seizing Szczekociny. In the afternoon, the 2nd Light Division had gotten amongst the retreating Poles supply columns, destroying much of it. By late evening, most of the enemy resistance to the 2nd Light had collapsed. Meanwhile, the 3rd Light Division was fighting its own defensive battle at Janow that morning. The division counterattacked and easily broke the Poles resistance, taking several thousand prisoners and large amounts of equipment. In the afternoon, the 3rd Light Division reorganized itself into several battlegroups to more effectively pursue the remaining enemy forces in the direction of Wloszczowa. The area the division had to traverse was made up of rough terrain and few good roads, but the division had made good progress by the end of the day.[24] The XIV Army Corps had yet to cross the Warta River. The 1st Panzer Division was rapidly closing in on Piotrkow from the south. Both wings of the 10th Army were rapidly crossing the Warta River and would be approaching the Widawka River by the end of the day. The majority of the 8th Army's units had reached the west bank of the Warta River on both sides of Sieradz. The 24th Infantry Division had taken Blaszki.

By the fourth day of the campaign, the Luftwaffe was having great success at attacking and destroying communication centers, Polish troop columns and rail transportation. Where the Luftwaffe was not having success at was bringing out the Polish air forces to fight and defend themselves. By this time, the Luftwaffe had realized that the Poles had redeployed their forward air units to other hidden bases at the beginning of the campaign to avoid being overwhelmed by the Luftwaffe's numerical superiority. There was still a definite lack of large air operations by the Poles and it was not known whether the Poles were waiting to make one large decisive strike or were moving to bases east of the Vistula River. The armies had reported in capturing several airfields that were apparently not in operational use during the first days of the war.

The army group received later that morning an assessment by OKH stating that the rapid advance by the army's forces had prevented the Poles from massing troops to form a solid line of defense and that only about 25% of the active Polish divisions had been able to fully form. Despite this success, there were still large pockets of organized Polish resistance. To the front of Army Group South, the largest groupings of enemy forces were around the city of Lodz and in the area of Ra-

---

[24]National Archives: T314/550/000238-241; Records of the XV Army Corps.

dom – Kielce. The Polish forces were seen to be rapidly abandoning the Poznan province and moving these formations to shore up their Warta – Widawka River lines. After completing the destruction of the Polish forces around the Krakow region, the 14th Army should continue its offense to cross the Dunajec and Biala Rivers. The 1st Mountain Division would continue to be the spearhead for the 14th Army's thrust toward Lwow.

OKH directed that the following units would be used to occupy the Poznan province; Group Ginanth with the 252nd Infantry Division, 183rd Landwehr Infantry Regiment, 13th Borderguard Command with Borderguard Regiment Schade, 12th Borderguard Command and Armored Train #4. A new boundary line between Army Group North and Army Group South was established that ran along the Obernik – Gnesen – Tremessen – Gostynin line. Air reconnaissance indicated that the Poles were attempting to concentrate forces at Radom from units transferred from East Galacia.

By noon, the 10th Army was changing the XV Army Corps direction, with the 29th Motorized Division to thrust toward Radom with its right flank on Kielce and the IV Army Corps marched on Konskie to cover their flank. The 8th Army was to regain its operational freedom of movement after its divisions had completed their crossing of the Warta and Widawka River lines.

Army Group South issued a new command order that afternoon that said the 8th Army was to continue its mission of guarding the 10th Army's flank and to engage the large enemy forces concentrating in the Lodz area. The 10th Army was to continue its maneuver against Radom as its major axis of attack and the 14th Army to continue its offense up to the Dunajec River.

By early evening, it was apparent that the Poles had been reduced to fighting rearguard actions as they attempted to organize a line of defense further to the east. The 1st Mountain Division's (14th Army) spearheads had reached Piwniczna and were reaching out toward Nowy Sacz. The 2nd Mountain Division was at Lacko where it had encountered strong resistance. The Poles had reinforced the units defending the town (mostly national guard) with a couple of battalions of mountain troops. Only after several attacks were the Poles dislodged from the town.[25] The 3rd Infantry Division of the Slovak Army was moving up to assist in the attack on Nowy Sacz if necessary.[26] The Slovak motor-

[25]National Archives: T314/595/000294; records of the XVIII Army Corps.
[26]Slovakia was the remnant of Czechoslovakia and an ally of Nazi Germany.

ized forces had moved into Zabsic. The XXII Army Corps had reached the Stomka – Kasina – Lubein – Peim line. The corps mobile units were sent to seize the town of Mylenice. The XVII Army Corps had reached the Sucha – Madowice – Zator line. The VIII Army Corps was approaching Krakow and was preparing for its attack on the city. The 10th Army continued its successful pursuit of enemy forces. With the destruction of the Polish 7th Infantry Division and parts of the Krakowska Cavalry Brigade, the XV and IV Army Corps continued their pursuit of scattered Polish units in their advance on Kielce. There were reports of Polish irregulars fighting behind the XV and IV Army Corps lines. Before the XIV and XI Army Corps, there was no enemy resistance worth mentioning. These two corps were approaching the Widawka River and prepared for the crossing.

The XIII and X Army Corps of the 8th Army had reached the west bank of the Warta River. The 17th Infantry Division (XIII Army Corps) was preparing to force a crossing at the Warta River in the late evening. After clearing out the towns of Abska and Ksieza, the 10th Infantry Division was faced with trying to seize a bridgehead across the Warta River at Sieradz. When the division approached the town, the Poles blew up the bridges. With the necessity of making a forced crossing, the division placed the 20th Infantry Regiment on its left flank, the 41st Infantry Regiment into the town and the 85th Infantry Regiment on the right flank. The engineers said the crossing should be made on the left flank close to the railroad bridge. The divisional artillery was situated to give maximum support and all was ready by 1:00 PM. There had not been any visible activity across the river by the Poles since the destruction of the bridges. There were several bunkers situated at the railroad bridge and the road bridge. These would have to be dealt with by the assault force. At dusk, the engineers began crossing in rubber dinghies with no visible reaction from the Poles. But, as soon as the infantry began to cross the Poles opened up with machinegun fire and artillery. The engineers and infantry that had already made it across began an assault on the barracks that were next to the railroad bridge. After a sharp fight, the barracks were cleared and the engineers began clearing the debris and the roadblocks the Poles had erected. Meanwhile, more troops of the 20th Infantry Regiment had been ferried across helping to expand the bridgehead. By daybreak two battalions of the 20th had been brought across. A further two infantry companies of the 41st Infantry Regiment had been brought across to guard the bridge, while the engineers made the necessary repairs to the bridge. Once done, the rest of the division with its heavy equipment could follow. By midmorning, an improvised bridge had been set and the rest of the division began crossing. The division was faced with having to breakthrough the bunker line north of Sieradz into which the Poles had retreated to earlier in the day.[27] The 24th Infantry Division (X Army Corps) had seized bridges across the Warta River at the town of Warta. The 30th Infantry Division had reached Gross Wartenberg and Ostrzeszow around 2:30 PM, and had continued its march to join the X Army Corps.

The estimate of Polish units facing Army Group South were as follows; before the 14th Army was the Polish 10th Motorized Brigade, the 61st, 21st and 23rd Infantry Divisions and in reserve the 3rd, 11th and 24th Infantry Divisions. Before the 10th Army were the 28th and 30th Infantry Divisions and the Wolynska Cavalry Brigade, with the 10th and 19th Infantry Divisions in reserve. Before the 8th Army were the 10th and 25th Infantry Divisions. In the Poznan area, the 17th, 14th and the 26th Infantry Divisions were identified along with the Wielpolska Cavalry Brigade.

By late evening on the 14th Army's front, the Polish 10th Motorized Brigade was holding up the XXII Army Corps progress with some hard fighting. The 44th and 45th Infantry Divisions also ran into stiff resistance from the Polish 21st Infantry Division after the Poles had been reinforced with some reserve infantry battalions. The 7th Infantry Division had to make repeated attacks before ejecting the Polish forces out of the bunker positions in front of Wegierska Gora. To the 10th Army's front, the Poles were unable to hold the Warta River line and their forces were already withdrawing with the Krakowska and Wolynska Cavalry Brigades covering their retreat. The 2nd Light Division was still pursuing remnants of the Polish 7th Infantry Division on toward Szczekoiny. The XI and XIV Army Corps were engaged with the Polish 30th Infantry Division in its fighting withdrawal to the Widawka River. Before the 8th Army, contact was being maintained with the retreating Polish 10th and 28th Infantry Divisions.

Army Group North – 5 September

The planned movement of the 4th Army on to 3rd Army's left flank continued throughout the day. The boarding of trains for the planned movement of the 10th Panzer and 21st Infantry Divisions and the Lehr Reconnaissance Battalion continued through the day. Units to be moved

---

[27]National Archives: T312/37/7545478; Records of the 8th Army.

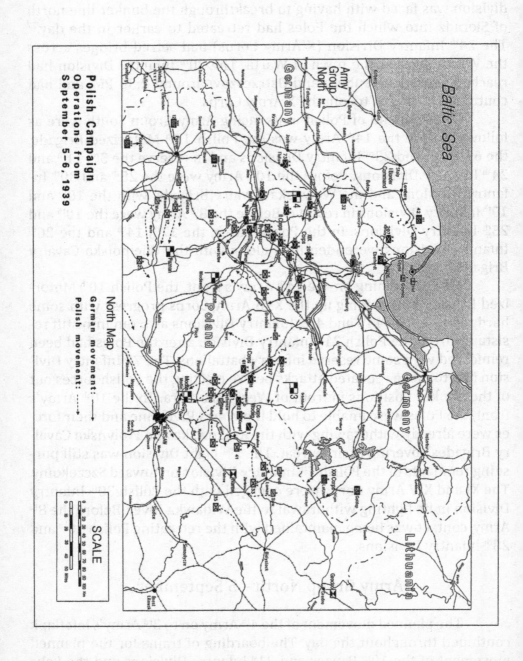

Polish Campaign
Operations from
September 5-6, 1939

North Map

German movement:
Polish movement: ----→

SCALE
0 10 20 30 40 50 60 70 80 90 100 Km
0 10 20 30 40 50 Miles

later were the 20th Motorized Division, 8th Machinegun Battalion and two heavy artillery battalions. Also, General Brauchitsch wanted Fortress Command Lötzen to be reinforced with additional border command units so it will be able to assist the regular army in its offense toward Lomza. The high command wanted the offensive to begin as soon as possible with what forces that were on hand. Bock strongly advised against that, saying that a weak attack out of East Prussia would give away the larger encirclement planned with the motorized units and that it would be better to wait for all the planned units to arrive at their starting positions. In a telephone conversation between Brauchitsch and Bock, Bock successfully argued the point and Brauchitsch acceded to what Bock and the army group wanted to do. Later, a letter sent to Army Group North from OKH officially set the outline of what was to be done. In the meantime, details on how the 4th Army was to conduct its offense towards Warsaw the next few days were still being worked out. OKH wanted the mass of the 4th Army to proceed down both sides of the Vistula River while the 3rd Army applied pressure on Warsaw. However, Army Group North wanted the 3rd Army to start swinging to the southeast and east of Warsaw to make a larger envelopment of Polish forces west of the Vistula River. After much debate with OKH, OKH agreed to let the army group use the forces now in transport (the 10th Panzer and 21st Infantry Divisions) with the new Group Lötzen to form a temporary strike force formed around the XXI Army Corps headquarters. Combined they would provide the force that Bock wanted to use to start the larger envelopment and encirclement of the Polish forces east of the Vistula River. This new force was designated "Group Falkenhorst" and its attack was scheduled for 7 September.

The elimination of Polish stragglers in the corridor continued. While awaiting transfer to East Prussia, the XIX Army Corps was ordered by the 4th Army to conduct one more sweep of its operational area for any organized Polish forces. Using the 3rd Panzer Division in its position as an 'anvil', the 23rd Infantry and 20th Motorized Divisions started their attack from their positions along the Crzana River at 10:00 AM. It did not take long for the divisions to move through the area and it only produced a small handful of prisoners and equipment. Satisfied that its operational area was now relatively enemy free, the XIX Corps resumed its task of moving to East Prussia. The 23rd Infantry Division would be left to secure the area until the civilian command had taken over.[28]

---

[28]National Archives: T314/611/000628-631; Records of the XIX Army Corps.

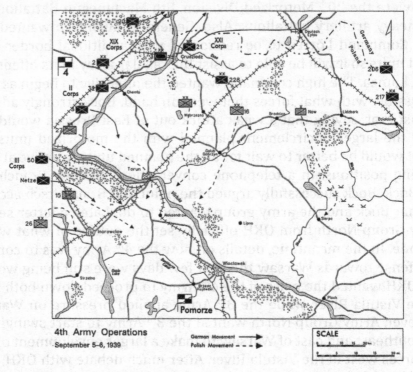

4th Army Operations
September 5–6, 1939

German Movement ⟶
Polish Movement ⟶

SCALE

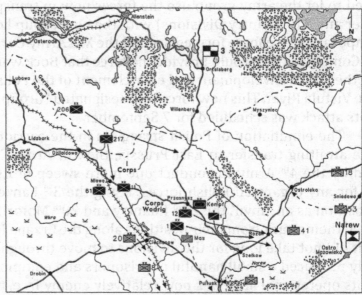

3rd Army Operations
First Corps and Corps Wodrig
September 5–6, 1939

German Movement ⟶
Polish Movement ⟶

SCALE

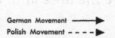

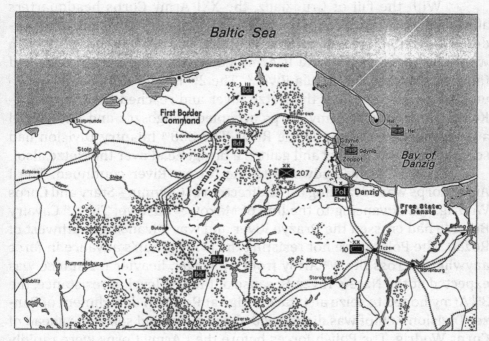

**Offensive of the First
Borderguard Command**

Operations from
September 5–6, 1939

German Movement ⟶
Polish Movement ⇢

SCALE

0   5   10   15   20 km

0   5   10   15   20 Mi.

With the fall of Grudziadz, the XXI Army Corps headquarters along with its korpstruppen and the 21st Infantry Division, were ordered for redeployment to East Prussia. The 228th Infantry Division would be reassigned to the II Army Corps after the entire corps had finished crossing the Vistula River.[29] The 2nd Border Command continued its advance south of the Netze River and reached the Obernicki – Kolmar line. The III Army Corps occupied Bydgoszcz and had seized a bridgehead across the Netze River. The 208th Infantry Division had seized the town of Nakel and gained a bridgehead over the Netze also.

The 3rd Army's advance to the Narew River continued. The I Army Corps was advancing in the direction of Golymin – Stary and Corps Wodrig was advancing to the line of Makow – Gasewo. The 1st Cavalry Brigade had crossed the Orazye River and was advancing southwest of Rozan. The Poles were not resisting the army group's advance in force anywhere across the 3rd Army front. However, heavier resistance was expected at the Narew River. Because of the low level of resistance, the 3rd Army hoped to seize an intact bridge at Rozan. A detachment of Panzer Division Kempf was dispatched ahead to try and seize one ahead of Corps Wodrig. The Polish forces before the I Army Corps were rapidly retreating and it was doubtful they could be overtaken.

The army group's plans for 6 September were for the 3rd Army's 21st Infantry Division to take up a position on the right flank of Group Falkenhorst's main jumping off point to cover its flank. The earliest that the 10th Panzer Division, Lehr Reconnaissance Battalion and Brigade Lötzen could be in position for its offense would be the evening of 7 September.

Army Group South – 5 September

The night of 4th/5th September passed quietly. When dawn had broken on the 5th, the 14th Army continued its previously established plan of operations. The 3rd Mountain Division forged ahead from its Dobra position passing through Porapka and Skrzydina while battling with Polish rearguard units in their mountain positions. By the afternoon, the 3rd Mountain had reached the more open terrain at the foothills of the mountains near Wierzbanowa. To the 3rd Mountains left, the 2nd Panzer Division drove to the north in the morning hours with the mass of the division coming to within 4 kilometers south of Myslenice. There the di-

---

[29]National Archives: T314/660/000118; Records of the XXI Army Corps.

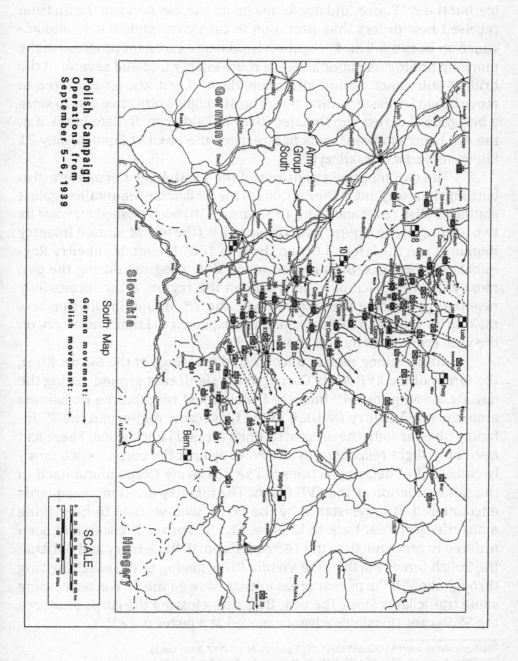

Polish Campaign
Operations from
September 5-6, 1939

South Map

German movement: ━━━▶
Polish movement: ╌╌╌▶

SCALE
0 10 20 30 40 50 60 70 80 90 100 km
0   10   20   30   40   50 Miles

vision ran into a large Polish force blocking the advance into Myslenice. After a sharp violent battle, the Poles were sent reeling back to Myslenice, but the 2nd Panzer did not follow up its success because the division received new orders that afternoon to turn east immediately and advance on Bochnia. The 4th Light Division made excellent progress in the morning finding its major advance route enemy free and several of the bridges still intact. At mid-afternoon, the 4th Light was also ordered to move in a more easterly direction. The 4th Light's objective was to seize a bridgehead across the Dunajec River at Zakliczyn. By late in the day, the 4th Light's forward units had reached the town of Lipnica, only 21 kilometers east of Zakliczyn.[30]

The two mountain divisions of the XVIII Army Corps were also battling their way out of the foothills of the Beskadian Mountains against staunch Polish resistance. The 1st Mountain Division pushed forward its two leading battlegroups, with Group Kress (the 99th Mountain Infantry Regiment) on the left and Group Utz (the 100th Mountain Infantry Regiment) on the right. Both groups made slow progress during the day, mostly from the lack of major roads in the region. After successfully negotiating crossing the Dunjec River, the 2nd Mountain Division was making its approach to Nowy Sacz and expected to launch an attack on the vital crossroads by late afternoon.[31]

After making mostly uncontested crossings of the Skawa River, the forces of the XVII Army Corps gained significant ground during the day. By evening the 44th Infantry Division had reached the Radziszow area, the 45th Infantry Division in the Glagoczow region and the 7th Infantry Division with the mass of its units around Lanckorona. There had been only slight resistance by the Poles against the corps, which mostly consisted of delaying actions.[32] The VIII Army Corps found itself in the same situation as the XVII Corps. The infantry division's vanguards encountered little resistance by the Poles, who seemed to be making a disorderly retreat back to Krakow. The 5th Panzer Division had been ordered to move north to the 14th Army's north flank to try and outflank the Polish forces north of the Vistula River fleeing to the east. Crossing through the VIII Corps rear areas initially slowed the 5th Panzer, causing some traffic jams along the way. But, after clearing the corps rear area the 5th Panzer Division's advance moved at a faster pace.[33]

[30]National Archives: T314/665/000011-15; Records of the XXII Army corps.
[31]National Archives: T314/594/000946; Records of the XVIII Army Corps.
[32]National Archives: T314/573/000379-380; Records of the XVII Army Corps.
[33]National Archives: T314/366/001005; Records of the VIII Army Corps

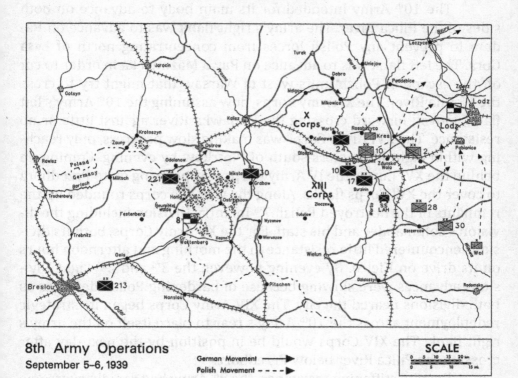

8th Army Operations
September 5–6, 1939

German Movement ——▶
Polish Movement ––▶

SCALE
0   5   10   15   20 km
0   5   10   15 mi.

The 10th Army intended for its main body to advance on both sides of the Pilica River. The army's right flank was to advance on Radom to prevent any Polish forces from concentrating north of Lysa Gora. The left flank was to advance on Rawa Mazowieka in order to cut off the escape of Polish units west of Warsaw that might try to cross the Vistula River. The XI Army Corps, now assuming the 10th Army's left flank, moved forward crossing the Widawka River against little or no resistance. The XVI Army Corps was making slow progress, only reaching within eight kilometers south of Piotrkow by evening. Coming up behind the XVI Corps, the IV Army Corps was pressing on to Przedborz to cover the XVI Corps flanks. Along the way, the corps rounded up the remnants of the destroyed Polish 7th Infantry Division including the division's commander and his staff. For the XV Army Corps, both its divisions encountered little resistance in the morning and afternoon hours on its drive on Kielce. By evening however, the 3rd and 2nd Light Divisions advances were slowing because of hardening Polish defenses as both divisions neared the city. The XIV Army Corps began its strategic redeployment across the 10th Army's rear to place itself on the army's right flank. The XIV Corps would be in position by the next day after crossing the Pilica River below Przedborz.[34]

Despite stiffening resistance, the 8th Army had rapidly overcome the Warta River defense line and was driving on the city of Lodz. The 10th Infantry Divisions (XIII Army Corps) penetration of the bunkers south of Lodz provided a good example of how this was achieved. The assault on the bunker positions was to start at 5:00 AM, but the divisional commander postponed the start of the attack until 8:00 AM so that all the proper preparations were made. The artillery opened fire promptly at 8:00 AM, first firing on known Polish artillery positions to suppress their fire, then on the bunker positions. Leading the attack was the 20th Infantry Regiment with the 41st Infantry Regiment following on the left flank. The artillery from the divisional batteries, especially the 105 mm howitzers, proved most effective. As was found later, the Polish artillery batteries were either destroyed or greatly disrupted by the division's artillery. Only a few of the enemy's light guns seemed to have survived the barrage. The initial momentum of the attack carried the third battalion of the 41st Regiment into capturing the village of Mniechow, but strong flanking machinegun fire from an enemy fortified position brought the attack to a halt. The Poles then counterattacked

---

[34]National Archives: T312/76/7595739-5740; Records of the 10th Army.

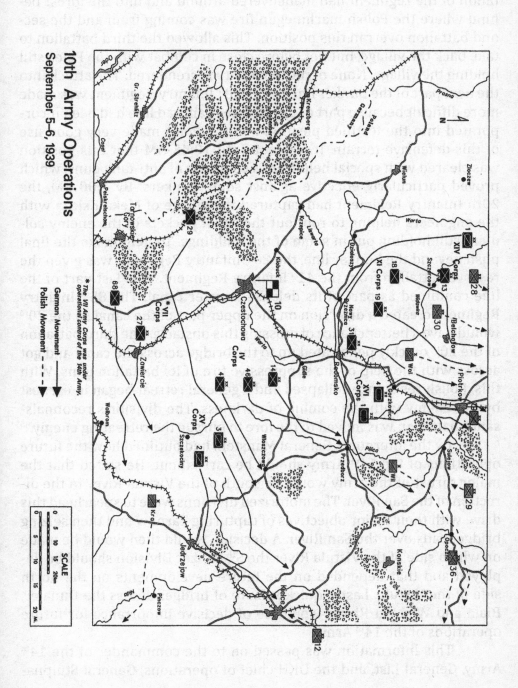

10th Army Operations
September 5-6, 1939

German Movement
Polish Movement

* The VII Army Corps was under operational control of the 14th Army.

SCALE
0   5   10   15   20km
0   5   10   15   20 Mi.

retaking the village. Mniechow was retaken again after the second battalion of the regiment had maneuvered around and into the forest behind where the Polish machinegun fire was coming from and the second battalion overran this position. This allowed the third battalion to take back the village, but not before close in combat with the Poles still holding the village. None of the defenders surrendered. The attack into the next part of the bunker line by the 20th Infantry Regiment was made more difficult because part of the elevated railroad line had been incorporated into the fortified position and the Poles made very good use of this defensive terrain. It was not until 10:45 AM that this position was cleared with special help from a company of anti-tank guns, which proved particularly effective against some bunkers. By 1:00 PM, the 20th Infantry Regiment had captured the village of Meka Ksieza with the engineers helping to root out the small pockets of the enemy soldiers still holding out in some of the buildings. To help make the final push beyond the bunker line, the 20th Infantry Regiment was given the reserve battalion from the 41st Infantry Regiment. This last part of the line contained as part of its defense a water canal. The 85th Infantry Regiment created a diversion on the upper part of the canal so the 20th would have a better chance of crossing this obstacle. The third battalion of the 20th quickly penetrated up to the bridge across the canal and got across with the help of the suppressive fire of its battalion guns. With this, Polish resistance collapsed and a general retreat began in earnest by the enemy with the coming of darkness. The division's reconnaissance battalion was moved to the fore to pursue the retreating enemy.[35]

By the afternoon, General Manstein had outlined how the future operations of the 14th Army should be carried out. He stated that the major thrust of the army would be south of the Vistula River in the direction of the San River. The motorized divisions were to spearhead this drive with their major objectives of capturing Tarnow and then seizing bridgeheads over the San River. A decision would then would be made on which side of the Vistula River the 5th Panzer Division should be deployed and that depended on the future developments on the north side of the Vistula. Lastly, quick seizure of bridges across the Dunajec, Biala and Wistoka Rivers would be of decisive importance for future operations of the 14th Army.

This information was passed on to the commander of the 14th Army, General List, and the OKH chief of operations, General Stülpna-

[35]National Archives: T312/37/7545479-5482; Records of the 8th Army.

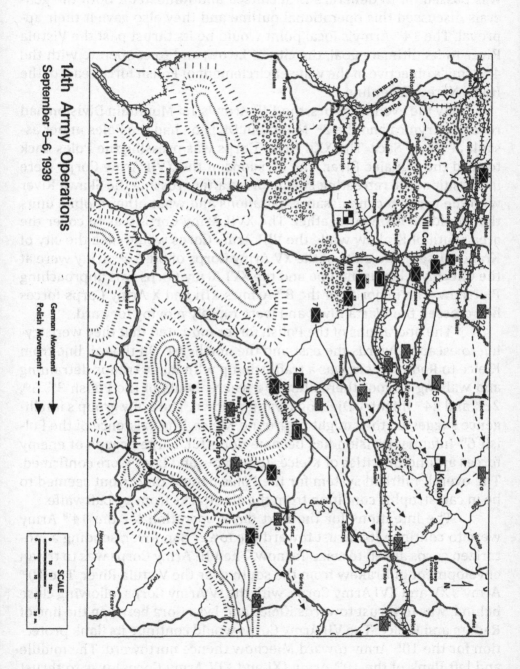

14th Army Operations
September 5–6, 1939

German Movement ——
Polish Movement ----

SCALE

gel. Both agreed in principle to this outline and then the information was passed on to General's Brauchitsch and Rundstedt. Both the generals discussed this operational outline and they also gave it their approval. The 14th Army's focal point would be its thrust past the Vistula River to its ultimate goal, the city of Lwow, and to cooperate with the 4th Army's objective of the wide encirclement of Polish forces east of the Bug – Narew River line.

By the evening hours, the 14th Army's 1st Mountain Division had reached Krynica and the 2nd Mountain Division had the Poles under assault at Nowy Sacz. The XXII Army Corps was pressing the Poles back toward the Dunajec River. The divisions of the XVII Army Corps were in pursuit of the retreating Polish forces after crossing the Skawa River with the corps reconnaissance battalions and what other mobile units that could be thrown together. The XVII Army Corps was to cover the area south of Krakow while the VIII Army Corps would take the city of Krakow itself. The units of the XV Army Corps of the 10th Army were at the Checiny – Lopuszno line and the XVI Army Corps was approaching Piotrkow. The majority of the 8th Army's XIII and X Army Corps forces had crossed the Warta River and were rapidly moving forward.

The operations of the Polish forces indicated that they were trying to escape towards the east and the northeast. On the rail line from Kielce to Radom there was a traffic tie-up with many troops detraining and walking on foot thereafter. The whereabouts of the Polish 3rd, 5th, 22nd and 24th Infantry Divisions was unknown. The army group's intelligence suggested they might be around Kielce. The existence of the Polish 6th Infantry Division has become doubtful. Large groups of enemy forces around the cities of Kielce, Tomaszow and Lodz were confirmed. The overall railroad system for the Poles behind their front seemed to be in catastrophic condition from the air attacks from by Luftwaffe.

The intentions for the next day's operation for the 14th Army were to continue its thrust toward the lower San River, sending a motorized corps ahead to seize Tarnow. The VIII Army Corps was to try an envelopment of Krakow from the south over the Vistula River. The 10th Army's XV and XVI Army Corps, with the IV Army Corps following close behind, was to thrust towards Kielce and Lysa Gora between the line of Radom and Kielce. The VII Army Corps would continue its flank protection for the 10th Army toward Miechow thence northward. The middle and left flank of the 10th Army (XI and XIV Army Corps) was to thrust their motorized forces ahead north of the Pilica River in the direction of Rawa Mazowieka in order to prevent the withdrawal of enemy forces around Lodz. The eventual seizure of bridges at Gora Kalwarja was most desirous. The 8th Army should continue its attack along the Lodz – Orzokow line.

Chapter 4

Combat Operations 6th – 12th September
The Exploitation

Army Group North – 6 September

There was some initial confusion in the morning hours at Corps Wodrig's headquarters as to whether or not the town of Rozan was still occupied by enemy forces. Rozan was a major traffic crossroads and the corps had hoped to use its vital bridge across the Narew River to funnel most of its major formations in its advance to the east. The first units to approach Rozan were those of Panzer Division Kempf and it initially reported that there were no enemy units in Rozan or in the forts guarding the approaches to the town from the west. Panzer Division Kempf then moved north (as per its orders) and when the advance units of the 12th Infantry Division approached the town and forts they were fired upon by Polish machinegun and artillery fire. The corps commander, Lieutenant General Wodrig, hoped that a bridgehead across the Narew could be established without a fight, but with the latest information, he decided to go to Rozan himself to see what the actual strength of enemy was at Rozan and what forces it might necessitate to force a crossing. General Wodrig, with his chief of staff, Major Boeckh-Behrens, arrived at the 12th Infantry Division headquarters and were briefed by the divisional commander, Lieutenant General Leyen, that they were not sure if there were any Poles defending the forts or town. Wodrig went to the forward positions to see for himself if there were any enemy units in the town and forts. After scanning the positions for some time, he could not detect any movement. It was now midday and General Wodrig did not want to waste any more time, so he ordered a reconnaissance in force to be launched in the afternoon to find the exact positions the Poles were on this side of the Narew River. This force consisted of the 1st Cavalry Regiment from the 1st Cavalry Brigade, which would probe to the south of the town; the 27th Infantry Regiment would probe around the outer forts and if possible the town, and the 89th Infantry Regiment would launch probing attacks north of Rozan. The 1st Infantry Regiment, which had just arrived from the 1st Infantry Division, would serve as the immediate reserve if needed. The attack was set for 2:00 PM, but was to be delayed until 4:00 PM because all units were not properly set.

The units finally moved forward a little past 4:00 PM. They quickly moved over the open terrain in front of the forts and occupied the forts themselves. After consolidating their gains, a small battle group was formed from the 1st Infantry Regiment and three horse squadrons from the 12th Division's reconnaissance battalion. This force moved forward on into the town, encountering no enemy units, but found that the Poles had burned the bridge across the Narew, making it unpasasable. It was soon discovered why the Poles had abandoned their positions so rapidly. The 1st Cavalry Brigade had discovered and crossed a passable ford below Rozan. The 1st Cavalry quickly expanded the bridgehead on the east bank, threatening the flank security of the Polish forces holding Rozan. With this threat, the Polish position was untenable, so they abandoned their position in Rozan to take up new blocking positions on the Bug River. By late evening, quick repairs were made to the damaged bridge and with the addition of several pontoon bridges thrown across the river; the 12th and 1st Infantry Divisions began a rapid pursuit of the fleeing Poles.[1]

The I Army Corps had little contact with Polish forces this day, except for the cavalry screen that was covering the withdrawal of the Pole's 8th and 20th Infantry Divisions to the Narew River. The Polish 8th Infantry Division did put up a short fight at the town of Gurdusk, but the 11th Infantry Division quickly routed the Poles and sent them fleeing towards Ciechanow.[2]

The III Army Corps forces turned east after moving south out from Bydgoszcz to pursue the retreating enemy forces. The Netze Brigade moved to the south of the 50th Infantry Division to cover that divisions flank while the division moved along the south bank of the Vistula River towards Torun. The corps other division, the 208th, had crossed the Netze River and was driving south to cover the gap between the 4th Army and the 2nd Border Command. Later in the day, the 50th Infantry Division was engaged in some hard fighting in the forest southeast of Bydgoszcz against Polish units trying to evade the German forces.

On the north side of the Vistula River, the III Army Corps began its advance to the east to drive before it any Polish forces it might encounter towards Warsaw. Movement of the 3rd Panzer Division over the Vistula at Mewe was proceeding at a slow pace. The problem arose because the pontoon bridge supports were sinking in the soft sandy soil

---

[1]National Archives: T314/750/384-387; Records of Corps Wodrig
[2]National Archives: T314/34/423; Records of the I Army Corps.

on both banks of the river. The supports had to be continually raised, which slowed the amount of men and matériel that could be moved over it.[3]

The army group intended that on the 7th, the next day, the 4th Army to continue its advance down both sides of the Vistula River and for the XIX Corps to continue strategic movement to East Prussia. The 3rd Army's I Army Corps was to place its forces over the Narew River on both sides of Pultusk and Corps Wodrig was to continue its thrust past Rozan towards the southeast after breaking out from its bridgehead. Group Falkenhorst was to begin its offensive towards Lomza with the 10th Panzer Division.

Army Group South – 6 September

The 14th Army was finally successful in its struggle to break free of the mountainous region, with its general front line running from Nowy Sandez to Mogliany to Zabierzow. In the afternoon, the city of Krakow had fallen to forces of the XVII Army Corps. It had been anticipated that the VIII Army Corps would probably capture the city by advancing from the west. However, when the 44th Reconnaissance Battalion (44th Infantry Division) found that there was no sign of enemy units to its north, the divisional commander gave the 132nd Infantry Regiment permission to probe as far as Krakow. The regiment formed a mobile column and drove north without encountering any Polish forces. By 3:00 PM, the column had entered the city. The regiment was ordered to secure the city and its vital bridges across the Vistula until the 28th Infantry Division (VIII Army Corps) could reach them. The VIII Army Corps was, itself, still encountering pockets of resistance to its front, so it did not anticipate being able to relieve the 132nd Infantry Regiment until the next day. The 5th Panzer Division was directed to force march its way north and to re-cross the Vistula River and then proceed along the rivers north bank in anticipation of cutting off fleeing Polish forces north of Krakow.[4]

The XVIII Army Corps had pushed east beyond Nowy Sacz against little resistance. The 4th Light Division was advancing onto Tarnow from the southwest, trying to gain control of the Zakliezyn – Tarnow road. The division had come under repeated attacks by enemy forces throughout the day trying to escape over the Dunajec River.

[3]National Archives: T312/37/7545311; Records of the 8th Army.
[4]National Archives: T314/366/1006; Records of the VIII Army Corps.

The 4th Light had, by the end of the day, secured the bridge at Zakliezyn across the Dunajec, cutting off the major escape route for many of the Polish units hoping to evade the German forces that were still west of the river below Tarnow.[5]

The army group wanted further clarification on 10th Army's situation and in especially that of the XVI Army Corps. Army group headquarters sent Captain Ferchl to 10th army headquarters at Krucina and he radioed back what he found. He reported that by noon enemy resistance at the Widawka had collapsed and the enemy forces were in general retreat before the 10th Army's left flank. As to the XVI Army Corps, its 1st Panzer Division had been driving north toward Piotrkow when, it was attacked by Polish forces from the south and east. These attacks were, however contained and thrown back into the forested areas southeast of the city. The 4th Panzer Division had come under attack by elements of the Polish 29th Infantry Division in the Wolborz – Bekow area and these attacks were also repulsed. The 31st Infantry Division was moving up to guard the corps left flank and had reached a point ten kilometers west of Piotrkow by noon. By the end of the day, the Poles appeared to be rapidly retreating before the 10th Army. The XV Army Corps had reached the Lysa Gora area and was preparing for crossings at the Nida River. The VII and IV Army Corps were rapidly marching up to help secure the flanks of the XV Army Corps. The XVI Army Corps continued its rapid advance past Piotrkow despite several enemy attacks on her flanks.

For the 8th Army, the Polish rearguard units facing the X Army Corps were rapidly abandoning the Warta River line and were falling back to the Szadek – Poddebice region. The 17th Infantry Division bypassed Lask and was advancing on Pabiance. The 10th Infantry Division had seized Szadek without encountering much enemy resistance and was driving onto Lodz. The 30th Infantry Division was rapidly marching to take up a position on the left flank of the 8th Army. It appeared that the Poles intended to reform their battered divisions in the Lodz – Radom area and form a strong defensive line there. But because of the 8th and 10th Armies rapid advances plus the Luftwaffe's incessant air attacks, this appeared not to be working out as well as the Poles had planned.

The army group's intentions for the next days operations were for the XVI Army Corps to continue as the 10th Army's advance guard, it would march towards Radom with the VII and IV Army Corps providing

---

[5]National Archives: T314/595/254; Records of the XVIII Army Corps.

flank protection for the XVI Corps. The XV Army Corps was to drive toward the Pulawy – Deblin line and to secure the Warka River line. The center and left flank forces of the 10th Army were to continue the thrust on the Pilica River and Rawa Mazowiecka with the aim of preventing enemy forces from escaping east of the Lodz region. The 8th Army was to continue with its right flank on Pabianice and its left flank on Ozorkow in order to attack and pin down Polish forces around Lodz. South of the Vistula River, the 14th Army was ordered to secure the lower San River and have the XXII Army Corps were to drive to Tarnow in order to secure a bridgehead over the Dunajec River. The VIII Army Corps was to continue its drive toward Szczucin to secure the 14th Army's flank north of the Vistula River. After the 10th Army had reached and secured the Vistula River in strength, units were to be sent from the 10th Army (including motorized units and bridging columns) to strengthen the 14th Army's drive beyond the San River.

Army Group North – 7 September

The 4th Army reported that the II Army Corps was breaking out of the Gollub bridgehead and driving to Drewenz without encountering much enemy resistance. The III Army Corps, however, was encountering heavy resistance from the enemy to its front. The 50th Infantry Division was heavily engaged with units of the Polish 15th Infantry Division in the Schulitz Forest west of Torun. The 50th finally reached the Torun – Inorowclaw road by evening, therefore clearing the forest. The division failed to reach the city of Torun in an effort to cut off the retreating Polish 27th Infantry Division. The Polish 27th had already eluded the II Army Corps after crossing the Vistula the previous day and now their comrades from the Polish 15th had bought enough time to save what was left of the 27th to fight another day. Group Netze continued to advance on the 50th Infantry Division's right flank, pursuing elements of the Polish 15th and 26th Infantry Divisions and maintaining contact with forces of the 2nd Border Command. The 208th Infantry Division was marching rapidly to catch up with the III Army Corps and was also rounding up stray Polish stragglers along its march route.

The Westerplatte fortress had finally fallen to the forces of the 1st Border Command. General Eberhardt praised the effort of the 1st Border Command troops involved, especially the engineers. With the capture of the Westerplatte, the military authority over the Polish Corridor would be handed over to the newly created civilian command

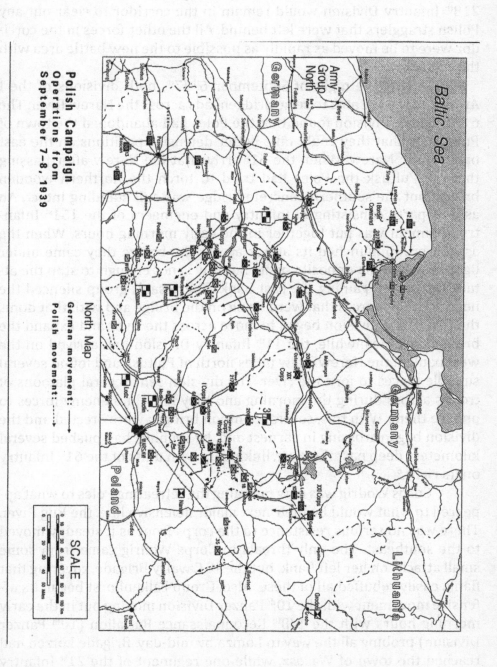

Polish Campaign
Operations from
September 7–8, 1939

North Map

German movement:
Polish movement:

SCALE

(soon to be renamed Command Posen with its headquarters in the city of Poznan). Only a few units of the 4th Army remained in the area. The 218th Infantry Division would remain in the corridor to clear out any Polish stragglers that were left behind. All the other forces in the corridor were to be moved as rapidly as possible to the new battle area with the 4th Army.

During the night of September 6th/7th, both divisions of the I Army Corps were able to seize bridgeheads across the Narew River. The 61st Infantry Division found that the Poles had abandoned the town of Pultusk so that they could take better defensive positions on the east bank of the Narew. When the 61st arrived at the Narew after passing through Pultusk the Poles had tried to torch the northern wooden bridge, but the southern concrete bridge was still standing intact. An assault party consisting of infantry and engineers of the 151st Infantry Regiment was put together in the early morning hours. When the assault group launched its attack across the bridge they came under light fire from the opposite bank, but it was not enough to stop the attack force from gaining the east bank. The assault group silenced the nearby enemy forces that were firing on the bridge and with that done, the rest of the division began to move across the river and expand the bridgehead. Meanwhile, the 11th Infantry Division had arrived on the west bank of the Narew a few miles north of Pultusk and found several suitable places to ford the river. The division sent several platoons of troops across during the morning and they found no enemy forces to oppose them. With this, several pontoon bridges were erected and the division began crossing in earnest and, by evening, had pushed several kilometers deep past the river, linking up with units of the 61st Infantry on its right.[6]

Corps Wodrig was now pursuing the retreating Poles to what appeared to what would be their next major defensive line, the Bug River. There was no serious resistance to the corps front as it steadily moved to the southeast. The only threats to Corps Wodrig came from some small attacks on her left flank, but the 1st Cavalry Brigade, covering that flank, easily rebuffed all of these. Also, Group Falkenhorst began its offensive movement with the 10th Panzer Division moving out in the early morning hours with the 1/8th Reconnaissance Battalion (10th Panzer Division) probing all the way to Lomza by mid-day. Brigade Lötzen had reached the town of Wasosz, while one regiment of the 21st Infantry Division had crossed the Kolno River at Czerwone. The Lehr Reconnais-

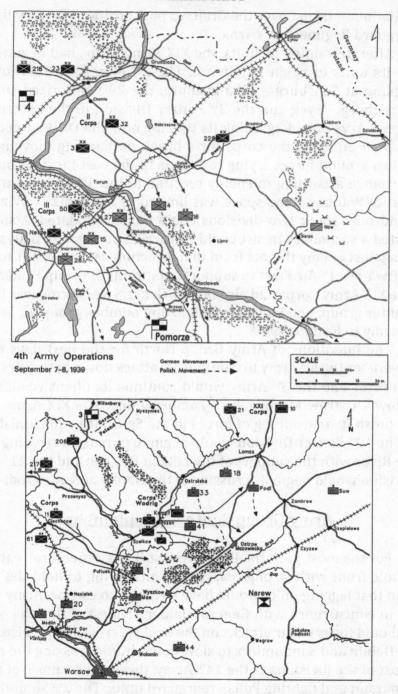

4th Army Operations
September 7–8, 1939

German Movement →
Polish Movement - - - ▶

SCALE
0 5 10 15 20 km
0   5   10   15   20 Mi.

3rd Army Operations
September 7–8, 1939

German Movement →
Polish Movement - - - ▶

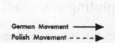

SCALE
0 5 10 15 20 25 km
0   5   10   15   20 Mi.

sance Battalion thrust over the Grajewo past positions held by the 41st Borderguard Regiment at Wizna.[7]

After detraining its units, the XIX Army Corps had begun forming up its units to begin its offense. The 2nd Motorized Division was assembling at Sensburg – Johannisburg, the 20th Motorized Division near Treuburg – Lyck and the 3rd Panzer Division in the Lötzen - Nikolalken – Arys area. Regarding its use, for now the OKH agreed with Bock's plan on using the corps for a broad outflanking movement of the Polish ground forces trying to escape to the east for now, but that might change according to enemy reaction to the 3rd Army's thrust to the east of Warsaw. Road space was limited in the Lomza – Wizna region and only about two divisions could be accomodated. Also, OKH suggested a secondary thrust could be carried out against Bialystok to guard against enemy threats from that direction. Movement of some of the Luftwaffe's 1st Air Fleet to support operations of Group Falkenhorst and the XIX Army Corps had also begun. General Kesselring was to take one fighter group, one Stuka group and one bomber group for support of the army to East Prussia.[8]

The intentions of Army Group North for the next days operations were for the 4th Army to continue its attack down both sides of the Vistula River and the 3rd Army would continue its offensive along the Wysakow – Ostrow Mazowieka – Zambrow line. The XIX Army Corps would finish its regrouping of forces in the Sensburg – Johannisburg – Lyck. The 10th Panzer Division would begin to pursue its crossing of the Narew River with the support of the Lötzen Brigade and the 21st Infantry Division would begin its crossing of the Narew at Nowogrod.

Army Group South – 7 September

For the most part, the Poles were still in a general retreat along the whole front with strong rearguard units trying to hold the flanks open so that lagging units would have a chance to escape. Army Group South, in concurrence with General Halder, requested that the 4th Air Fleet should focus its air attacks on the bridges crossing the Vistula between Deblin and Sandomierz to slow down traffic crossing the river. For most of the divisions of the 14th Army, this day was more of a matter of pursuit and fighting Polish rearguard units. The 2nd Mountain Division had, after completing it's crossing of the Dunajec River, found

---

[7]National Archives: T314/750/388-391; Records of Corps Wodrig.
[8]National Archives: T314/611/626-627; Records of the XIX Army Corps.

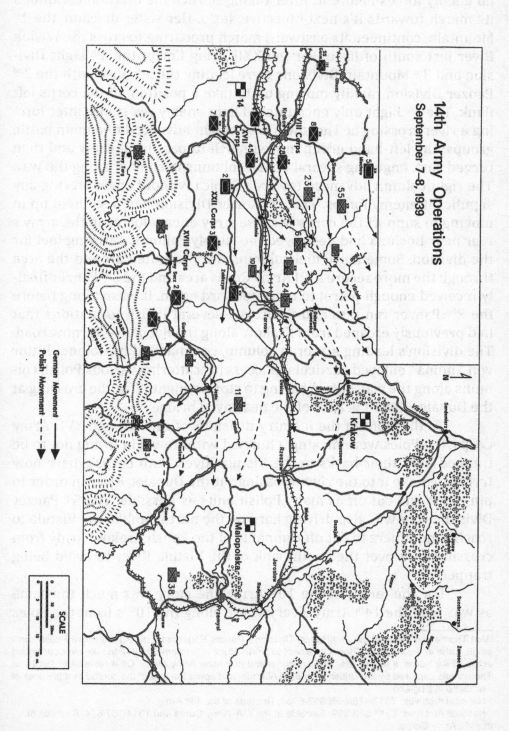

14th Army Operations
September 7–8, 1939

German Movement →
Polish Movement ⇢

SCALE

no enemy forces before it. After taking Gorlice the division continued its march towards it's next objective, Jaslo. Her sister division, the 1st Mountain, continued its eastward march preparing to cross the Wislok River just south of Jaslo. For the XXII Army Corps, the 4th Light Division and 3rd Mountain Divisions were leading the advance with the 2nd Panzer Division rapidly moving up to take a position on the corps left flank. The 4th Light only encountered light enemy resistance after forcing a river crossing at Tuchow. The 4th Light advanced two main battle groups; the left-hand group moved north to pass by Tarnow and then turned east, engaging several Polish columns in combat along the way. The right column advanced towards Debica without encountering any significant enemy forces. The 2nd Panzer Division had been held up in moving to support the corps because stray enemy forces in the army's rear near Bochnia had destroyed the supply columns carrying fuel for the division. Some more fuel columns were rerouted around the area through the more secure XVII Army Corps area and the 2nd Panzer finally received enough petrol to move forward again. It wasn't long before the 2nd Panzer ran into and destroyed several Polish formations that had previously escaped from Krakow along the Bochnia – Tarnow road. The division's leading armored column, commanded by Colonel Ritter von Thoma[9], enjoyed particular success in scattering various Polish columns along the way before having to stop by nightfall at the crossing at the Dunajec River because of the destroyed bridge.[10]

To the front of the infantry divisions of the VIII and XVII Army Corps, the Poles were making a hurried withdrawal in trying not to be trapped with their backs to the Vistula River. Both corps where now trying to make it to the river crossings at the Dunajec River in order to pin down and cut off as many Polish units as possible. The 5th Panzer Division itself was also driving hard on the north bank of the Vistula to reach Sandomierz to cut off remnants of the Polish Krakow Army from crossing back over the south bank of the Vistula River to avoid being trapped.[11]

For the forces of the 10th Army, the story was much the same as was with the 14th Army. Everywhere along the 10th's front the Poles

---

[9]Von Thoma commanded the 2nd Panzer Division's Panzer Regiment 3 during the entire Polish campaign. Later in the war, von Thoma was sent to North Africa in September 1942 to take over command of the Afrika Korps, a month later he took command of Panzer Army Afrika. On 4 November 1942 von Thoma was captured by the British west of El Alamein and spent the rest of the conflict in a prisoner of war camp in England.
[10]National Archives: T312/476/8066952-6955; Records of the 14th Army.
[11]National Archives: T314/573/389; Records of the XVII Army Corps and T314/367/674; Records of the VIII Army Corps.

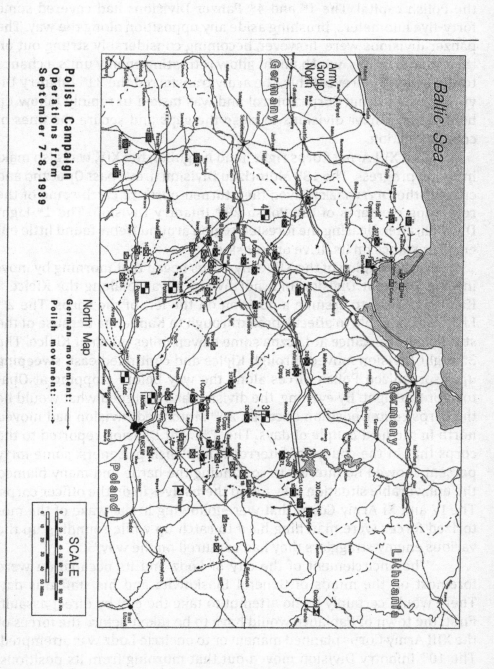

Polish Campaign
Operations from
September 7-8, 1939

North Map

German movement: →
Polish movement: ---→

SCALE

0 10 20 30 40 50 Miles

Baltic Sea

Army Group North

Germany

Germany

Poland

Lithuania

were in headlong retreat, except for the occasional rearguard actions. The XVI Army Corps was making astounding progress in its march on the Polish capital. The 1st and 4th Panzer Divisions had covered some forty-five kilometers, brushing aside any opposition along the way. The panzer divisions were, however, becoming considerably strung out on their march routes, which might allow retreating enemy units a chance to slip away. To prevent this, the army transferred the 31st Infantry Division to XVI Army Corps control and was tasked to rapidly follow up behind the panzer divisions to close the gaps and secure the lines of communication.

The XVI Army Corps right hand neighbor, the XIV, was also making good progress. The 13th Motorized Division drove past Opoczno and crossed the Drzrwiazka River, then turned north to catch some of the retreating elements of the Polish 29th Infantry Division. The 1st Light Division, after clearing the forested region around Deba, found little enemy resistance on its drive on Konskie.

A regrouping of the XV Army Corps began that morning by moving the 2nd Light Division in a northward advance along the Kielce – Kamienna road to assume a position on the left of the corps. The 2nd Light was not able to affect a breakthrough to Kamienna because of the stiff Polish resistance at Laczna some eleven miles north of Kielce. The 3rd Light Division moved through Kielce and continued east, sweeping up disorganized Polish forces along the way before stopping at Opatow for the night. By evening, the division had assumed what would be the corps center position once the 29th Motorized Division had moved north in the next couple of days. The 3rd Light Division reported to the corps that in the course of interrogating Polish prisoners, some forty percent showed no interest in continuing the battle and many blamed the unfavorable situation they found themselves in on the officer corps. The IV and XI Army Corps that were following in the wake of the motorized forces were marching hard to catch up while rounding up the various enemy stragglers they had captured on the way.[12]

The encirclement of the city of Lodz and its occupation were foremost on the minds of General Blaskowitz and his staff this day. There would certainly be no attempt to take the city by direct assault. First, the town of Pabiance would have to be taken before the forces of the XIII Army Corps planned maneuver to encircle Lodz was attempted. The 10th Infantry Division moved out that morning from its positions, fighting rearguard forces of the Polish 2nd Infantry Division all the way

[12]National Archives: T314/550/244-245; Records of the XV Army Corps.

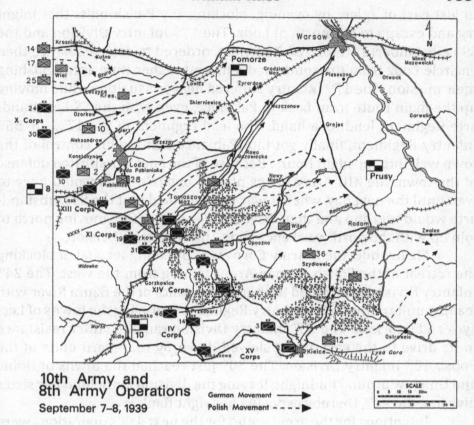

**10th Army and
8th Army Operations**
September 7-8, 1939

German Movement →
Polish Movement ⇢

SCALE
0   5   10   15   20km
0   5   10   15   20 m.

to just east of Zgierz by evening, blocking any Polish units that might try and escape to the north of Lodz. The 17th Infantry Division and the SS Leibstandarte Motorized Regiment, ordered to seize Pabiance then encircle Lodz from the south, had a much tougher time accomplishing their mission. The 17th Infantry suffered heavy casualties while moving up the main route from Lask to Pabiance, even with the SS Leibstandarte Regiment lending a hand. The lead regiment of the 17th, the 55th Infantry Regiment, finally got into Pabiance fighting for control of the town well into the night hours. Because of the enemy's spirited defense of the town, the XIII Army Corps plan to encircle Lodz would have to wait until the next day, when it was now planned that the SS Leibstandarte would regroup and then drive further east before moving north to join up with the northward encircling 10th Infantry Division.

Meanwhile, the X Army Corps was pursuing its goal of blocking the retreat of the Polish Poznan Army coming from the west. The 24th Infantry Division continued its march just south of the Bzura River with leading units of the 102nd Infantry Regiment capturing the towns of Leczyca and Ozorkow. The 30th Infantry Division ran into stiffer resistance in its drive to the east, being slowed down by rearguard units of the Polish 10th Infantry Division. The 30th just reached the towns of Dobie and Uniejow around midnight, leaving the division far behind her sister division, the 24th, thereby exposing her right flank.[13]

Intentions for the army group for the next day's operations were for the 14th Army to quickly reach the lower San River crossings and to seize bridgeheads. The 10th and 8th Armies would continue their thrust up to the Vistula River between Pulawy and Warsaw. The enemy's situation seemed, to the army group, to be becoming more disorderly in their retreat to the east and southeast.

Army Group North – 8 September

In the city of Bydgoszcz, there was some civilian unrest and some German units came under fire during the night. The source of the gunfire was never determined.

The 4th Army began its redirected march direction down both sides of the Vistula River and only encountered weak enemy resistance. Air reconnaissance discovered one Polish division marching in irregular order on the road between Kruschuitz, Sompolno and Dabre.

On the right wing of the 3rd Army, the I Army Corps was hasten-

---

[13]National Archives: T312/37/7545242-7545247

ing its effort to reach the crossing of the Bug River at Wyszkow. The bridges at that location were, however reportedly already destroyed. The Corps Wodrig was approaching the town of Ostrow – Mazowiecka and the 1st Cavalry Brigade was between both the I Army Corps and Corps Wodrig at the Brok River. Panzer Division Kempf, after passing through Rozan over Narew River, turned to the northeast towards Lomza with the intention of cutting off Polish forces retreating southwards from the Narew River. This mass of Polish troops was what was left of the Polish 18th Infantry Division trying to hold back the XXI Army Corps. When Panzer Division Kempf drove some 15 miles northeast without encountering any major enemy forces, the division was ordered by the corps to turn back to the south and rejoin the corps on its advance to Ostrow-Mazowieka. The bridgehead at Wizna (13 miles east of Lomza) was determined to be unusable by large forces because of the difficult terrain. Therefore, Brigade Lötzen and 20th Motorized Division would cross the Narew River at Lomza and the 10th Panzer Division would try and force a bridgehead directly below Wizna.[14]

Brauchitsch arrived at the army group's headquarters in the morning to be apprised of its current situation. Bock told the army commander in chief that operations were running smoothly, but he did not agree with Brauchitsch's idea of pivoting 3rd Army's axis of advance on Ostrow-Mazowieka as this would not give much room for Group Falkenhorst and the XIX Army Corps for maneuvering. After much discussion, Bock finally convinced Brauchitsch to turn the direction of the 3rd Army in a more southerly direction. With that, orders were issued for the future operations for the army group for the next few days. It stated that the 3rd Army was to continue offensive operations over the Bug River between Wyszkow and Malknia to cut off any enemy formations retreating east of Warsaw. The XIX Army Corps was to advance towards Siedlce and then southeastward and that the corps was now under the direct control of the army group. Meanwhile, the 23rd and 73rd Infantry Divisions were to be prepared for rail transport so that they could be moved to eastern East Prussia as soon as possible. Later, Bock amended the order to move the 73rd, as he felt that the division should stay in the Polish Corridor for security reasons. Bock also considered halting the II Army Corps advance because it might interfere with the friendly forces advancing onto Warsaw.

The army group's intentions for the next day were for the 21st Infantry Division to cross the Narew River at Nowogrod to clear out any

---

[14] National Archives: T314/750/390-393; Records of Corps Wodrig.

remaining enemy forces in that area. The XIX Army Corps, consisting of the 10th Panzer and 20th Motorized Divisions and the Lehr Reconnaissance Battalion were to assume positions on the left flank of the 3rd Army. The XIX Corps was to push through the Wizna-Zambrow region towards Siedlce making the Warsaw-Bialystok railline the next day's goal. The 10th Panzer Division was to cooperate with Brigade Lötzen at Wizna to help overcome the bunker position on the east bank of the Narew River.

Army Group South – 8 September

The swift progress of the armies in pursuit of the evasive enemy forces, and with the combination of the air reconnaissance reports led the army group to the conclusion that the Poles were going to try one last defensive stand behind the Vistula River line. This assessment was passed on to OKH, and with additional information from Army Group North; OKH issued new guidelines for the continuation of offensive operations. For Army Group South, there were to be two strong armies on the south flank to continue the offensive east of the Vistula River. The 10th Army was to continue its major axis of attack along the Warsaw to Kamienna River with its main focal point between Pulawy and Deblin. A secondary axis of advance was to run towards the Chelm – Lublin area. The 14th Army was to continue pushing the XXII Army Corps towards the Przemysl area. The XVIII and XVII Army Corps were to cross the San River above the mouth of the Wislok River in a brisk advance and the VIII and VII Army Corps to cross the Vistula River and the lower San River. The 8th Army would continue its assignment of flank guard for the 10th Army. The new divisional order of battle for Army Group South was as follows:

14th Army's advanced forces	XXII Army Corps (4th Light & 2nd Panzer Divisions)
Follow-up forces	XVIII Army Corps (1st, 2nd, 3rd Mountain Divisions)
Reserves	56th, 57th & 239th Infantry Divisions
10th Army's advanced forces	XIV Army Corps (1st Light, 13 Motorized Divisions) XV Army Corps (2nd, 3rd Light & 29th Motorized Divisions) XVI Army Corps (1st & 4th Panzer Divisions)
Follow-up forces	VIII Army Corps (8th and 28th Infantry Divisions) VII Army Corps (27th, 68th & 62nd Infantry Divisions) IV Army Corps (4th & 14th Infantry Divisions)

8th Army's advanced forces	XI Army Corps (19th, 31st & 46th Infantry Divisions)
	XIII Army Corps (10th, 17th & 18th Infantry Divisions)
	X army Corps (24th & 30th Infantry Divisions)
Reserves	213th & 221st Infantry Divisions

Certain details were still to be worked out depending on how well operations went on the west side of the Vistula River and the bridgeheads that could be established on the upper Vistula River. The army group asked OKH for additional materials it would need if the revised order of operations were to be carried out (mostly bridging equipment and construction units). The army group also wanted to obtain the use of the Presov – Sanok rail line to help facilitate the transportation of supplies on the army group's right flank.

On the 14th Army's front, the Poles were still in general retreat. The XVII and VIII Army Corps were pursuing a force of two infantry divisions and a cavalry brigade down both banks of the Vistula River. The 2nd Mountain Division was approaching Jaslo by evening and was hoping to seize the bridges intact across the Wisloka River intact. The 1st Mountain Division was already across the Wisloka by evening after making a forced crossing against light Polish resistance at the town of Debowiec. The 4th Light Division was now facing lighter opposition in its drive past Debica and on towards Rzeszow. It was hoped that the 2nd Panzer Division could rapidly catch up with the 4th Light after its transition over Dunajec River.

On the 10th Army's front, most of the army's motorized units were also actively pursuing the Polish armies. The XV Army Corps on the army's right flank found the enemy in full withdrawal trying to make it to the safety of the Vistula River. The 3rd Light and 29th Motorized Divisions were only encountering weak enemy resistance by Polish forces to their front. Only the 2nd Light Division was encountering stiffer resistance in its battle with enemy units in and around Suchedniow, but by evening the division had bypassed the town and had seized Kamienna. The 13th Motorized Division of the XIV Army Corps had its advance guard force (the reinforced 93rd Motorized Regiment) seize the town of Odrzywol against strong enemy forces. One of the divisions columns, consisting of the III/66th Infantry Regiment and the II/13th motorized Artillery Regiment, had to fight off several Polish forces struggling to escape to the east.

The two panzer divisions of the XVI Army Corps, the 1st and 4th were rapidly gaining ground. The 4th Panzer Division's leading battle group, the 5th Panzer Brigade, had reached Mszczonow by midmorning without encountering much resistance. General Reinhardt, the divisional commander, felt that the division might have a chance of reaching Warsaw by the end of the day. He ordered the 5th Panzer Brigade to make an effort to reach the city before nightfall. By late afternoon, when the forward elements of the 5th Panzer Brigade reached the outskirts of the city they were met by murderous artillery fire. The Poles were not going to give up their capital so easily. Because of Reinhardt's effort to reach Warsaw quickly, the 4th Panzer Division became considerably strung out along the Rawa-Mazowiecka – Warsaw road. The divisions rear echelon units were coming under constant attack by Polish forces trying to escape the other pursuing German forces. Because of these threats to the 4th Panzer's security, the 10th Army ordered the 31st Infantry Division and the SS Leibstandarte Motorized Regiment to close the gap between the 4th Panzer and the XI Army Corps. Meanwhile the 1st Panzer Division had a much easier advance. It had not encountered many enemy forces that day in its drive to the Vistula River.[15]

On the 8th Army's front, the scattered enemy units were still fighting with the 10th Infantry Division around Strykow and Niskulkow. The 24th Infantry Division's vanguard regiment, the 32^{nd,} came under attack by strong Polish forces in the area just north of Glowno. The regiment easily repulsed this attack, driving the attackers back into the forest where the attack had originated. The regiment followed the retreating Poles into the forest, capturing several hundred prisoners and three armored cars. The 32nd continued its northeast advance, crossing the Mroga River while constantly fighting with Polish rearguard units. Meanwhile, the northernmost unit on the 24th Infantry Division's flank, a *kampfgruppe* (battle group) consisting of the 102nd Infantry Regiment, the XI Corps motorized artillery battalions and the 30th Engineer Battalion (borrowed from the 30th Infantry Division), was probing along the south bank of the Bzura River looking for large enemy formations. In Bielawy, it only encountered a weak enemy force that was easily brushed aside. The *kampfgruppe* reported of no significant enemy forces on either side of the Bzura River. In the afternoon, the 26th Infantry Regiment (30th Infantry Division) had a major engagement with remnants of the Polish 25th Infantry Division between Uniejow and Poddebice. The regiment chased the enemy north to Uniejow, where the retreating Poles destroyed the bridge over the Warta River to escape the pursuing Germans.

[15]National Archives: T312/75/7595392; Records of the 10th Army.

Faced with making a direct assault on the city of Lodz, the 17th Infantry Division made preparations in the morning to launch an attack by the two regiments facing the city, the 21st and 95th. Much to the relief of the division, the Poles sent a delegation sometime after noon from the city's government to negotiate the surrender of the city. The delegation indicated that the city leaders were afraid of the death and destruction that might be wrought if and when the Germans launched an attack to take the city. So after consulting with the military commander of Lodz, the Polish commander agreed to hand over the city to the Germans if allowed to leave the city unmolested. The Polish commander was certainly aware that the Germans were closing a ring around the city to the east and he wanted to get what formations he had left to help form a new defensive line with the rest of the already retreating Polish forces behind the Rawka River. The 17th Infantry Division sent a staff officer back with the delegation to work out the details. The only stipulation that the division and corps made was that there be a guarantee that its troops would not be fired upon by provocateurs as had happened when other German forces had occupied other large cities and towns in the first week of the campaign. The city delegation could not make such a guarantee, so the negotiations dragged on until the evening hours, when both parties finally saw that the best time for the troops to move in would be at night when the majority of the population was off the streets. The word was passed on to the division to be ready to move into the city by midnight, but this time could not be kept being that the two infantry regiments were not ready, so the time was moved up to 5:00 AM the next morning. At the appointed time, both regiments marched through the city without incident. Both regiments continued on to Nowosolna, just east of Lodz to continue its pursuit of the retreating enemy forces while the 55th Infantry Regiment remained to secure the city itself.[16]

Army Group North – 9 September

After a brief halt in the town of Plock, the 4th Army continued its offensive drive down both sides of the Vistula River with the III Army Corps on the south side and the II Army Corps on the north side after a brief halt in the town of Plock. It appeared from air reconnaissance that the Poles had already destroyed the bridge over the Vistula at Wlocawek, making cooperation between the two corps more difficult.

[16]National Archives: T312/37/7545241-7545243; Records of the 8th Army.

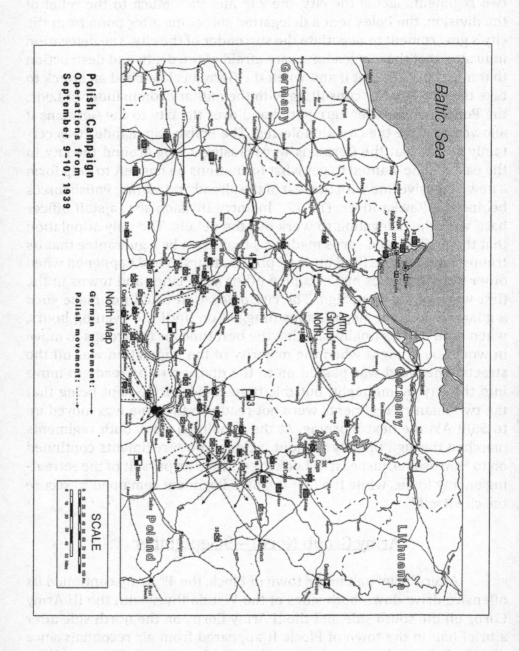

On the 3rd Army's front, the 61st Infantry Division was in heavy fighting during its crossing of the Bug River at Wyszkow. The division made a two regiment assault south of the city, with the 162nd Infantry Regiment on the left and the 176th Infantry Regiment on the right. The division's 152nd Infantry Regiment was held in reserve. Both regiments were reinforced with the first and second artillery battalions from the divisional artillery regiment and the division's engineer battalion. At 9:00 AM, both regiments launched their attacks across the Bug River with little return fire from the Poles. Only after a few squads had landed on the opposite bank did the Poles launch several attacks on the bridge-heads. These attacks were beaten back with difficulty and it was the divisional artillery that broke many of these attacks. By the afternoon, both regiments had managed to reinforce and expand both bridge-heads across the Bug River. By evening the 162nd had swung around to the north and captured the bridge opposite of Wyszkow. This done, the division began moving its heavy equipment across the river.[17]

The 11th Infantry Division made an easy crossing over the Kamienya River and was advancing on Bocynic. The Panzer Division Kempf was approaching Malklinia. Corps Wodrig with the 1st Cavalry Brigade crossed the Brok River and was driving on Stotzeck. The 21st Infantry Division had overcome the Poles guarding the Nowogrod position and was moving south towards Ostrow-Mazowiecka. The 10th Panzer Division was across the Narew River and was advancing toward Szepielowo. There was some consternation that the two motorized divisions, the 20th and 2nd, were having some problems with their approach march to the battle line. Refugees were clogging the roads so ruthless clearance of the roads had been undertaken.

By evening, OKH made changes in the direction of the campaign for the army group. With the number of Polish forces seemingly to have doubled that were crossing the Vistula and the Narew Rivers, the army group was directed to try an envelopment of the enemy forces further east of the Vistula River. The plan would set the army group to the general direction south towards Siedlce and with the Army Group South's cooperation cut off enemy forces in the area of Lukow and Deblin. In furtherance, the east wing of the army group with its motorized forces would advance down the Bug River to meet the forces of Army Group South coming up from the north in the Zamosc – Chelm region. This new strategic direction was more in line with what General Bock had been advocating all along. The commander of Army Group North had

---

[17]National Archives: T315/1009/136; Records of the 61st Infantry Division.

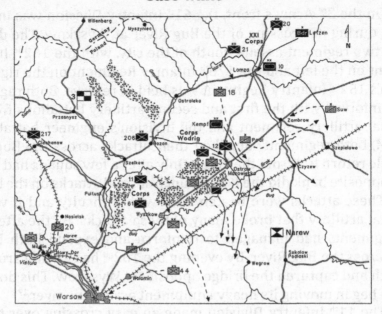

3rd Army Operations
September 9–10, 1939

SCALE

German Movement →
Polish Movement --→

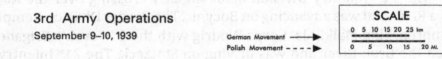

10th Army and
8th Army Operations
September 9–10, 1939

German Movement →
Polish Movement --→

felt that OKH had been short sighted in its strategic thinking from the start of the campaign. That evening, Bock gave the order directly to General Guderian, the commander of the XIX Army Corps, to launch the corps in an offensive move down the Bug River as far as Brest-Litovsk and to meet up with the motorized forces from Army Group South that would be driving up from the south.

By evening the 2nd and 20th Motorized Divisions were finally getting through the traffic jams that had delayed them earlier in the day. The 10th Panzer Division had become entangled in a second bunker line just south of its Narew River crossing. General Guderian went forward himself to see what was holding up the 10th Panzer's advance. What he found was a confused state of affairs amongst the combat units. When he arrived at noon he found no assault preparations being made to break the deadlock. The rifle companies of the 86th Motorized Infantry Regiment had refused to move forward without tank support and the regimental staff seemed to be very disorganized. There also seemed to be no coordination between the armor and artillery. Guderian ordered an immediate probing attack against the bunker line with several infantry companies. The attack itself was to be proceeded by a quick bombardment by the division's artillery. The attack began at 1:30 PM and made slow but steady progress. General Guderian then ordered elements of the 71st Light Flak Battalion and the Panzer I and II's of the 8th Panzer Regiment to support the attack (the heavier Panzer III's and IV's were not available because they were still crossing the Narew River some miles back). The guns of the flak battalion proved most particularly effective against the enemy bunkers and by 5:00 PM the 10th Panzer had captured the length of this fortified line. By 6:00 PM the 8th Panzer Regiment was prepared to resume its march south to Brest-Litovsk.[18]

The 21st Infantry Division was not able to make a forced crossing at Nowogrod at the Narew River because of the stiff Polish resistance there. The XXI Army Corps sent one of its reserve heavy artillery battalions and some engineers to aid the 21st in its planned attack for the next day.

The army group's intentions for 10 September were to have the 4th Army continue its offensive down both banks of the Vistula River towards Warsaw. The army group emphasized that the 4th Army should push forward as rapidly as possible with motorized forces toward Modlin, with the intention of capturing this key river crossing and fortified

[18]National Archives: T314/611/635-640; Records of the XIX Army Corps.

position. The I Army Corps and Corps Wodrig were to continue their attacks over the Bug River, then begin a rotation toward the west at the Warsaw – Siedlce roadway line. Panzer Division Kempf was to thrust over the Brok River and then push southward. The XXI Army Corps was to complete its crossing of the Narew River and advance on to Lomza and the XIX Army Corps to cross the Wizna River and drive towards Brest-Litovsk.

Army Group South – 9 September

After seizing Gorlice on the previous day, the 2nd Mountain Division advanced to Jaslo and captured the town after a short battle with the rapidly retreating Polish forces. The fighting for the bridge at the Jasiolka River was particularly viscous, with many casualties in the division's 82nd Engineer Battalion. The 1st Mountain Division quickly seized Dukla and the Dukla Pass with its improvised motorized battalion leading the way. Both divisions began a pursuit of the Polish forces retreating toward the Przemysl – Jaroslaw area by late evening.

The 5th Panzer Division, which had been previously been ordered to assist the 10th Army in its battles around Radom, was to turn back towards Sandomierz to assist the VII Army Corps in crossing the Vistula River. To prevent any traffic problems between the VII Army Corps and the VII Army Corps, the boundary line between the two corps was shifted to the south along the Bus – Stopnica road.

On the 10th Army's front, there were violent battles as the Poles tried to breakout of the Radom pocket, but they were successfully beaten back by the XV and XIV Army Corps. The strongest attacks were against the XV Army Corps, where the Poles renewed their assaults to break out around 10:00 AM. The attack against the 2nd Light Division's positions held only after, with the help of Luftwaffe bombers, the 67th Panzer Battalion counterattacked and the Poles were thrown back with considerable losses at Ilza. The 3rd Light Division was also trying to stop large groups of Polish forces from slipping across the Kamienna, but was not successful since the division was so spread out. It was hoped that the 5th Panzer Division could assist the XV Army Corps, but it had been recalled back to the 14th Army. Instead, the 29th Motorized Division was ordered by the corps to assist the 3rd Light. The 29th Motorized swept north during the day and managed to breakup the enemy formations trying to regroup, capturing many prisoners. Meanwhile the 1st Light Division, with its vanguard battlegroup of the 65th Panzer and 15th Machinegun Battalions, was rapidly driving south of Radom,

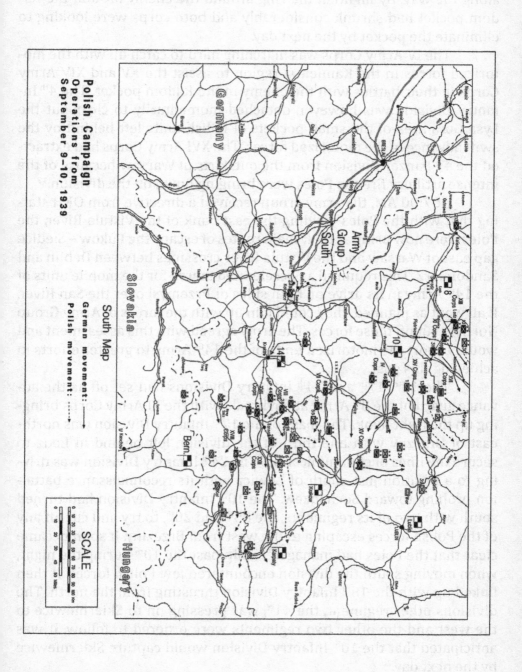

encountering little resistance and rounding up hundreds of prisoners along the way. By nightfall the ring around the enemy around the Radom pocket had shrunk considerably and both corps were looking to eliminate the pocket by the next day.

The IV Army Corps was marching hard to catch up with the motorized forces in the Kamienna region to assist the XV and XIV Army Corps in their battles with the enemy in the Radom pocket. The 4th Infantry Division was however, detached momentarily to clear out the Lysa Gora area of the small pockets of Polish units left behind by the swift advance of the motorized forces. The XVI Army Corps had extracted the 4th Panzer Division from the outskirts of Warsaw because of the intense artillery fire the Poles were bringing down on the division.[19]

At 7:00 AM, the army group received a directive from OKH stating that with the Poles yielding the east bank of the Vistula River, the Poles were now using as their main routes of escape the Lukow – Siedlce gap east of Warsaw and the Vistula River crossings between Deblin and Sandomierz. This required an accelerated march for the mobile units of the 14th Army in its drive on both sides of Przemysl over the San River. If all went as planned, they could join up with the forces of Army Group North to cut off these forces. The army agreed with this assessment and would exhort the motorized units of the 14th Army to greater efforts in achieving this goal.

The 10th, 17th and 24th Infantry Divisions had set off as the advance guard of the 8th Army at daybreak, with the XI Army Corps bringing up the right flank. The mass of the 17th Infantry Division was northeast of Brzezny with one third of the division left behind in Lodz to secure the lines of communication. The 24th Infantry Division was driving to a position just south of Lowicz with its reconnaissance battalion probing toward Sochadzew. The 10th Infantry Division had turned south with two of its regiments, the 85th and 20th, to try and cut off any of the Polish forces escaping to the west from Brzeziny. It soon became clear that the Poles had managed to slip past the 10th during the night, when moving south the division encountered few Polish forces. It then linked up with the 18th Infantry Division thrusting from the north. The divisions other regiment, the 41st, was pressing on to Skierniewice to the west and the other two regiments were ordered to follow. It was anticipated that the 10th Infantry Division would capture Skierniewice by the next day.[20]

---

[19]National Archives: T312/75/7595404-7595406; Records of the 10th Army.
[20]National Archives: T312/37/7545489-75490 and 7545556; Records of the 8th Army.

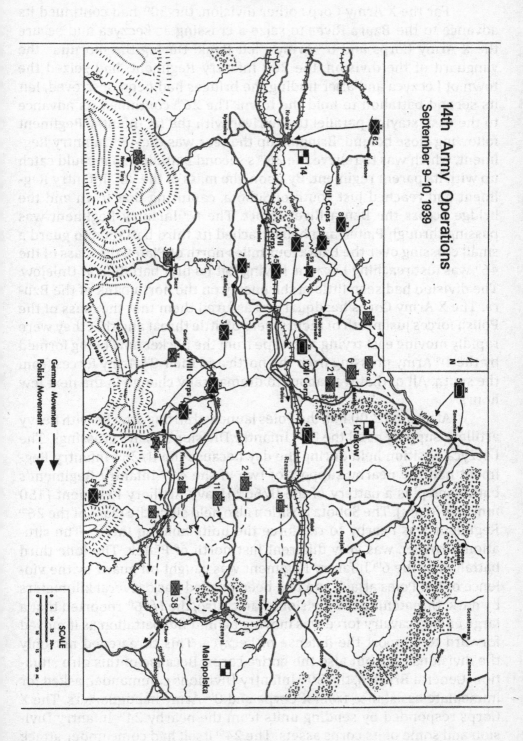

14th Army Operations
September 9-10, 1939

N

German Movement
Polish Movement

SCALE
0 5 10 15 20m
0 5 10 15 20 KL

For the X Army Corps other division, the 30th had continued its advance to the Bzura River to seize a crossing at Leczyca and secure the X Army Corps and 8th Army's left flank. During the morning, the vanguard of the division, the 26th Infantry Regiment, had seized the town of Leczyca and after finding the bridges had been destroyed, left its second battalion to hold the town. The 26th continued its advance to the east, staying parallel to the river with the 6th Infantry Regiment following close behind. Bringing up the rear was the 46th Infantry Regiment, which was to relieve the 26th's second battalion so it could catch up with its parent regiment. By noon, the mass of the 26th Infantry Regiment had reached just south of Sobota, capturing that town and the bridge across the Bzura River intact. The 6th Infantry Regiment was passing through Piatek and had detached its third battalion to guard a small crossing over the Bzura four miles north of Piatek the mass of the 46th was just reaching Leczyca, having left its first battalion at Uniejow. The division had seen little of the enemy on the north bank of the Bzura. The X Army Corps headquarters assured them that the mass of the Polish forces just north of them where of little threat and that they were rapidly moving east trying to escape from the pocket now being formed by the 4th Army pressing from the north and their 8th Army forces from the south. All of that was about to dramatically change in the next few hours.

At around 2:00 PM, the Poles launched strong attacks with heavy artillery support at all the 30th Infantry Division's Bzura crossings. The Leczyca position held during the day because the II/26th Infantry Regiment had the nearby support of two of the 46th Infantry Regiment's battalions plus a battery of the II/66th Heavy Artillery Regiment (150 mm howitzers). The Sobota position also held since the mass of the 26th Regiment was nearby to reinforce the units holding there. The situation however, was very different just north of Piatek. The lone third battalion of the 6th Infantry Regiment was caught off guard by the violence of the Poles attack and had been pushed back several kilometers by dark, threatening the divisions flank. Also, the I/46th reported that a large enemy cavalry force was moving behind the battalion as it moved forward to support the defense of Leczyca. This threatened not only the divisions rear, but also the entire corps. Because of this dire situation, General Briesen, the 30th Infantry Divisions commander, asked for immediate assistance from X Corps and 8th Army headquarters. The X Corps responded by sending units from the nearby 24th Infantry Division and some of its corps assets. The 24th itself had come under attack

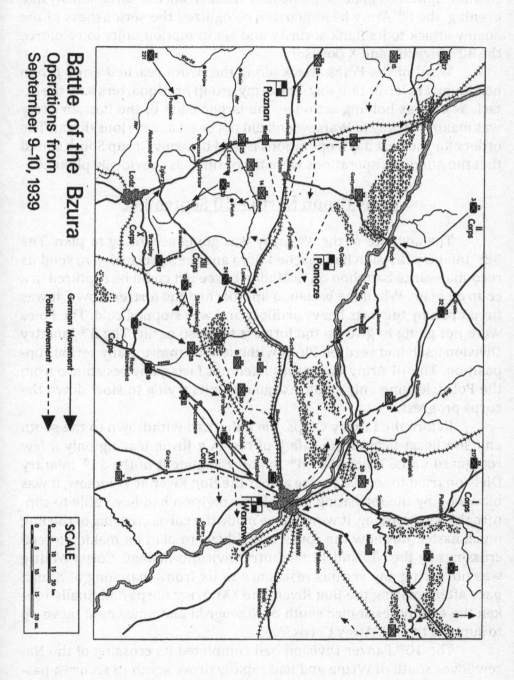

Battle of the Bzura
Operations from
September 9-10, 1939

German Movement ———
Polish Movement - - - - ▶

SCALE

0   5   10   15   20 km

0   5   10   15   20 mi.

at its Lacowiecz bridgehead, but all these attacks were easily repulsed, so there appeared to be no immediate threat from this direction. By late evening, the 8th Army headquarters recognized the seriousness of the enemy attack to its flank security and set in motion units to reinforce the 30th Division and X Corps.[21]

Word of the Poles attack along the Bzura reached army group headquarters latter that day. The army group headquarters saw the attack as only as holding action as the larger mass of the Poznan Army was making its way to Warsaw and did not see it as a serious threat. The orders for the next day's operations issued by Army Group South stated that the offensive operations were to continue as previously planned.

Army Group North – 10 September

The advance of the 4th Army was going according to plan. The 32nd Infantry Division had reached Gora and then proceeded to send its reconnaissance battalion on to Modlin to see if it could be captured in a coup de main. When the battalion approached the fortress town, it was fired upon by the forts heavy artillery and was stopped cold. The Poles were not going to give up the fortress town so easily. The 3rd Infantry Division itself had secured Plock without encountering any serious opposition. The III Army Corps was itself not facing any resistance from the Poles, leaving only small rearguard units trying to slow down the corps progress.

Before the I Army Corps, the Poles had withdrawn to the south and southeast behind the safety of the Bug River, leaving only a few rearguard units. When the 44th Infantry Regiment of the 11th Infantry Division tried to seize a bridge across the Bug River at Wyszkow, it was blown up by the retreating Poles. If the division had been able to capture this key crossing, it would have made the corps crossing of the Bug much easier. But now the corps would have to plan on making forced crossings by the 61st and 11th Infantry Divisions instead. Corps Wodrig was not facing any serious resistance to its front, marching at a high pace after crossing the Bug River. The XXI Army Corps had finally broken the enemy resistance south of Nowogrod and now could move up to support the XIX Army Corps.[22]

The 10th Panzer Division had completed its crossing of the Narew River south of Wizna and had rapidly drove south to secure a pas-

---

[21]National Archives: T312/37/7545254-7545256; Records of the 8th Army.
[22]National Archives: T312/31/7539032; Records of the 3rd Army.

sage over the Brok River at Wysokie. The panzer division could now gain the freedom of movement that General Bock had been looking for during the past few days. The only worry was that the follow up divisions only had one major road to use and that the XIX and XXI Army Corps may become entangled in their employment.

In the opinion of the army group, the Poles were going to make one more stand behind the Brest – Bug line. Some Polish forces were thought to be gathering along the Slonim – Brest line to secure the rail line for an eventual escape route and perhaps to launch a future counterattack if the opportunity presented itself. In this case, the army group ordered that the Lötzen Brigade march on Bialystok and capture the city to secure this flank. The rest of Group Brand would be used to secure the lines of communication back to East Prussia. Through information coming from air reconnaissance, it seemed much of the Polish forces were now heading east to try and avoid any encirclement. This made it more imperative for the 3rd Army to apply more pressure on the motorized forces of XIX Army Corps to move as rapidly as possible on Brest-Litvosk to close the trap. The army group was even encouraging the motorized forces to move at night.

It was noted that larger and larger areas of Polish territory were being left unguarded in the army groups rear and that the army group had very few formations it could detach for occupation duties. The 73rd Infantry Division, which had been holding in the Pomerania region, had been ordered by OKH to begin entraining to be shipped to the western front and the 23rd Infantry Division, which was already enroute to East Prussia, was about to be turned around also. The army group had intended to use the two formations for rear area occupation, but for now Army Group North could only use what odd units that were at hand (such as the border command units). It was hoped that the army high command would send some sizeable units to hold these areas until combat operations had been completed.

The intention for the next days operations for the army group were for the 4th Army's main effort to be on its south flank with Lubien as the objective. It was apparent that only weak forces opposed the 4th Army on the north bank of the Vistula, so rapid seizure of the vital bridges at Modlin should take place in the next few days. The 3rd Army would move the I Army Corps and Corps Wodrig on an advance to the Minsk-Siedlce line. The XXI Army Corps was to march on to Sniadowo and if necessary, leave one battalion in Lomza to help secure the rear. In general, all the enemy forces were in retreat. The air reconnaissance reports indicated that through the day, most enemy units were retreating towards the area between Warsaw and Siedlce. It appeared that the Poles were trying to set up a new defensive line from the Bug River to the Kamionka Lakes then south to the Dniester River to Lwow.

Army Group South – 10 September

The 1st and 2nd Mountain Divisions had succeeded in dispersing the enemy rearguard forces (composed mostly of the Polish 11th Infantry Division) in battle towards the San River in the Sanok – Javornik region. The 2nd Mountain Division had been particularly successful in capturing crossings at the San River after some fighting in Korczyra and Humniska and overwhelming the enemy units guarding the San River crossing at Jablonica. The 3rd Mountain Division was on the march from Gorlice to Jaslo. The 4th Light Division had taken Radymno (north of Przemysl) and the 2nd Panzer Division continued its steady drive towards Jaroslaw. The 2nd Panzer had the intention of capturing Jaroslaw by the end of the day, but because of the mine barriers and difficult terrain aiding the Polish rearguard units, this slowed the 2nd Panzer considerably in the morning hours. By midday, the division had finally broken free of these hindrances and, by evening the 2nd Motorized Infantry Regiment had reached the outskirts of Jaroslaw. The regiment quickly stormed the city and by 9:00 PM, had secured Jaroslaw and in the process taking many prisoners. The Poles had managed, though to destroy the San River bridge, but this did not prevent the 5th Reconnaissance Battalion of the division from getting across to the east bank of the river that night. Before dawn the 5th Reconnaissance had already probed as far as some 15 kilometers northeast of the city.[23]

Following behind the XXII Army Corps, the XVII Army Corps was rounding up numerous Polish units wondering around on its march route. The 7th Infantry Division was approaching Jodlowa and the 44th and 45th Infantry Divisions were moving through Debica and would be moving on to Rzeszow. The two divisions of the VIII Army Corps were engaged in fighting with enemy rearguard units throughout the day. After quickly building an eight-ton bridge over the Vistula River at Opatowisc, the mass of the 28th Infantry Division crossed the river and before dark had reached as far as Szczucin with its 49th Infantry Regiment. The 8th Infantry Division had seized the bridges at Nowy Korczyn and was pursuing the rapidly retreating Poles, capturing many prisoners

---

[23]National Archives: T314/595/255; Records of the XVIII Army Corps.

from the Polish 23rd Infantry Division. The VII Army Corps had reached Staszow and was marching south.

On the 10th Army's front, the 29th Motorized Division was just south of Zwolen and was continuing its drive north. The 3rd Light Division had momentarily stopped just east of Ilza and the 2nd Light Division had paused north of Kamienna before continuing its offensive north to Radom. These divisions reported an ever-increasing number of enemy soldiers being captured in and around Radom. With the XIV Army Corps, the 1st Light Division was advancing past Radom and pushing on to the Vistula River and the 13th Motorized Division had marched north of Radom heading for the town of Deblin. The IV Army Corps was following closely on the heels of both the XIV and XV Army Corps, clearing out pockets of resistance bypassed by the motorized units. The 1st Panzer Division reported that its reconnaissance battalion had seized a small bridgehead east of Gora Kalwarja across the Vistula River.

The 31st Infantry Division was at first ordered to swing to the east towards Otwock to try and seize a crossing across the Vistula River and to block any Polish forces from leaving or entering Warsaw from the south, but since the 1st Panzer Division was rapidly approaching from the south, it would be left to that division to form the blocking force there. The 31st continued its advance to link up with the 4th Panzer Division, but the heavy street fighting encountered by the 82nd Infantry Regiment at Nadarzyn delayed the division. Meanwhile, the 4th Panzer Division had removed its advance combat group from the west suburbs of Warsaw, withdrawing it through the 33rd Motorized Infantry Regiment, leaving the 33rd to screen that part of the city. The 4th Panzer Division was ordered to send the 5th Panzer Brigade to the west and northwest of the city to block any of the Polish forces from escaping the now forming Bzura pocket. The 5th Panzer Brigade attacked in the direction of Mlociny and Blonie, running into several enemy units that were trying to escape to the safety of Warsaw. The 5th Panzer Brigade destroyed and scattered all the enemy units it found in its path. The SS Leibstandarte Motorized Regiment had also joined in on this attack, covering the 4th Panzer Division's south flank. By evening, the 4th Panzer and Leibstandarte had reached a line running from Pilaszkow to just south of Kopytow.[24]

On the 8th Army's front, the vanguard of the 10th Infantry Division began the morning operations by driving up to Skierniewice in preparation of its capture. At 11:00 AM, the advance battalion moved in

---

[24]National Archives: T312/77/7596961-7596964; Records of the 10th Army.

to capture the town encountering little resistance from the enemy and along the way capturing a Polish regimental artillery commander and his whole staff with all four of the artillery batteries. However, it was not long before the battalion came under heavy artillery fire from beyond the Rawaka River to the east. With this and the stiffening resistance from the Polish infantry in front of Skierniewice, the advance ground to a halt. It was too late in the day to bring up another battalion for reinforcing the attack and the 30th Infantry Division to the west was holding the other two division's regiments back because of the setbacks earlier in the day. The 8th Army headquarters had ordered the 10th Infantry Divisions 20th Infantry Regiment, the III/10th Artillery Regiment and the II/53rd motorized Artillery Regiment to the west to help relieve pressure on the 30th Infantry Division's right flank. This effectively stopped the 10th's effort to capture Skierniewice until the crisis was settled.

The situation for the 30th Infantry Division was gradually stabilized as the day wore on. The Poles had increased the pressure on the II/26th Infantry Regiment and the I and II/46th Infantry Regiment holding Leczyca and, after several reports of Polish cavalry moving into the rear areas of their positions, the battalions retreated to just south of the town. This retreating force linked up with the 6th Machinegun Battalion. With the support of the corps heavy artillery, the battalions were then able to hold their positions for the rest of the day.

The lone III/6th Infantry Regiment had to retreat until it reached Piatek, where its sister battalions joined together to halt the advancing Polish forces threatening the divisions center. After securing the bridgehead across the Bzura at Sobota, the 26th Infantry Regiment began its move to the west to support the 6th Infantry Regiment at Piatek. By evening, the Leczyca position had been firmly secured despite the continual attacks by the Poles. However, the Piatek position had to be abandoned from the constant attacks launched against it by the Polish 2nd Infantry Division. The 6th and 26th Infantry Regiments retreated several kilometers before halting two kilometers south of Piatek. Meanwhile, the 17th Infantry Division had moved into position behind the 30th Infantry Division in case of any enemy breakthroughs.

The other division under attack, the 24th, was having little difficulty in fending off enemy attacks at its Lowicz bridgehead. Despite heavy attacks by the Polish 16th Infantry Division, the 31st and 32nd Infantry Regiments were able to hold their bridgehead positions across the Vistula. The divisions other regiment, the 102nd, was not molested at all at the bridgehead it was holding at Sochaczew.

Meanwhile, the 221st Infantry Division was moving to secure the 8th Army's open west flank between Poddebice and Leczyca. By 7:00 AM, the division's reconnaissance battalion had reached Uniejow with the mass of the division closely following behind. The reconnaissance battalion tried to move beyond Uniejow, but it ran into a strong Polish force blocking its forward movement. The divisional commander, Lieutenant General Pflugbeil, decided to wait until the two forward regiments were moved into proper attack positions before attempting a link with the 30th Infantry Division.[25]

By evening, General Blaskowitz and his staff had realized what the Poles were trying to achieve in this sudden attack on the army's north flank. They now saw that the enemy had attacked their northern flank with the force of two to three infantry divisions and two cavalry brigades from the Poznan Army. The intention of the attack appeared to be to drive past the 30th Infantry Division and to retake the city of Lodz. The 8th Army felt that the seriousness of the attack warranted not only reinforcements from what the army had itself, but was also requesting from the army group the assistance of one of the motorized corps to help deal with this threat.

The army group itself saw an opportunity in this crisis to capture or destroy this large group of Polish forces before it became too much of a further threat to future operations. The army group issued a new set of orders to become effective as of 1:00 AM on 11 September. The 10th Army was to detach the XI Army Corps from its command and move the corps to the left flank of the X Army Corps in the area of Lodz and to launch an attack towards Kutno. The 31st Infantry Division was to move in the direction of Blonie. The 213th and 221st Infantry Divisions were to be rapidly brought up to cut off any incursions by the Poles along the Ner River line. Army Groups North's III Army Corps was to bring more pressure on the retreating Polish forces down the south side of the Vistula River. All the other forces were to continue their operations as already planned.

In the afternoon, an order from the Führer directed that the Luftwaffe would direct more attacks against the city of Warsaw itself. The Luftwaffe told the army group that most of these attacks would be directed at the bridges in Warsaw across the Vistula and in the suburbs of Praga to cut off any of the enemy forces from retreating into the city from the east. The Luftwaffe added that the 4th Panzer Division and the SS Leibstandarte Regiment be withdrawn from the west edge of War-

[25]National Archives: T312/37/7545265-7545268; Records of the 8th Army..

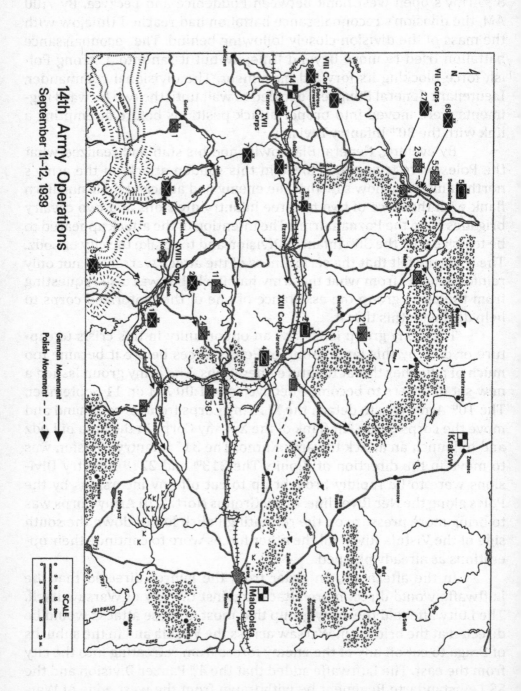

14th Army Operations
September 11-12, 1939

German Movement →
Polish Movement ⇢

SCALE
0 5 10 15 20mi.
0 5 10 15 20 25km.

saw so that these units would not be hit by stray bombs.

Army Group North – 11 September

The 4th Army was meeting more resistance by both its corps as they moved down the east and west banks of the Vistula River. The 32nd Infantry Division made an effort to quickly seize the Modlin fortress by pooling all of the division's trucks and transporting the 4th Infantry Regiment through Zackorzyn and into the approaches of Modlin. The 4th Infantry quickly deployed and launched a hasty attack, but the Poles were ready for the Germans and repelled the assault, especially with the help of the fortress heavy guns. The 4th Infantry Regiment would have to wait until the rest of the division arrived before another assault could be attempted, which would be another day because the advance of the 32nd Division was being held up by the Poles fierce defense of Plonsk. The 3rd Infantry Division had successfully captured Plock and was preparing to try and gain a bridgehead across the Vistula for future operations.

The XIX Army Corps itself was now beginning to gain its full operational freedom of movement as Bock had envisioned. The 10th Panzer Division had already reached as far as Bransk and was rapidly moving south towards Brest-Litovsk and the 3rd Panzer Division was marching hard to catch up with the 10th Panzer after crossing the Narew River. The 20th Motorized Division was in a daylong running battle with retreating Polish forces south of Zambrow. The vanguard of the division, the 76th Motorized Infantry Regiment, had to fight its way forward along the Zambrow-Czyzew route with the 69th Motorized Infantry Regiment following. The divisions other units came under attack from what appeared to be broken groups of the Polish 18th Infantry Division from the west and cavalry forces from the east. These attacks were easily repulsed, but the divisional staff was worried about larger groups of the enemy may be roaming in its rear areas. But the XIX Army Corps headquarters assured the division that it should not worry about the flanks and to continue its attack to the south. By the afternoon, the division had cleared Zambrow of any remaining enemy forces and to help secure the divisions flanks. The 3rd and 10th Panzer Divisions sent reinforcements in the form of two motorized rifle battalions, one tank battalion and one artillery battalion towards the 20th's eastern flank. The XXI Army Corps diverted the 206th Infantry Division to cover the 20th's west flank around the Brok River. This seemed to have smashed any

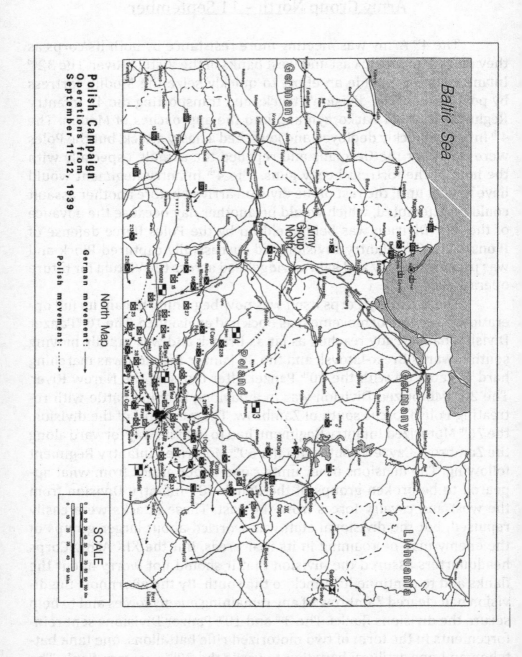

Polish Campaign
Operations from
September 11-12, 1939

German movement: →
Polish movement: ⇢

North Map

SCALE

of the remaining Polish forces that were on the loose around the Zambrow region. Meanwhile, the Lehr Reconnaissance Battalion that had been attached to the 20th Motorized Division, had moved ahead of the 76th Motorized Infantry Regiment to the Bug River crossing at Tonkiele, where the Lehr found that the bridge was still intact, but guarded by a small Polish unit. Unfortunately for the Germans, the Poles destroyed the bridge later in the day, dashing any hopes of capturing the bridge in a coup de main. However, the 20th's own reconnaissance battalion had already seized a railroad bridge at Siemiatyose at the Bug and was proceeding south. Towards the evening hours, elements of Polish forces were reported to be 6 kilometers north of Czyzew trying to fight their way south back to their own lines, but they were dealt with by sending back a battalion of the 76th Motorized Infantry Regiment and these enemy units were quickly rounded up by the battalion. The 20th Motorized Division finally secured the road between Zambrow and Czyzew, freeing the division to proceed south the next day.

The XIX Army Corps requested that the XXI Army Corps infantry divisions be sent over to help clear out any other Polish forces that might still be wandering in the rear areas so that its motorized forces could move forward and not have to worry about sending any units back. This would mean however, leaving a significant gap between the 3rd Army and the XIX Army Corps. But to the army group, this was deemed an acceptable risk since no significant enemy forces were detected between the region of Bielsk Podolaski and Siedlce. There was going to be a gradual shift eastward by both army groups over the next couple of days, hence the problem would solve itself.[26]

The Lötzen Brigade had encountered large groups of Polish stragglers and that was slowing its effort to catch up with the motorized units of XIX Army Corps. The army group was worried that these roaming groups of enemy units would hinder the operations of the XIX Corps, since this was to be the main supply route for that corps.

The army group requested that OKH give a clear demarcation line for both army groups east of the Vistula, since both forces were rapidly closing in on that area east of Warsaw. OKH responded by giving Army Group North responsibility of the areas north of the line running from Warsaw to Lublin to Brest-Litovsk and Army Group South would take everything south of this line. Of course, OKH reminded both army groups this demarcation line would shift according to the outcome of future operations.

[26]National Archives: T314/611/639-642; Records of the XIX Army Corps.

The intentions for the army group for the next day's operations were for the III Army Corps to focus its main attack in the direction of Lubin – Kutno. The II Army Corps should continue to close in on Warsaw and Modlin from the north and northwest. The 32nd and 217th Infantry Divisions were to continue offensive operations while the 218th Infantry Division would now be tasked with masking the Modlin fortress. The XIX Army Corps was to continue its advance in the general direction of Brest-Litovsk. The 2nd Motorized Division was to move on through Kolno and on to Lomza, the 23rd Infantry Division was to move through Szsuzycyn and on to Stawiski. The 21st and 206th Infantry Divisions were to halt movement for the moment to allow the motorized divisions passage, moving south across their front. The Lötzen Brigade would be transferred back to under the command of Group Brand, so as to help facilitate the capture of Bialystok to secure the XIX Army Corps flank.

In an overall assessment of the enemy, there seemed to be little organized resistance of forces beyond the division level east of Warsaw and that elsewhere on the army group's front the Poles were in a general retreat.

Army Group South – 11 September

The 8th Army had begun preparations to counterattack against the enemy forces that had attacked its left flank the two previous days. For the divisions of X corps, it was still a tough day of defensive fighting and stabilizing its front. The 30th Infantry Division had to pull back from its defensive positions because of the unrelenting pressure the Poles had brought on the division. The division set up new defensive positions between Ozorkow, Biala and Strykow. Around 12:55 PM, the Poles launched a concentrated attack of two to three battalions against the 46th Infantry Regiment at Sierpow, but this attack was repulsed. The rest of the day the Poles seemed to be content to bombard the division with artillery. The 17th Infantry Division had now formed on the 30th's left flank and had launched its attack toward Ozorkow by late afternoon. The divisions 21st Infantry Regiment had captured Ozorkow by evening. The regiment was subjected to several counterattacks that night by the Polish 25th Infantry Division bent on taking back the town, but all their efforts were unsuccessful.

The XIII Army Corps itself had already by the afternoon launched its attack on the Polish eastern flank. The 10th Infantry Division first

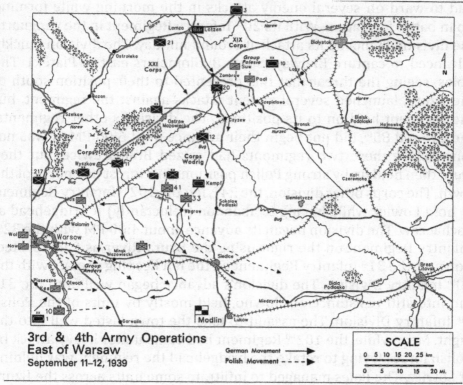

3rd & 4th Army Operations
East of Warsaw
September 11–12, 1939

German Movement →
Polish Movement →→→

SCALE

0 5 10 15 20 25 km

0 5 10 15 20 Mi.

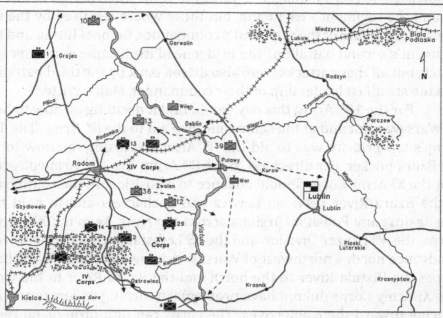

10th Army Operations
September 11–12, 1939

German Movement →
Polish Movement →→→

SCALE

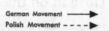

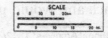

had to ward off several enemy attacks in the morning while forming up in battle formation. With its 20th Infantry Regiment in the vanguard, the division launched its attack at around midday. The division quickly advanced to capture Bielway (some 8 kilometers east of Piatek). The Poles, seeing the threat that this presented to their position south of the Bzura, launched several violent attacks against the regiment, but the regiment held on to its positions. The division's other regiments, the 41st and 85th, did not begin their advance until 6:00 PM. It was not long before these two regiments had seized Braloszewice, but they were then held up by strong Polish positions in a forest just north of the town. The corps other division, the 24th, left the 102nd Infantry Regiment to hold Lowicz while having to abandon (reluctantly) it bridgehead at Sochaczew. The division began its advance about 4:00 PM with the 32nd Infantry Regiment on the right using the Bzura River as flank protection and, the 31st Infantry Regiment on the left keeping contact with the 10th Infantry Division. The division's advance began well until the 31st ran into stiff resistance at Glowno, held mostly by units of the Polish 4th Infantry Division. The assault to take the town lasted well into the night. Meanwhile, the 102nd Regiment had come under heavy attack by Polish forces trying to retake the bridgehead the regiment was holding at Lowicz. The Poles managed to infiltrate some units across the Bzura around the regiment's east flank, but these where repulsed by the energetic leadership of the regiment's commander, Colonel Rittau and the regiment's second battalion. The bridgehead itself came under serious attack, but all these attacks were also driven back by the third battalion and the steadfast leadership of their commander, Major Witte.[27]

For the 10th Army, this day would find it deciding on how to hold its Warsaw front and at the same time give aid to the 8th Army. The 10th Army's top priority was to aid the 8th Army in closing the now forming Bzura pocket. For direct aid to the 8th Army, the 10th Army directed that the XI Army Corps should advance to a position on the south bank of the Bzura River between Lowicz and Sochaczew and to hold this line against any Polish incursions across the river. As to the XVI Army Corps, the 4th Panzer Division and the SS Leibstandarte Regiment were to advance north – northwest of Warsaw driving any enemy units back across the Vistula River to the north and the Bzura River to the west. The XI Army Corps did not have problems in turning its forces and advancing toward their objectives. The corps ran into little or no resistance and would probably close in on the Bzura by the next day. After

---

[27]National Archives: T312/37/7545494-7549496; Records of the 8th Army.

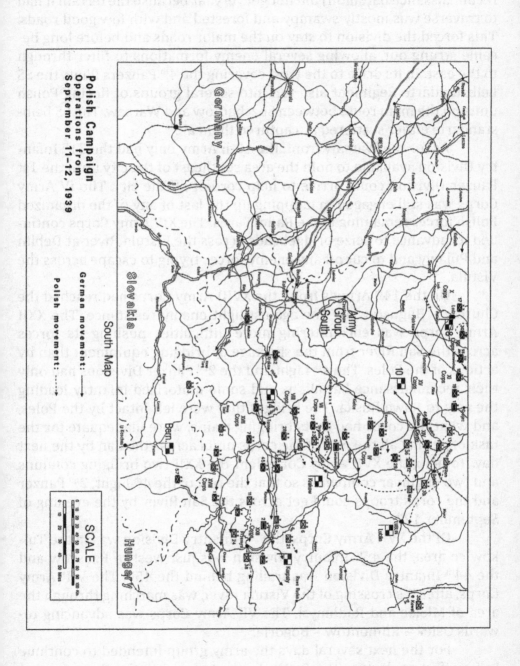

Polish Campaign
Operations from
September 11-12, 1939

German movement:

Polish movement:

South Map

SCALE

0 10 20 30 40 50 Miles

0 10 20 30 40 50 60 70 80 90 100 Kls.

reforming its forces for its advance, the 4th Panzer Division (minus its reconnaissance battalion) did not get very far because the terrain it had to traverse was mostly swampy and forested and with few good roads. This forced the division to stay on the major roads and before long became strung out, allowing several enemy formations to filter through to the east. In its drive to the west covering the 4th Panzers flank, the SS Leibstandarte Regiment also ran into several groups of fleeing Polish units on the main route between Sozchaczow and Warsaw. The SS Leibstandarte either scattered or captured them all.[28]

As for the Warsaw front, the 10th Army only had the 31st Infantry Division available to hold the area southeast of the city until the 1st Panzer Division could arrive to help cordon off the city. The IV Army Corps was still engaged in mopping up the last of any of the organized Polish forces remaining in the Radom area. The XIV Army Corps continued its advance to seize bridgeheads across the Vistula River at Deblin and Pulawy and to cut off any enemy forces trying to escape across the Vistula.

On the 14th Army's front, the XVIII Army Corps had reached the Churow – Bugustowska line against light enemy resistance. The XXII Army Corps was encountering more difficulties pushing its forces across the San River from the shortage of bridging equipment than by actions of the Poles. The 4th Light and the 2nd Panzer Divisions had only their reconnaissance battalions and some motorized infantry leading the way to Rawa Ruska. The bridges that were left intact by the Poles, and what the corps had in its bridging trains, were inadequate for the task of getting all the rest of the corps units across the San by the next day. To help, the XVII Army Corps lent the XXII two bridging columns and two engineer companies so that the rest of the 4th Light, 2nd Panzer and the corps troops could get across the San River by the evening of September 12th.

Of the XVII Army Corps, the 7th Infantry Division was in the Tulkowice area, the 45th Infantry Division was just west of Rzeszow and the 44th Infantry Division was trailing behind the 45th. The VIII Army Corps, after it's crossing of the Vistula River, was marching through the area of Mielec and Radomysl. The VII Army Corps was advancing towards Osiek – Klimontow – Bogorja.

For the next several days the army group intended to continue in its effort to destroy the Polish forces trapped in the Bzura pocket and to mask the city of Warsaw until adequate forces could be brought

[28]National Archives: T312/77/7596964-7596967; Records of the 10th Army.

up to take the city. The 29th Motorized and 1st Light Divisions were to be brought up from the 10th Army to assist the 8th Army to clear the Bzura pocket. The 10th Army was to continue its offensive operations toward the Krasnik – Lublin area past the Vistula River and to prevent formations of the Polish Army from escaping across the Vistula River. The 14th Army was to continue its advance by crossing the San River with the XXII Army Corps in the lead on the left flank thrusting towards Tomaszow and Rawa Ruska. The XVIII Army Corps was to advance past the San River with an eye on capturing the city of Lwow. It was noted that some of the combat units had been engaged in constant combat since the beginning of the campaign and that they were in need of a short period when the troops could be rested, material was in need of reconditioning and there were some critical shortage of some provisions. Only the swift destruction of the Polish forces west of the Vistula River could give the requisite pause that was needed.

For the overall enemy situation, the Poles were still trying to get as many of their forces east of the Vistula River to form a new defensive line based on the Bug and Dniester River lines. On the 10th Army's front, there were still pockets of resistance at about regimental strength in the Kamienna – Konskie – Jedlinsk region. The enemy forces that attacked the 8th Army appeared to be about the strength of two infantry divisions and two cavalry brigades. These forces seemed to be screening the movement of the larger Polish forces that had escaped from the Poznan region. The enemy forces before the 14th Army remained unchanged. The rail traffic east of the San and Vistula Rivers was substantially smaller than the previous three days and this was brought about in no small part by the constant air attacks by the Luftwaffe on key transportation nodes. Also, the presence of enemy aircraft had significantly subsided.

Army Group North – 12 September

The 3rd Army was now rapidly advancing south. In the morning, Corps Wodrig was approaching Siedlce and would be at the Siedlce road by the next day. Panzer Division Kempf, forming the outer flank for the 3rd Army, had now moved through Wegrow and Kaluzyn. The division turned to the west after passing through Kaluzyn to try and cut off any Polish forces trying to escape from the 3rd Army. Panzer Division Kempf would continue its drive to Garwolin by the end of the day if possible. The 1st Cavalry Brigade also turned west towards Warsaw to

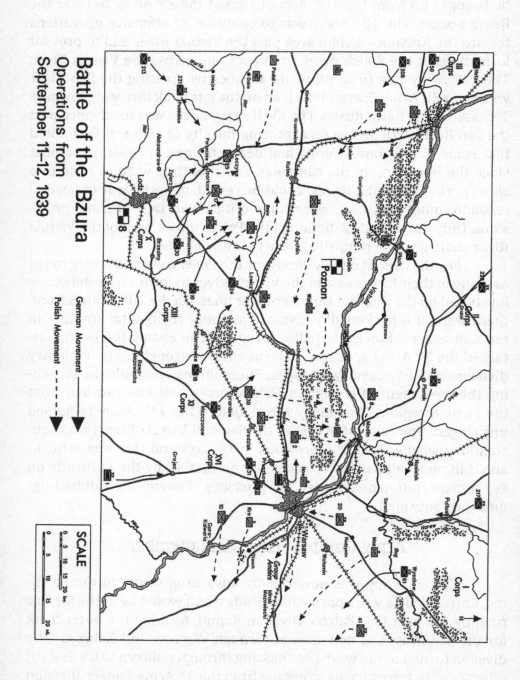

Battle of the Bzura
Operations from
September 11–12, 1939

German Movement
Polish Movement

SCALE

0   5   10   15   20 km

0   5   10   15   20 mi.

cover the 3rd Army's flank against any enemy forces that might try and attack out of Warsaw. The 10th Panzer Division had pressed forward to reach within 40 kilometers of Brest-Litovsk and the 3rd Panzer Division was rapidly moving to catch up with the 10th Panzer Division.

While continuing its drive to the south, the 20th Motorized Division (with the assistance of units of the 10th Panzer Division) had to forcibly eject some retreating Polish units from its path along the Rosochate and Krzeczkowo route in the morning. At first it looked as though the enemy was going to put up a fight, but with the appearance of tanks from the I/8th Panzer Regiment the enemy scattered only after firing a few shots. Later that morning, the division ran into more Polish stragglers trying to make their way back to their own lines. The 76th Infantry Regiment was set upon by these enemy forces along the Czyzew – Ciehanowiec route, but the 20th Motorized Division's 120th Reconnaissance Battalion turned back and assisted in routing the Poles. By the afternoon, the 20th had transferred the 8th Panzer Regiment and the three battalions 86th Infantry Regiment back to the 10th Panzer Division after the corps became satisfied that there was no more danger from other stray Polish units wondering in the rear areas. The 20th Motorized however, came under artillery fire from its right flank later that day and the 20th was not sure if this was enemy or friendly fire. After several radio messages and a personal reconnaissance by a staff officer from the XIX Army Corps headquarters in a Fiesler Storch, it was found that it was indeed units of the XXI Army Corps having mistaken the 20th Motorized for enemy forces. This was the 206th Infantry Division coming over to cover the XIX Army Corps flank.[29]

Because of this friendly fire incident, the 21st and 206th Infantry Divisions were ordered through the XXI Corps headquarters not to advance beyond the Zambrow – Siedlce road until all the units of the 20th Motorized Division had moved through and beyond Czyzew. Because of this order, the 206th Infantry Division remained fairly inactive this day except for rounding up disparate groups of Polish stragglers. The 21st Infantry Division was also mopping up remnants of what was left of the Polish 18th Infantry Division in a forest outside of Czerwony Bor. The division then moved south to the Ostrow – Mazowiecka – Zambrow road, picking up more enemy stragglers along the way.[30]

In the afternoon, a message from OKH confirmed that the III Army Corps would be placed under tactical control of the 8th Army until

[29]National Archives: T314/611/643-648; Records of the XIX Army Corps.
[30]National Archives: T314/660/65-66; Records of the XXI Army Corps.

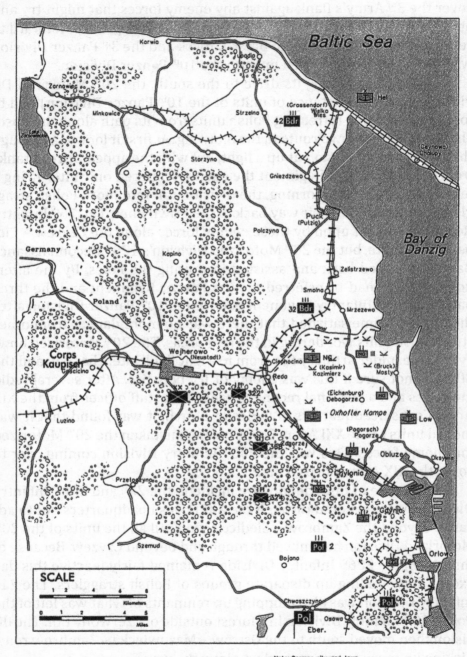

Offensive of the First Borderguard Command

German and Polish positions
Morning of
September 12, 1939

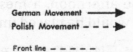

German Movement →
Polish Movement - - →
Front line - - - -

Note: German city and town names are in parentheses.

the encircled Poles at Kutno (the Bzura pocket) had been destroyed. The 3rd Infantry Division was to block the crossing at Plock while the other two divisions of II Army Corps move to block Modlin and to seal off the northern perimeter of Warsaw.

The intention of the army group for the next day's operations were to have the I Army Corps and Corps Wodrig to seal off the eastern perimeter around Warsaw. The I Army Corps would turn west towards Warsaw at Minsk Mazowiecka to isolate Warsaw on its eastern side. The Corps Wodrig would pivot to the southeast at Siedlce and seal off Warsaw along the lower Vistula River. The XIX Army Corps would continue its offensive towards Brest-Litovsk and the XXI Army Corps would be tasked to advance towards Bialystok.

The only cohesive enemy units still identified before the 4th Army were the rearguard forces of the Polish 15th Infantry Division. The only identified units between the 4th and 8th Armies were the Polish 14th, 17th, 25th and 26th Infantry Divisions and the Wielpolska and Kresowa Cavalry Brigades. Before the II Army Corps the enemy situation remained unclear, except the Modlin fortress appeared to be occupied by remnants of the Polish 8th Infantry Division. Before the 3rd Army, the I Army Corps and Group Wodrig had only about one organized infantry division and a cavalry brigade and several disorganized infantry brigades. These forces appeared to be the remnants of the Polish 4th, 19th, 28th and 29th Infantry Divisions. Before the XXI and XIX Army Corps only the remnants of the Polish 18th Infantry Division had been encountered.

Army Group South – 12 September

The night of 11/12 September passed quietly for the 8th Army. For the beginning of this day's operations, the XI Army Corps front was situated along the Zyradow – Skierniewice rail line. The XIII Army Corps was in general forward of the Lowicz – Zgierz road with the 24th Infantry Division west of Bogozna and the 10th Infantry Division just west of Glowno. The X Army Corps was holding the line from Zgierz to Braloszewwice and the 221st Infantry Division was in position at Poddebice.

The X Army Corps spent this day resting and consolidating its positions and preparing for the resumption of offensive operations. The Poles launched several small attacks across the corps front during the day, but these were all easily thrown back. The only real excitement of the day for the corps was a frantic inquiry from the 8th Army head-

quarters about a reported breakthrough by enemy forces around Strykow towards Lodz. The corps commander, General Ulex, sent a message back to army headquarters that their staff had no indication of an
enemy breakthrough in that sector. To make sure though, General Ulex
sent staff officer Colonel Adelhoch to personally check on the situation
at Strykow. After arriving on the scene and assessing the situation, he
radioed back that all was well in that sector. Apparently, the problem
began when units of the 6th Machinegun Battalion were pulling out of
the line so that the 10th Infantry Divisions 85th Infantry Regiment could
take over this section of the line. The 85th was slow in taking over the
new positions, so this left a gap in the line for a few hours. The air reconnaissance for 8th Army had detected the backward movement of the
6th Machinegun Battalion and mistook it for an advancing Polish column
moving down the road to Lodz. General Ulex sent Colonel Adelhoch's
report back to a much-relieved 8th Army headquarters.[31]

For the XIII Army Corps, one division had a day of little activity while the other was engaged in some desperate defensive battles.
The 24th Infantry Division, rather reluctantly, abandoned its positions
at Lowisz to contract the corps defensive line some four miles south to
a new position between Domaniewice and Belchow. The Poles made
no serious effort to hinder this movement. For the 10th Infantry Division, the situation was much more serious. All day long the Poles con-
tinuously attacked the line held by the 41st Infantry Regiment and in
the afternoon the 85th was subjected to numerous assaults as well. One
particularly vicious battle saw one village change hands no less than
five times during the course of the day. Only the exceptional leadership
shown by the battalion and company commanders kept the troops fo-
cused on the task at hand, despite the mayhem around them. By nightfall both regiments were exhausted. Much to the division's relief, the
20th Infantry Regiment was transferred back to the division after being under temporary command of the 24th Infantry Division. For the
divisions of the XVI Army Corps, it was another day of simultaneous-
ly trying to hold its defensive positions against escaping Polish forces,
while attempting to close off the Bzura pocket to the east. The 1st Panzer Division continued its advance north, attacking and dispersing several enemy units from the Polish 10th Infantry Division that was moving
across its front making for the Vistula River. The 31st Infantry Divisions
82nd Infantry Regiment fought a particularly desperate defensive battle
west of Warsaw against a mixed force of Polish infantry and tanks mov-

---

[31]National Archives: T314/441/958-959; Records of the X Army Corps.

ing out of Mokotow to the south. The 82nd had to call in help from the just departed 33rd motorized Infantry Regiment, which arrived in time to hold back the enemy and destroying some eighteen of the attackers twenty-four armored vehicles.[32] For the 4th Panzer Division and the SS Leibstandarte motorized Infantry Regiment, it was also a seesaw battle of attempting to advance while aiding the 31st Infantry Division in trying to hold its positions west of Warsaw. As it advanced on Blonie, the SS Leibstandarte had to extend its left flank more than two kilometers to reestablish contact with the 31st Division. The Poles tried to keep this corridor open to aid their comrades in escaping the noose tightening around them. The Poles launched several attacks, but they were all driven back. Later in the day the 17th Infantry Regiment, on a request from the XVI Corps, advanced north to link up with the SS Leibstandarte at Pruszkow to help seal this gap. The 4th Panzer Divisions advance was made difficult by having to parcel out several of its battalions to help with the corps emergencies throughout the entire front. By evening, most the crises had been handled and it was hoped that the division could gather itself back together to continue the advance to the north and northwest by the next day.

Lastly, for the XI Army Corps, the 18th Infantry Divisions drive to the Bzura River was slowed by some well-placed Polish machinegun nests in the forest north of Skierniewice. By the end of the day, though, the 18th was closing in on Lowicz and the 19th Infantry Division was keeping pace on the 18th's right flank with only light resistance to its front.[33]

For the 10th Army, the effort to clear out what was left of the enemy forces in the Radom area was wrapped up this day. Only the XIV Army Corps divisions faced any significant enemy forces in the final sweep of this area. The 1st Light Division had trapped some Polish formations in a forest northwest of Kozienice and fought a daylong battle to clear them out. Only some stragglers appeared to be deeper in the forest and they would be rounded up the next day. The 13th Motorized Division was engaged in rounding up disparate enemy forces south of the Kozienice – Radom road, bringing in some 600 prisoners.

The IV Army Corps set about its mission for the day, to round up any stray Polish formations in its area, and then advance on to the Vistula River to seize bridgeheads and then to carry out any further operations that may be needed east of the river. The 4th Infantry Divi-

---

[32]The 33rd motorized Infantry Regiment had been placed under the command of the 4th Panzer Division from the 13th Motorized Division on 4 September..
[33]National Archives: T312/37/7545351 and 7545499; Records of the 8th Army

sions reconnaissance battalion managed to cross the Vistula and seize the town of Annopol some 20 miles east of Ostrowiec after a brief fight with the Polish forces guarding the bridge. By the end of the day, the divisions I/10th Infantry Regiment had crossed the river setting up a defense perimeter against any Polish counterattacks and had sent the division's reconnaissance battalion probing east of Annopol.

At first, the XV Army Corps was going to be sent to the southeast on the 10th Army's southern flank and placed under the command of the 14th Army. However, by midday this order had been rescinded and the 3rd Light and 29th Motorized Divisions were now to be sent to help with the 8th Army's crisis at the Bzura. General Hoth, the corps commander, quickly contacted the divisional commanders (Major General Kuntzen for the 3rd Light and Lieutenant General Lemelson for the 29th) and worked out new march routes for their new destinations.[34]

By the afternoon, the 10th Army reported to army group headquarters it had completed the destruction of the Polish forces around the Radom area and had reportedly captured 52,000 men, 130 artillery pieces, 38 armored vehicles and large numbers of machineguns and rifles. Because enemy resistance in front of the 10th Army seemed to be getting weaker and weaker, most of the 10th Army's motorized divisions were to be diverted back to the fighting at the Bzura pocket. Only the 13th Motorized Division and the IV Army Corps were to continue the offensive to the east beyond the Vistula River for now.[35]

The 14th Army's pursuit of the Polish forces continued unabated. The VII Army Corps was moving up to the Vistula River and preparing for its crossing. The VIII Army Corps was making rapid marches against slight enemy resistance and would be north of Rzezow by evening. The XVII Army Corps was also making rapid progress and anticipated in marching through Rzezow by the end of the day. The army's vanguard, the XXII Army Corps, was making excellent progress after completing its crossing of the San River with the 4th Light Division at Krakowice and the 2nd Panzer Division moving past Lubaczow. The SS Germania motorized Infantry Regiment would close up behind to secure the bridgehead at Jaroslow by the end of the day.

The XVIII Army Corps was encountering more enemy resistance in its advance to the east. The 1st Mountain Division advanced motorized combat group had driven past Churow and Sambor and it expected to reach the outskirts of Lwow by early next morning. The divisions

---

[34]National Archives: T314/550/254-255; Records of the XV Army Corps
[35]National Archives: T312/77/7596967-7596970; Records of the 10th Army.

other combat and rear services were battling elements of broken Polish formations trying to elude capture along its march route between Sanok and Churow. The division estimated that there was the equivalent of about three Polish divisions as far back as Sanok still trying to make their way east to avoid capture. The 1st Mountain Division also reported that the physical damage inflicted by the Luftwaffe's attacks on various towns and sections of rail lines on its march route was particularly impressive. Even more impressive was that captured Polish troops confessed to being greatly frightened and confused after attacks by the Luftwaffe's forces bombing and strafing. The 2nd Mountain Division was encountering the same problems that the 1st Mountain was also having in trying to reach Przemysl. Many enemy groups were trying to regain their lines and in consequence, the rear service units of the 2nd Mountain were under constant threat from these roaming groups of Polish stragglers. During the day, the I/137th Mountain Infantry Regiment was sent back to help maintain order and to fend off attacking enemy units along the divisions lines of communication.[36]

For the continuation of the next day's operations, the army group directed that the 8th Army was to continue its offensive operations to destroy the remains of the Polish forces trapped in the Bzura pocket. Also detailed to support the 8th Army's effort, the Flieger Führer Zbv[37] under the command of General Richthoven, was placed under the 8th to give direct air support. The 10th Army would continue its offensive with its remaining forces in pursuit of Polish forces east of the Vistula River towards the Lublin – Krasnik region. The 14th Army would continue its thrust towards Lwow and to move major forces to the Polish – Rumanian border to prevent the escape of enemy forces in that direction. Also, reserve forces were to be kept close at hand in the south for pacification of the Galacia region when the fighting was over. Also of note, OKH ordered that the 3rd Mountain and 62nd Infantry Divisions were to be placed in the army high command reserves until further notice.

By the estimate of the army group's staff, the enemy situation before the 14th Army seemed to have remained unchanged. The 8th Army still faced a large Polish force in the Bzura pocket, now estimated to be about four to five infantry divisions and two cavalry brigades in strength. The road and rail traffic east of the San and Vistula River was substantially smaller than the previous week and there was no noticeable traffic in the Lwow – Stanislov – Brody region indicating that

---

[36]National Archives: T314/595/256-257; Records of the XVIII Army Corps.
[37]Zbv: zu besonder verband – on special duty.

the Poles had just about exhausted any reserves they might have in the area. In addition, the Polish Air Force's sorties had greatly diminished.

Chapter 5

Combat Operations 13th – 28th September
The Annihilation

<u>Army Group North – 13 September</u>

Because of the changing operational needs of the 3rd and 4th Armies, OKH gave orders to the army group to pass control of the II Army Corps, with its corps and army troops, from the 4th Army to the 3rd Army as of midnight 12 September. The 4th Army had begun moving its headquarters staff to East Prussia to assume command of the XXI Army Corps, Group Brand and the 23rd Infantry Division. With this arrangement, the army group would have a strong eastern wing to protect its eastern flank. With these new adjustments to the command structure and order of battle, the army group adjusted its forces directions with the aim of trapping Polish forces east of the Polish capital. The 3rd Army would concentrate its forces more to the east of Warsaw, leaving only minor forces to mask Modlin and the north of Warsaw for now. The 3rd Army would wheel its major forces to pivot at Siedlce then move southwesterly towards Garwolin and, thence, to the Vistula River where it could link up with the forces of Army Group South to encircle Warsaw.

To help with the flank security for the XIX Army Corps, the XXI Army Corps was ordered to move towards Bielsk and Bialystok to cover the XIX Army Corps left flank. Group Brand, along with the 23rd Infantry Division, was to drive towards Bialystok itself to secure that region. Group Brand though, first had to subdue the fort at Ossoweic on the Narew River, which was occupied by the Poles, before it could move on. In the Czerwony Bor region, the XIX Army Corps was still engaged in a running battle in its rear area with remnants of the Polish 18th Infantry Division. The XIX Corps wanted to quickly eliminate this threat so it could move the 20th and 2nd Motorized Divisions forward to the corps next objective, Brest-Litovsk. It required the entire day for both divisions and the 206th Infantry Division to round up the Polish stragglers. An example of the problems it was causing the corps became clear when, that morning, one of the 206th Division's field kitchens was set upon by a roaming band of Polish troops. Two German soldiers were wounded before the Poles were driven off. By the end of the day, the Germans had captured about 5,000 – 6,000 Poles with large numbers of weapons, vehicles, horses and other equipment. However, some groups

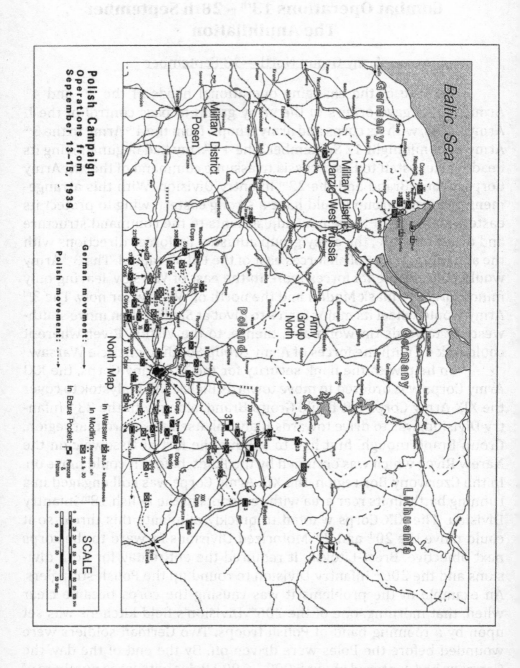

of Polish cavalry managed to breakthrough to the east.[1]

Now only 35 kilometers northwest of Brest-Litovsk, the 10th Panzer Division paused at the town of Wysokie Litewskie, severing the main rail line between Belsk Podlaski and Brest-Litovsk. The division, not finding any significant Polish forces towards its front, sent its reconnaissance battalion to the southeast probing for any sign of major Polish formations. The reconnaissance battalion drove all the way to the Lesna River a few kilometers north of Brest reporting that the bridge was still intact and there was no sign of Polish forces. Even though it appeared that the way was clear to the city, the division's commander, General Schaal, held the mass of the 10th Panzer around Wysokie Liteskie to await the arrival of the rest of the XIX Corps divisions.[2]

Meanwhile, the 3rd Army's corps continued to tighten its grip on the Polish capital. Panzer Division Kempf struggled during the day in its effort to cut off retreating Polish forces moving south and trying to reach the Vistula River. The panzer division had moved far ahead of the rest of Corps Wodrig leaving a gap of about 30 kilometers between it and the corps two infantry divisions. This was allowing Polish formations an escape route to the south. The division itself had a hard time holding its own area against infiltrating Polish units and protecting its own lines of communication. The Corps Wodrig ordered Panzer Division Kempf to regroup and hold only the major roads leading to the southeast from Warsaw, while a reinforced infantry regiment from the 1st Infantry Division would force march towards the panzer division to close the gap. This stopgap measure did not stop the Poles from filtering through the German lines, especially on the night of September 13th/14th. Only the arrival of substantial infantry forces from the 1st and 12th Infantry Divisions could put up an effective barrier to staunch the flow.

Meanwhile, the I Army Corps was in a running battle with Polish forces between Minsk- Mazowiecki and Wolomin. The Poles were throwing up large cavalry screens east of Warsaw to try and slow down the advance of the 11th and 61st Infantry Divisions progress. Even with this, the two divisions still pushed forward closing to within 25 kilometers of Warsaw. The 11th Infantry Division reported on capturing large amounts of war material still loaded on rail cars along the Minsk-Mazowieki to Siedlce rail line. This included several artillery batteries and ammunition.

---

[1] National Archives: T314/611/655-658; Records of the XIX Army Corps
[2] National Archives: T314/611/655-658; Records of the XIX Army Corps.

The 4th Army, now left with only two corps under its command, continued to apply pressure on the Polish forces around Modlin and the Bzura Pocket. The II Army Corps had successfully gained bridgeheads across the Narew River with the 32nd Infantry Division crossing at Debe and the 217th Infantry Division crossing at Serock. The Poles, fearing that the Germans were heading straight towards Warsaw, tried to stop both divisions by bringing up reinforcements from their 8th and 20th Infantry Divisions, launched several attacks against the Germans during the day. All these attacks, however, failed to stop the Germans progress towards the south.[3]

Army Group South – 13 September

The divisions of the 14th Army continued to apply pressure on the Poles across a broad front in the hope that this would pin down the major enemy formations in large pockets that were forming around Przemysl and those north of the San River. With the deep thrusts of the XXII and XVIII Corps, the army group was certain that these Polish formations could be caught and destroyed before they could escape to the east.

Late on the evening of 12 September, the spearhead of the 1st Mountain Division had reached the outskirts of Lwow. The battlegroup commander, Colonel Schörner, who commanded the 99th Mountain Regiment and two battalions of the 98th Mountain Regiment, called together the battalion leaders during the night to discuss what to do the next day. The colonel and the battalion commanders decided that the battlegroup was too weak to seize Lwow by itself directly and that the best course of action would be to wait until the rest of the division arrived. Meanwhile the battlegroup would move to north of the city to block its northerly approaches so as to block any Polish reinforcements from arriving from that direction. Colonel Schörner radioed the division headquarters with the next day's plans and the division sent back its approval for his course of action.

For the assault, Colonel Schörner, divided his command into three groups: the first under Schörner himself, with the I and II/99th Mountain Regiment, the II/98th Mountain Regiment and the 1/85th Engineer Battalion, would lead the attack around the north of the city, while Group Kress, with the III/98th and III/99th Mountain Regiments, would follow and Group Franck with the rest of the battlegroups forc-

[3]National Archives: T314/81/232-234; Records of the II Army Corps.

es would hold the western approaches of the city. The attack moved out at 7:00 AM, with Schörners group rapidly taking the villages of Lewandowka and Bogdarovka, crossing the major Lwow-Janow highway and by 9:30 AM, it had approached its first major obstacle, the Steinburg heights. The Poles certainly knew the importance of holding these heights to keep the northern approaches open to their forces to the north. When Schörner launched the attack on the heights, at 10:15 AM, his forward units did not get far, as the Poles fought them to a standstill. While additional firepower in the form of artillery and flak guns were brought up to help breakthrough to the other side of the heights, Colonel Schörner ordered the groups left flank battalion, the II/98th, to try and maneuver around the north side of the Polish positions where the Steinburg heights ended. The attack on the Steinburg renewed at 1:30 PM with the Poles putting up a terrific fight, but eventually Schörners group managed to push the Poles off the heights gaining for the Germans the heights dominating all the Polish positions north and northwest of Lwow.

Meanwhile, the outflanking maneuver of the II/98th Mountain Regiment was more successful than Colonel Schörner thought it would be. The battalion had moved some 1.5 kilometers northwest and then east. Major Picker, the battalion commander, had expected more resistance to his front by the Poles. But they only encountered some enemy outposts and, by the late afternoon, had made it to the open plain north of the city. Then Picker's battalion quickly moved east to secure the two major highways running north out of Lwow by occupying the towns of Holosko Wielk and Zboiska. By the time the Poles had realized that these two towns were taken, the II/98th was firmly in positions in and around both Holosko Wielk and Zboiska. All subsequent attacks by the Poles during the day to retake them failed. With nightfall all the counterattacks by the Poles had stopped along the perimeter of Schörner's battlegroup.

The XVIII Corps' other division, the 2nd Mountain, was making its approach march to the San River, below Przemysl, and was hoping to cross the river by the next day. With the 7th Infantry making a direct attack on Przemysl from the west and pinning down the Polish forces around the city, it was hoped that the 2nd Mountain Division could outflank the Poles from the south, thereby, making their positions untenable.

To the north of XVIII Army Corps, the XXII Army Corps continued in its drive north to link up with the forces of Army Group North.

The 4th Light Division captured Rawa Ruska in the morning hours cutting the major road between Lwow and Lublin. By evening, the division had traveled some 60 kilometers in one day with the vanguard units arriving at the town of Mircze just short of the Bug River. The 2nd Panzer Division had rapidly moved forward also, arriving at the Lublin – Lwow road around mid-day. Then division turned north to capture Tomaszow. By evening the 2nd Panzer Divisions reconnaissance battalion was probing as far as Zamosc. Both divisions had encountered little or no Polish resistance during the day. What units they did encounter were surprised at the appearance of German forces so deep in their rear. The 4th Light and 2nd Panzer Divisions reported capturing numerous artillery guns, bridging columns and many munitions trains.

Following in the path of the XXII Army Corps, 44th and 45th Infantry Divisions were marching as rapidly as possible to keep up with the 2nd Panzer and 4th Light Divisions. The 45th Infantry Division was moving the mass of its forces across the San River at Jaroslaw, while the 44th Infantry Division was making its approach march to the San River just behind the 45th Infantry Division. On the south flank of the XVII Army Corps, the 7th Infantry Division was making a critical approach march to Przemysl, where it would have to pin down the Poles at Przemysl. The division also wanted to capture the bridges on the San River. The 7th Infantry Division pushed its reconnaissance battalion ahead to probe for the best approach route to the San River crossings and looked for any significant Polish forces that might still be on the west side of the river. It was at the town of Krywcza, some 16 kilometers west of Przemysl, that the reconnaissance battalion found that the Poles had set up a strong defensive position to block the Germans approach to the San River. By evening the 7th Infantry Division had moved into positions just west of Krywcza to drive the Poles back into Przemyzl the next day and make a grab for the San River bridges.

The VIII Army Corps also raced to seize bridgeheads across the San River in an effort to keep the Polish forces to their north from moving directly south. The two divisions found suitable crossings during the day, one at Lezajsk for the 28th Infantry Division and the other at Krzeszow for the 8th Infantry Division. Enemy resistance was not what delayed the VII Army Corps crossing of the Vistula River earlier in the day. Because of the soft sand on both banks of the river, the bridging equipment has to be continually shored up by the construction engineers, which caused traffic to stop every time adjustments had to be made. Only infantry units were allowed across during the morning

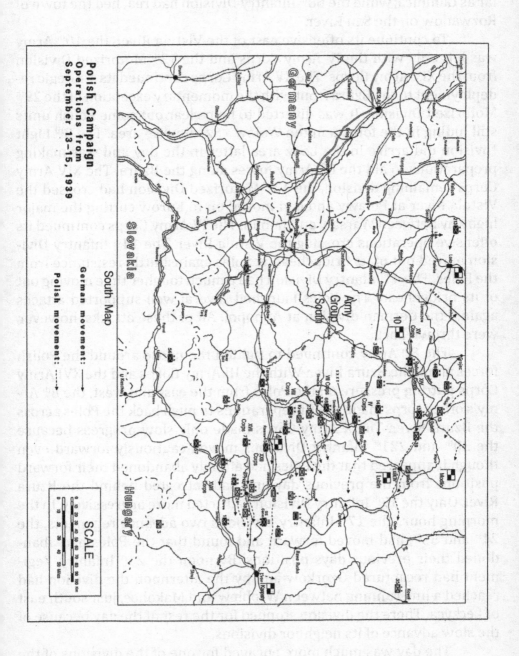

Polish Campaign
Operations from
September 13–15, 1939

South Map

German movement:
Polish movement:

SCALE

hours, which slowed the forward progress of both divisions out of the bridgeheads. By evening the 27th Infantry Division had only made it as far as Gamnica, while the 68th Infantry Division had reached the town of Rozwadow on the San River.

To continue its offensive east of the Vistula River, the 10th Army was left only with the IV Army Corps and the 13th Motorized Division from the XIV Army Corps. The XV Army Corps continued its strategic redeployment to the Bzura front with the momentary exception of the 29th Motorized Division. It was diverted to help clear out some Polish units still hiding in the forests in the Wolow - Szydlowice area. The 3rd Light Division did arrive in the Lodz area latter in the day and was making preparations to aid the 8th Army forces along the Bzura. The XIV Army Corps remaining division, the 13th Motorized Division had crossed the Vistula River at Pulawy and had moved on to Kurow cutting the major highway between Warsaw and Lublin. The IV Army Corps continued its offensive operations crossing the Vistula River. The 14th Infantry Division moved out of its bridgehead at Solec against little resistance from the Poles. The 4th Infantry Division had a much tougher time moving out of its bridgehead. The Poles launched several well-supported attacks against the German division at Annopol. All of these attacks, however, were thrown back.

The 8th Army continued to tighten the noose around the Polish forces along the Bzura River. With the III Army Corps and the XVI Army Corps putting pressure on the Poles from the east and west, the 8th Army's other corps made their preparations to push back the Poles across the Bzura River. The X Army Corps made only slow progress because the 30th and 221st Infantry Divisions moved cautiously forward even though it appeared that the Poles had already abandoned their forward positions from the previous day and had retreated behind the Bzura River. Only the 17th Infantry Division had acted more aggressively. In the morning hours the 17th Infantry Divisions two advance regiments, the 21st and 55th, had moved forward and found that the Poles had abandoned their previous days positions. By noon the 21st Infantry Regiment had recaptured Ozorkow and by the afternoon the division had reached a line running between Wroblew and Makolice, just south east of Leczyca. There the division stopped for the rest of the day because of the slow advance of its neighbor divisions.

The day was much more engaged for one of the divisions of the XIII Army Corps. During the early morning hours, the Poles had beset the 24th Infantry Division with numerous attacks in an attempt to breakthrough to the south. A Polish regiment made several assaults on the left flank of the 32nd Infantry Regiment but they were all repulsed. The division made a slow advance during the rest of the day against heavy resistance, managing only to cross the Zgierz – Lowicz road by the end of the day. The 10th Infantry Division remained in place, also rebuffing several assaults on their lines.

The XI Army Corps was still slowly working its way through the Polish positions south of the Bzura River. Both the 18th and 19th Infantry Divisions were meeting stiffer resistance, as they got closer to the Bzura. On the east side of the pocket the 4th Panzer Division and SS Leibstandarte Regiment continued their drive to the Bzura River. Both formations moved forward during the morning hours without encountering much resistance. By 3:00 PM they had reached the towns of Leszno and Blonie respectively. On the XVI Army Corps left flank two regiments of the 31st Infantry Division had also driven forward with little or no resistance, meanwhile the 17th Infantry Regiment relieved the Leibstandarte of its occupation of Blonie in the afternoon. And even though the majority of Polish forces north of the XVI Army Corps were retreating to the safety of the Modlin fortress during the day, the 4th Panzer still came under attack after dark by Polish units apparently seeking an escape route to the south. Meanwhile the rest of the 31st Infantry Division and other German units continued to hold their positions outside the city of Warsaw. To aid the 31st, the 1st Panzer Division began to gather itself together around Grojec before moving north.[4]

Lastly, the Luftwaffe launched its first major bombing attack on Warsaw since the beginning of the campaign. Bad weather had initially cancelled the attacks planned for the first week and other operational diversions since then had delayed any attack. Now that it looked like the Luftwaffe had gained air superiority over the skies of Poland, Hitler ordered the attacks to begin. The days attacks (called Operation Seaside) with 183 aircraft concentrated on Warsaw defenses and public utilities causing damage to many buildings and had started several large fires throughout the city. The Luftwaffe did not however, follow up on the days bombing the next few days because of the events that were to transpire on the Bzura front.

---

[4]National Archives: T314/441/946-965; Records of the X Army Corps.
T312/37/7545341; Records of the 8th Army.
T312/77/7596989-7596993; Records of the 10th Army.

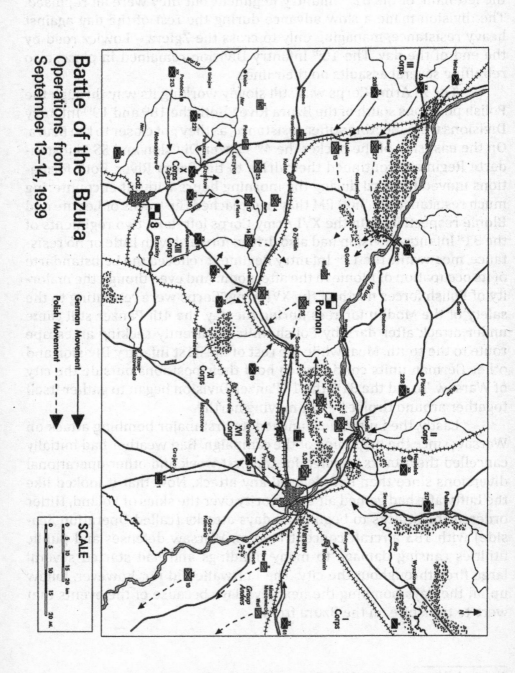

Battle of the Bzura
Operations from
September 13–14, 1939

German Movement
Polish Movement

SCALE
0   5   10   15   20 km.
0   5   10   15   20 mi.

Army Group North – 14 September

The 3rd Army renewed its efforts to tighten the closing ring around the north and east sides of Warsaw. The I Army Corps continued its drive east of the Polish capital against ever dwindling resistance from the Polish rearguard forces. It was very apparent to the Germans that the Poles were falling back to take up new defensive positions just outside of the Warsaw suburb of Praga. Corps Wodrig was driving its two infantry divisions harder to try and catch up with Panzer Division Kempf to aid it in its battles to prevent further Polish forces from retreating south of Warsaw. Unfortunately, the day's orders from the 3rd Army completely contradicted General Wodrig's intention for the two infantry divisions. The 3rd Army wanted both the 1st and 12th Infantry Divisions to turn immediately towards the west and to move up to the Vistula River to cover the south flank of the I Army Corps. General Küchler and his staff felt that it would require both divisions to secure the line. General Wodrig, however, still wanted at least one of the divisions to help the panzer division out of its precarious situation. After many heated communications between Wodrig and General Küchler, both generals reached a suitable compromise. The 1st Infantry Division would march on to the west, while the 12th would hold just southwest of Siedlice for the day to aid Kempf's panzer division. In order to help the panzer division the 3rd Army got the Luftwaffe to make supply drops by air of much needed fuel. The day's operations however, did not completely come off as planned. It was not long before the 1st Infantry Division had run into retreating units of the Polish 1st Infantry Division. The Poles put up enough fierce resistance to slow the German division way short of its day's goal. The 12th Infantry Division kept physical contact with Panzer Division Kempf while making security sweeps in and around the Siedlce area. For its part, the panzer division held its ground during the day with the help of the air dropped supplies from the Luftwaffe. This did not stop the southern flow of retreating Polish forces through and around Kempf's division. It would require the physical presence of the corps infantry divisions before the Germans could sufficiently stop the flow of Polish forces out of Warsaw.[5]

The II Army Corps continued to tighten its grip on the Modlin fortress. The 228th Infantry Division had edged closer to Modlin from the north despite the heavy artillery fire coming from the Modlin fortress. East of Modlin the Poles had earlier in the day launched several

[5]National Archives: T314/750/398-400; Records of Corps Wodrig.

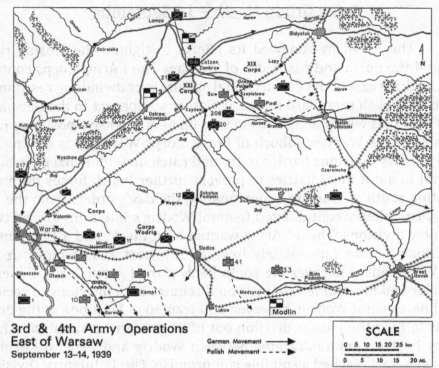

3rd & 4th Army Operations
East of Warsaw
September 13–14, 1939

German Movement →
Polish Movement - - - →

SCALE

0 5 10 15 20 25 km

0   5   10   15   20 Mi.

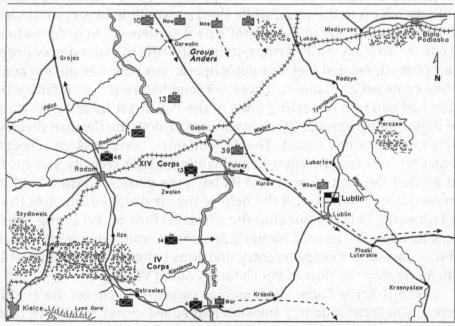

10th Army Operations
September 13–14, 1939

German Movement →
Polish Movement - - - →

SCALE

0 5 10 15 20km

0   5   10   15   20 Mi.

spoiling attacks against the 32nd Infantry Division, which had the effect of delaying the divisions planned assault to reach the Vistula River until 11:00 AM. When the 32nd finally began its drive toward the Vistula it only ran into isolated pockets of resistance. By 4:00 PM the 32nd Infantry Division had reached Jablonna, next to the river, effectively cutting off Modlin from any outside help north of the Vistula River. By the end of the day the 217th Infantry Division had arrayed its regiments between Radzymin and Nieport in preparation to begin the next days drive south to cut off Warsaw from the north.[6]

The XIX Army Corps continued its operations against Brest-Litovsk and to secure its lines of communication. Since the reconnaissance reports from the previous day indicated few or no Polish forces were between the 10th Panzer Division and Brest, an opportunity to seize the city could not be passed up, whether the division had any support from the corps or not. General Schaal ordered the 8th Panzer Regiment forward to try and seize the city from its northern approaches. The 8th Panzer Regiment moved steadily south without encountering any Polish forces until it reached the outskirts of Brest itself. There the advance group of one Panzer battalion and one company of infantry forged ahead through the city, while shooting up any Polish columns they encountered along the way. Having made their way to the city's center, they turned their attention to the Brest citadel itself. It was here that the Poles put up a fight. All attempts by the Germans were rebuffed. The 8th Panzer Regiment would have to settle for taking the city for now. It would have to wait for the rest of the division to make a proper assault on the citadel.

Meanwhile, the 3rd Panzer Division had crossed the Lesna River at Kamieniec Litewskie earlier in the day moving south-southeast to assume a left flank position next to the 10th Panzer Division. The 3rd Panzer was to continue moving south and east of the Bug River to form the outer most ring for the encirclement of the Polish forces by Army Group North. To reach the east side of the Bug River the division would first have to negotiate a crossing of the Muchawiec River near Zabinka. When the divisions forward units arrived at the crossing at 9:15 AM they found that the Poles had destroyed the bridge forcing the Germans to make an opposed crossing. The 3rd Panzer's forward forces had little difficulty in fording and pushing back the screen the Poles had along the river. On their approach to Zabinka itself the Germans came under fire from various Polish forces, engaging in combat with several armored

---

[6]National Archives: T314/81/236-237; Records of the II Army Corps.

cars and an armored train. Once the 3rd Panzer's units had taken Zabinka they paused, because the division's motorcycle battalion reported that there were large enemy forces mustering to the east of their position that might threaten their flank. Even though the reconnaissance battalion later found that the reported Polish forces were only units trying to escape to the east, away from the Germans, General Schweppenburg halted any forward progress for the day. He preferred to let the 3rd Panzer Brigade to catch up with the rest of the division, which was still crossing the Lesna River back some 24 kilometers.

Because of their rapid progress, General Guderian worried about both the 3rd and 10th Panzer Divisions fuel situation since both only had enough to last another two days. The XIX Army Corps supply service units were hard pressed in trying to keep up with the advance. The corps quartermaster said he would make an effort to bring up the needed fuel supplies along the same routes used by both the divisions in their initial advance, but the supply columns would be mostly unprotected and liable to attack by groups Poles trying to escape to the east.[7]

Overall, Army Group North continued to adhere to its strategic plan for the foreseeable future. This entailed having the 3rd Army cordon off Warsaw and Modlin and to keep further Polish forces from escaping to the south while the 4th. Army (with the XXI Army Corps and Group Brandt now placed under its command) would provide the XIX Army Corps with flank protection. The army group would also guard the north side of the Vistula River west of Modlin to keep any of the Polish forces trapped in the Bzura pocket from crossing back over the Vistula River to the north.

Army Group South – 14 September

There were two pockets of Polish forces now forming on the 14th Army's battlefront, one just east of Przemysl and the other in the forest between the Wieprz and Tanew Rivers. These were the only cohesive Polish formations left facing the army and if these were destroyed there would not be any major enemy left formations to stop the 14th Army's advance. This would also create a barrier to any of the other Polish forces to the north from attempting to escape to Rumania which appeared the goal now for most enemy formations in the south of Poland. With the XXII Army Corps seemingly not facing any serious opposition in its advance to meet up with the forces of Army Group North coming south

[7]National Archives: T314/611/659-662; Records of the XIX Army Corps.

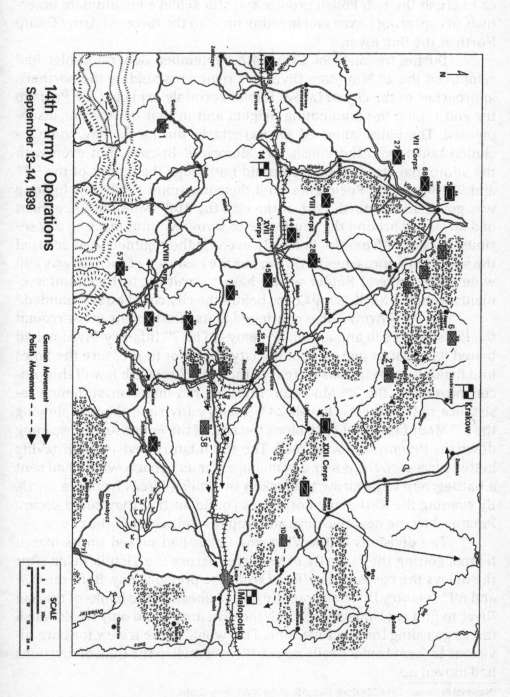

14th Army Operations
September 13–14, 1939

German Movement
Polish Movement

SCALE

via Brest-Litovsk, General List felt that he could use the rest of his forces to crush the two Polish groups and still achieve his ultimate objectives of capturing Lwow and meeting up with the forces of Army Group North at the Bug River.

During the night of 13th/14th September, General Kübler had reinforced the 1st Mountain Division's regiments holding the northern approaches to the city of Lwow. Kübler certainly expected the Poles to try and retake the dominating heights and in that he was not disappointed. The Poles launched several attacks during the day, some included tanks from the Polish 10th Motorized Brigade. But even with the additional armor the Poles could not budge the troops of the 98th and 99th Mountain Regiments from their positions. While this fighting was going on the north part of the city, the 100th Mountain Regiment had advanced around the south side of Lwow without meeting any serious resistance from the Poles. By evening the regiment had secured the southern approaches to Lwow, but the east side of the city was still wide open. General Kübler would have to wait for further reinforcements from the XVIII Army Corps before the city could be surrounded.[8]

The XVII Army Corps continued in its effort to pin and surround the Polish forces in and around Przemysl. The 7th Infantry Division had halted its advance just west of the city so as not to pressure the Poles into making a precipitous retreat to the east. The south jaw of this pincer movement, the 2nd Mountain Division, ran into ever stiffening resistance put up by the Polish 24th Infantry Division, thereby slowing the 2nd Mountain's ability to block the rest of the Polish forces escaping down the Przemysl – Lwow road. The 45th Infantry Division was having better success to the north, advancing as far as Lubaczow, and had sent a battlegroup to Jawarow to block in the Polish forces from the north. By evening the XVII Army Corps was confident that they could secure Przemysl by the next two days and trap the Poles east of the city.[9]

The divisions of the VII Army Corps had picked up its march tempo, getting the majority of its forces across the Vistula River after the delays the corps had suffered from the previous day. Both the 27th and 68th Infantry Divisions rapidly forged ahead to the banks of the San River to find crossings there. Both the divisions found only weak Polish forces guarding the San River line. This would make it easy for both divisions to form bridgeheads across the river when the bulk of divisions had moved up.[10]

[8]National Archives: T314/595/258; Records of the XVIII Army Corps.
[9]National Archives: T314/573/321-325; Records of the XVII Army Corps
10 National Archives: T314/343/197-198; Records of the VII Army Corps.

The VIII Army Corps experienced the same problem that had plagued the VII Army Corps the previous day when it tried to cross the San River. Because of the soft sand on both banks of the river the engineer's temporary bridges kept sinking into the sandy banks. The divisional engineers had to constantly add props to shore up the bridges, thus delaying the number of troops that were able to cross. This problem in particular plagued the 28th Infantry Division, which considerably delayed its advance out of its bridgehead. By the end of the day the division had only advanced 19 kilometers, well behind its anticipated goal for the day. The 8th Infantry Division had fared a little better, but when the division had advanced the short distance to the Tanew River, the division had to wait for the bridging equipment to be disassembled and brought up for the next crossings.[11]

The strategic relevance of the 10th Army had been significantly reduced since most of her motorized units had either been removed to aid the 8th Army's fight to reduce the Bzura pocket or were being placed in reserve by Army Group South. Essentially left with only three divisions that were crossing the Vistula River, the 13th Motorized Division continued its drive towards the crossroads at Kurow while the 14th and 46th Infantry Divisions had consolidated their positions at the Vistula before pushing on to their next objective.

The 8th Army's battle to destroy the remaining Polish forces in the Bzura pocket continued unabated. Now with the III Army Corps placing pressure on the Poles left flank and with the XVI Army Corps cutting the Poles eastern side from any outside help the final destruction of the pocket could begin. Pushing in the Poles from the west, the III Army Corps kept the Polish forces retreating all day, despite their strong resistance along the chain of lakes south of Wloclawek. With Group Netze covering the corps flank along the Vistula, the 50th and 208th Infantry Divisions engaged the Poles in hard combat, eventually forcing them out of their defensive positions along the Pakosc – Kruschwitz – Skulsk line.[12] The XI Army Corps steadily drove back the Poles towards the Bzura just north of Zgierz despite several counterattacks by the Polish forces.

Expecting to do the same, the XIII Army Corps was handed a setback by a much more determined Polish foe. While the 10th Infantry Division held the corps left flank to pin the Poles to their front, the 24th Infantry Division was expected to advance and outflank the Polish be-

[11]National Archives: T314/366/1014; Records of the VIII Army Corps.
[12]National Archives: T312/37/7545312; Records of the 8th Army.

hind the Bzura River. But before the 24th had moved forward, the Poles launched a concentrated attack against the 102nd Infantry Regiment pushing the regiment back. Calling for help, the regiment received aid from the 10th Infantry Division's 20th Infantry Regiment and divisional artillery. With this help the 102nd warded off repeated attacks that lasted throughout the day, dealing the Poles heavy losses. Meanwhile, the 24th's other two regiments had made very little progress, gaining at most a couple of kilometers against tough Polish resistance.[13] Toward the XIII Army Corps right, the XI Army Corps had at least advanced up to the Bzura River. Despite incessant attacks by the Poles both the 18th and 19th Infantry Divisions would be ready to cross the Bzura River the next day.

On the east side of the pocket, both the 4th Panzer Division and the SS Leibstandarte Regiment had reached the Bzura River after a hard day fighting. Operating in two battlegroups, the 4th Panzer's left group had driven down the Blonie – Sochaczew road without encountering any solid resistance until it had reached Sochaczew itself, where the Poles launched attacks trying to take back the town. One of these attacks threatened to overrun the Leibstandartes positions late in the day, but with the help of some reserve units and some stubborn defensive fighting by the SS regiment their front was eventually stabilized. Meanwhile the right group had also encountered growing resistance while moving down the Leszno – Brochow road but this did not keep them from reaching the Bzura River.

Still worrisome to General Blaskowitz and the 8th Army staff was the gap between the III and X Army Corps. They were worried that the Poles might attempt a breakout from the pocket on the still open side. This would cause all sorts of problems for the Germans since there were no combat units to back up the two corps. The Poles could wreak havoc on the 8th Army's rear echelon and supply lines. To their relief, evening reports from the army's air reconnaissance reported that all the Polish forces were steadily moving east into the pocket, greatly allying their fears.

To ensure a quicker conclusion to the reduction of the Bzura pocket, Army Group South had ordered further reinforcements to the 8th Army. On the afternoon of the 15th, General Rundstedt informed the 8th Army's chief of staff, Major General Felber by telephone that the 29th Motorized and 2nd Light Divisions were being sent from the 10th Army to assist the 8th Army. Furthermore, he was informed that the 1st and 3rd

---

[13]National Archives: T312/37/7545351 & 7545500; Records of the 8th Army.

Light Divisions were to be moved up to the 8th Army's command area the next day to be placed at their disposal.

The army group's assessment of the Poles situation at the end of the second week of the campaign was that their forces were becoming more dispersed and what organized forces that were left were making attempts to reach the refuge of Hungary and Rumania. The Polish leadership seemed to be trying to rally the other Polish forces much further to the east attempting to reorganize some kind of fighting withdrawal to continue resistance east of the Bug River.

Army Group North – 15 September

In telephone conversations between von Bock and General Brauchitsch, Bock discussed with the army commander in chief how he wanted to proceed with the army groups future operations. First, the 3rd Army would secure the Vistula River crossings at Wyszogrod and Modlin; second, drive the Polish forces from the Praga suburb of Warsaw and lastly, continue the 3rd Army's sweeping left flank movement with the I Army Corps and Corps Wodrig to close off Warsaw from the south on the army groups side of the Vistula River. Also, the XIX Army Corps should, after securing Brest-Litovsk, drive on and capture the city of Kowal in its furtherance to meet up with the forces of the 14th Army moving north through Galacia. In addition, Bock wanted to split part of the XIX Army Corps off to move on to Slonim to build an outer ring against any Polish forces from trying to escape in that direction. Brauchitsch concurred with Bocks outline and to proceed with as he had laid it out.

Tightening its grip on Warsaw, Küchler's 3rd Army continued to maneuver its divisions into position to isolate Warsaw on the north and east side of the Vistula River. Leaving the 228th Infantry Division to isolate the Modlin fortress, the 32nd Infantry Division turned and moved towards Warsaw along the Vistula River marching to within a few kilometers just north of the city. The 217th Infantry Division also continued its move south towards the Polish capital stopping just to the right of the 32nd Infantry Division. The 228th Infantry had mostly surrounded Modlin on the north side of the Vistula by the evening hours. While two of the 228th's infantry regiments moved down on the north side of Modlin the other infantry regiment crossed over the Narew River and had isolated the Polish forces in Nowy Dor from the east. Still fearing that remaining Polish units may try to re-cross the Vistula from the south at Wyszogrod, the II Army Corps sent troops to block the north side of the river at Wyzsogrod. The corps dispatched a company of the 9th Machinegun Battalion, the I/411th Flak Regiment and one anti-tank company to guard the crossing.[14]

Approaching Warsaw directly from the east, the forces of the I Army Corps steadily moved closer to the Praga suburbs. Both the 11th and 61st Infantry Divisions encountered little or no resistance that morning as they approached the outer defenses of the city. However, by mid-afternoon the forward troops had run into ever stiffening resistance as they neared the suburbs of Praga. Not wanting the troops to get involved in any urban fighting just yet, the corps ordered that no attacks were to be made into Praga itself until further notice. On the corps right flank the 1st Cavalry Brigade had not made contact with the 217th Infantry Division, but expected to link up and close the gap between the II and I Army Corps by the next day.[15]

With the likelihood of the I and II Army Corps completely sealing off Warsaw on the east side of the Vistula River in the next couple of days, this left the Corps Wodrig free for deployment for other missions. Once the corps had rescued the Kempf Panzer Division from its predicament, the corps was to maneuver its two infantry divisions and panzer division into positions to block enemy troops from exiting the capital and escaping to the south and southeast. The corps was to perform security sweeps in the area between Siedlce and Maciejowice. By evening the divisions were in place with the 12th Infantry Division between Wodynie and Stoczek, the 1st Infantry Division blocking the area from Stoczek to Zelechow and the Panzer Division Kempf still holding the line between Gonczyce and Maciejowice .

Now under the direct command of the 4th Army, the XIX Army Corps was struggling with its effort to capture the Brest-Litovsk fortress and the other forts around it. The 20th Motorized and 10th Panzer Divisions, along with elements of the 3rd Panzer, had made several incursions during the day against the fortress but they all failed to overcome the Poles. It seems that the Germans had underestimated the number of Polish troops still in the fortress, since the previous intelligence reports had indicated that large contingents of enemy troops had been leaving the city. Apparently, the Poles had retained a large garrison at the main fort and the satellite forts. An attack on the outer forts numbers IX and X by the 3rd Panzers motorcycle battalion was successful, but that

[14]National Archives: T314/81/238-239; Records of the II Army Corps
[15]National Archives: T314/34/444-446; Records of the I Army Corps.

is all they had gained. A more sustained assault by the 20th Motorized Infantry Division on the west side of the fortress across the Bug River had gained the western island without much of a fight. However, the Germans could get no further because of the heavy fire from the Polish flak and machineguns from the citadel itself. Witnessing these assaults himself, General Guderian called off any other planned attacks for the day. Knowing that the Luftwaffe had set up temporary bases close by, he wanted direct air support for his troops for the next day's assaults. He ordered the engineer battalion from the 10th Panzer Division and the corps 43rd Engineer Battalion be placed under the 20th Motorized Divisions command. The 20th Motorized was to take overall command for the next days attack and to coordinate the artillery fire from both divisions. Air attacks were arranged to take place between 7:30-8:00 AM and the ground attack would move in thereafter.

Meanwhile the rest of the 3rd Panzer Division and the 2nd Motorized Division continued to motor their way around Brest-Litovsk. The 2nd Motorized Division drove south of Bielsk then turned east to cross the Lesna River north of Brest to finally arrive by the evening hours near Zabinka. The division did not encounter any Polish forces the entire day. The bulk of the 3rd Panzer Division continued its march south moving down the east bank of the Bug River in the direction of Wlodawa. Both divisions were still having problems getting the supply services to forward adequate fuel to move both their entire divisions. Both divisions had immobilized some of their non-critical units so as to continue their forward movement. General Guderian warned both the army and army group headquarters that if the supply situation were not remedied soon both divisions would have to stop all forward movement.[16]

The 4th Army's other corps, the XXI was still in the process of securing the Bialystok region. Brigade Lötzen had occupied Bialystok itself against little resistance from the Poles. After crossing the Narew River in the vicinity of Suraz and Bokiny, the 21st Infantry Division marched forward to the Zabludow – Bialstok road by evening. Crossing the Narew River at Ploski east of the 21st Infantry Division, the 206th Infantry Division moved steadily northward without encountering any substantial Polish troops. It appeared from the reconnaissance reports to the XXI Army Corps that there were large numbers of Polish troops gathering in the Bialowieska Forest just northwest of Bialystok. This explained where all of the Polish forces had moved to and why the

---

16National Archives: T314/611/664-667; Records of the XIX Army Corps.

corps had encountered little or no enemy forces to their front during the day.[17]

Army Group South – 15 September

When the army group received air reconnaissance reports that morning that the Poles were building new bridges across the Vistula River at Modlin, there was a renewed fear that the Poles might try and escape across the Vistula and out of the Bzura pocket. Even though these fears were unfounded, the Army Group South staff closely watched for any other signs that the Poles might try to escape to the north side of the Vistula. In relation to this, OKH ordered that the 3rd Infantry Division halt its progress temporarily for the fear that the division might be isolated. OKH based this decision on what General Brauchitsch saw and heard when he had visited the 8th Army headquarters the previous day. However, after further discussions between General Manstein and General Stülpnagel, Manstein argued that the continued advance by the 3rd Infantry Division played a crucial part in the closing of the Bzura pocket. Convinced that Manstein was correct in his assessment, OKH gave the go ahead for the division to continue its advance. General Halder wanted the 3rd Army to bring more pressure on the Polish forces operating on the north side of the Vistula River to distract the Poles from the XVI Army Corps effort to clear out the enemy forces between Modlin and Warsaw.

Generals Rundstedt and Manstein telephoned General Blaskowitz to urge him to greater efforts to eliminate the Bzura pocket as quickly as possible. Blaskowitz assured both generals that with the proper reinforcements he would accomplish this in a few days. He then gave a summary of how the 8th Army would proceed with the next few days' attacks. The XVI and XI Army Corps would continue to press Poles on their right flank blocking the escape route to Warsaw. The XV Army Corps would move up behind the XVI Army Corps to finish clearing out any of the Polish formations south of Modlin and to block Modlin itself. XIII and X Army Corps were to launch simultaneous attacks over the Bzura River driving the enemy forces against the Vistula River. The III Army Corps would drive the Poles in on their west flank.

The actual days operations started on the left flank at Leczyca when the 221st Infantry Division moved up to the south bank of the Bzura River early in the morning hours. The division discovered that the

---

[17]National Archives: T314/660/121; Records of the XXI Army Corps.

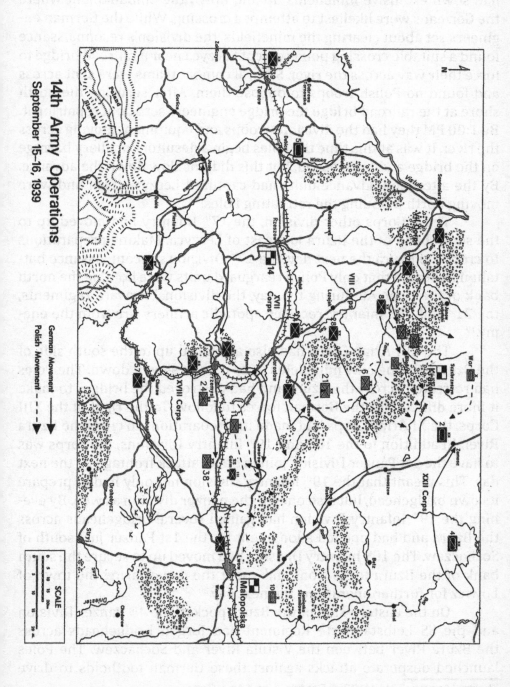

14th Army Operations
September 15–16, 1939

German Movement →
Polish Movement - - - →

SCALE
0 5 10 15 20mi
0 5 10 15 20 ki.

Poles had not repaired the main bridge across the Bzura and that they had sown extensive minefields up and down the embankment where the Germans were likeliest to attempt a crossing. While the German engineers set about clearing the minefields, the division's reconnaissance found a suitable crossing point west of Leczyca near a railroad bridge to force their way across the river. Several combat teams were sent across and found no Polish troops to oppose them. After securing the north shore at the railroad bridge the bridge engineers set about repairing it. By 1:00 PM they had the divisions troops and equipment moving across the river. It was at this time the Poles begin a desultory artillery barrage on the bridge and bridgehead, but this did not slow down the advance. By the afternoon advance units had captured Leczyca itself and were moving north pursuing the retreating Poles.[18]

The X Corps other division, the 17th Infantry had moved up to the south bank of the Bzura just east of Leczyca. Making preparations to cross the Bzura the next day, the 17th Division's reconnaissance battalion indicated that only Polish rearguard units were holding the north bank of the river. All during the day, the divisions' forward regiments, the 21st and 95th Infantry, received sporadic artillery fire from the enemy.[19]

The XIII Army Corps had also advanced up to the south side of the Bzura, finding only minefields in its path to slow it down. The Poles had retreated across the Bzura and had destroyed the bridges to make it more difficult for the German forces to follow. To the right of the XIII Corps, the XI Army Corps had made its preparations to cross the Bzura River. In addition to the 18th and 19th Infantry Divisions, the corps was to have the 1st Panzer Division join in on its attack frontage by the next day. This meant that the 19th Infantry Division not only had to prepare its own bridgehead, but also one for the panzer division as well. By evening the 19th Infantry Division had gained several bridgeheads across the Bzura and had opened a lodgment for the 1st Panzer just south of Sochaczew. The 18th Infantry Division had moved up to secure the south bank of the Bzura to its front and spent the day clearing the town of Lowicz for further operations the next day.[20]

On the eastern side of the Bzura pocket, the 4th Panzer Division and the SS Leibstandarte Regiment had forged bridgeheads across the Bzura River between the Vistula River and Sochaczew. The Poles launched desperate attacks against these German footholds to drive

[18]National Archives: T314/441/1259; Records of the X Army Corps.
[19]National Archives: T312/37/7545562; Records of the 8th Army.
[20]National Archives: T314/477/40-41; Records of the XI Army Corps.

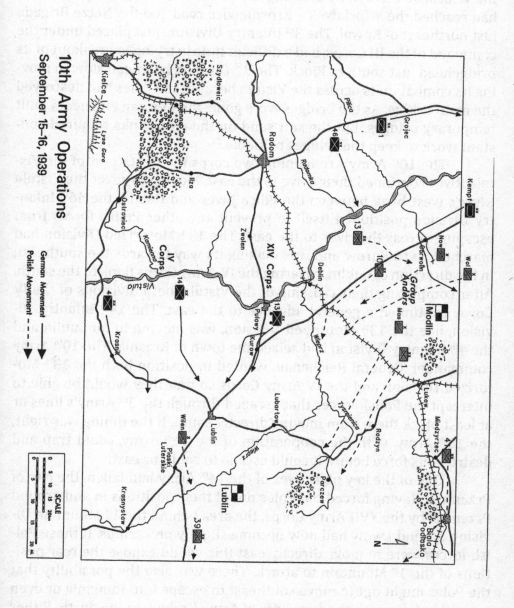

10th Army Operations
September 15-16, 1939

German Movement →
Polish Movement ---→

SCALE
0 5 10 15 20km
0   5   10   15   20 ml.

them back, but these all failed. On the western side of the pocket the III Army Corps continued to drive the weak Polish rearguards to the east, while the Netze Brigade battled strong Polish forces still holding out in the Wloclawek forest. By evening, the 50th and 208th Infantry Divisions had reached the Wloclawek – Krosniewice road and the Netze Brigade just northeast of Kowal. The 3rd Infantry Division, just placed under the command of the III Corps, had a difficult time in trying to breakout of its bridgehead just south of Plock. The 3rd Division had been slow in moving its combat units across the Vistula because the Poles had destroyed the main bridge. As the bridges were gone, the German engineers built temporary bridges, but the soft sand on the riverbanks required constant work to keep the bridges passable.[21]

The 10th Army's remaining two corps that were east of the Vistula River continued their drive to the east. Moving to cover the Vistula River's west bank between the Pilica River and Deblin, the 46th Infantry Division positioned itself to prevent any other Polish forces from escaping across the river to the east. The 13th Motorized Division had marched on to Kurow and was making its way towards the southeast, in the direction of Lublin, covering the IV Army Corps flank to the south. After completing their crossing of the Vistula, both divisions of the IV Corps continued a general advance to the east. The 14th Infantry Division, like the 13th Motorized Division, was moving in on Lublin and the 4th Infantry Division had seized the town of Krasnik. The 10th Army commander, General Reichenau, wanted to position both the 13th Motorized Division and the IV Army Corps so that they would be able to intercept the Polish forces that escaped through the 3rd Army's lines or at least block them from moving directly south. If the timing was right, the 10th Army, with the cooperation of the 14th Army, could trap and destroy this force before it could escape to south or east.

One of the key objectives of the 14th Army had fallen, the city of Przemysl. Having forced the Poles out of their positions in and around Przemysl by the XVII Army Corps, the area behind the 1st Mountain Division around Lwow had now become slightly precarious. If these Polish forces were to move directly east this would expose the rear positions of the 1st Mountain to attack. There was also the possibility that the Poles might opt to move southeast to escape into Rumania or even try and link up with the remnants of Army Krakow to the north. Either way, all were a threat to the 1st Mountains links to the corps and could disrupt the division's tenuous hold on Lwow. To help keep the lines of

[21]National Archives: T312/37/7545313; Records of the 8th Army.

communication open to the 1st Mountain Division, the XVIII Army Corps sent the recently arrived 57th Infantry Division marching from Churow to Sambor to cover the extreme right flank, while the 2nd Mountain Division moved to gain the major road between Przemysl and Lwow to force the retreating Poles to the east. The 1st Mountain Division sent what units it could spare to form a blocking force twenty-two kilometers west of Lwow along the Grodeker Lakes region. The Germans had set up the lake line of defense just in time. It was not long before the Polish forces that were being herded east tried to break through the German's thin defensive line. Most of the attacks were turned back, but a few groups of Polish troops managed to infiltrate through the north part of the line, moving into the forest just to the north of Janow. This move threatened the 1st Mountain units holding the area north of Lwow. Fearing that the 1st Mountain's positions might be compromised, the 14th Army turned around units of the 2nd Panzer Division to march south to reinforce the 1st Mountain Divisions hold on Lwow.[22]

With the abandonment of Przemysl by the Poles, the main effort of the XVII Army Corps was now to try and cut off the large Polish group (made up of remnants of the 11th, 24th and 38th Infantry Divisions) making their way to the east. Leaving only a small force to occupy Przemysl, the 7th Infantry Division moved north to cross the San River at Radymno. Hopes that the 7th Infantry could intercept the Poles around Jaworow were soon dashed as intelligence had indicated that the Poles were moving faster than anticipated. In an effort to get a blocking force to Jaworow before the Poles arrived, the 7th Infantry Division formed a temporary reinforced motorized battalion, under the command of a Major Muhl, to race ahead. Together with the SS Germania Regiment (just to the south), it was hoped that these two forces could stop the retreating Poles. Unfortunately, this action did not work as planned. When Group Muhl reached Jaworow large groups of Polish formations were already moving east around Jaworow and despite the Majors and his groups best efforts, they could do little to slow the Poles down. The SS Germania to the south also had little success in stopping the Poles. Both units were under constant attack and were now virtually isolated and would have to wait for relief from the 7th Infantry Division till the next day. Meanwhile, the 45th Infantry Division had encountered heavy resistance at Oleszyce just west of Lubaczow. By the time the division had cleared the town the corps had ordered the 45th to turn north in response to the previously mentioned threat from the Krakow Army.

---

[22]National Archives: T314/595/258; Records of the XVIII Army Corps.

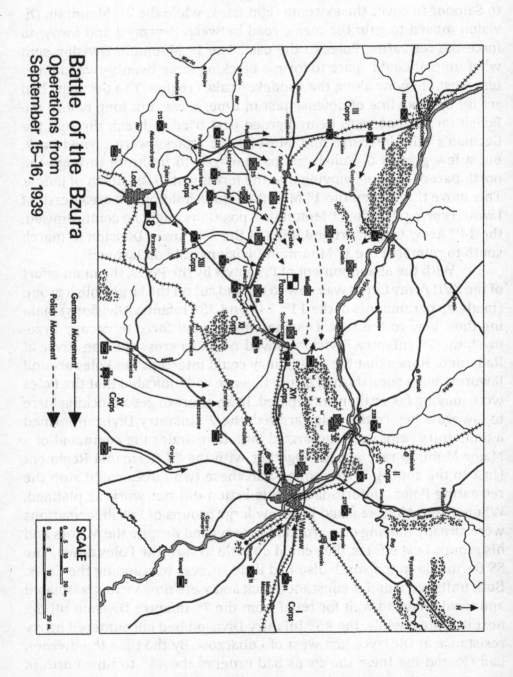

Battle of the Bzura

Operations from
September 15–16, 1939

German Movement

Polish Movement

SCALE

0   5   10   15   20 km

0   5   10   15   20 M.

The 44th Infantry Division was rapidly brought forward to take over the 45th's position and to continue to drive east.[23]

To prevent remnants of Army Krakow from forcing its way south across the Tanew River, the VIII Army Corps rapidly maneuvered its two divisions to block such an attempt. The 28th Infantry Division had a battalion move ahead to try and seize a bridgehead across the Tanew River by the morrow. With the same intent, the 8th Infantry Division managed to move its forces up to the Tanew River, though against stiff resistance from the Polish forces marching south. But the two divisions' efforts paid off, driving the Poles to the east. In the afternoon, the VIII Army Corps had received a command from the 14th Army to continue its offensive moves across the Tanew and into the forested region east of the river. This would force the remaining Polish forces into an ever-tightening encirclement created by the VII, VIII and XXII Army Corps.[24]

Pressing the Army of Krakow from the west, the VII Army Corps had completed its crossing of the Vistula River moving through the forest between Janow Lubelsk and Nisko. With occasional clashes with Polish cavalry to slow them down, the 27th and 68th Infantry Divisions moved steadily through the forested region. The only problem corps reported were of the stray Polish units in its rear setting upon isolated rear service units and having to chase them down.[25]

Army Group North – 16 September

With the end of the Bzura battle in sight, General Halder and the OKH staff looked ahead to what would be the culmination of the campaign; the capture of Warsaw. Over the past week the German high command had noted that many of the Polish forces that had evaded capture by the 8th and 10th Armies had gained the safety of the Polish capital. OKH's estimates of the number of Polish troops remaining in Warsaw were about 100,000 troops. This would make it largest concentration of Polish forces left in the field. To take the capital though, it would mean a long and costly siege and this presented a problem for the Germans. If the Poles held out long enough, there would be the possibility of emboldening the British and French forces to launch an attack against the Germans weak western front while most of their forces were still tied down in Poland.

---

[23]National Archives: T314/573/325-329; Records of the XVII Army Corps.
[24]National Archives: T314/366//1015; Records of the VIII Army Corps.
[25]National Archives: T314/343/198; Records of the VII Army Corps.

With this in mind, General Halder sent a message to Army Group North urging them to try and force an early surrender of the city if possible. General Bock felt that this was not possible at this time, because all of the intelligence the army group had gathered on the Poles in Warsaw from radio broadcasts and other sources indicated that the Poles were still very much in a defiant mood and the troops' morale was still high. Before launching any attacks into the city, Bock wanted to tighten the 3rd Army's grip on the city and bring up the forces he would need so he could start a proper siege. Also, Modlin was still holding out and its forces remained a threat to the army groups rear. Despite these objections OKH still insisted on trying to negotiate surrender, so Bock passed this request to the 3rd Army to send a representative into the city. This was done, but the Poles flatly refused to have any negotiations at this point. With this refusal Bock and the army group continued making its plans for an extended siege.

With the collapse of the first day's negotiations General Küchler's 3rd Army continued to tighten its grip on the Polish capital. Küchler had intended that the I and II Army Corps make an assault into and through the Praga suburbs and perhaps move up to the Vistula River itself. However, the day's assaults were cancelled because of the aforementioned negotiations. The staff at Army Group North headquarters was still apprehensive that the Poles in the Bzura pocket might attempt to regain the north bank of the Vistula River between Wyszogrod and Modlin. They wanted the 32nd and 217th Infantry Divisions available for redeployment in just such a case. However, Küchler and the 3rd Army staff were themselves certain that the Polish forces in the Bzura pocket would be unable to effect a crossing in their now weakened state. The I and II Army Corps attack on Praga would, therefore, take place as scheduled the next day. The 3rd Army's plan to assault the fortress Modlin was also moving forward to take place by 19 September. The 228th Infantry Division was to be reinforced by the 2nd Artillery Command Staff, two regimental artillery staffs, five heavy artillery battalions and the 9th Machinegun Battalion.[26]

Corps Wodrig continued it's clearing of any stray Polish formations east of Warsaw. Late in the morning, General Küchler ordered the corps to stand down from any further offensive operations and that Panzer Division Kempf would be removed from the corps command by the next day. General Wodrig was not happy about the panzer division

[26]National Archives: T314/34/446-450; Records of the I Army Corps.
T314/81/242-243; Records of the II Army Corps

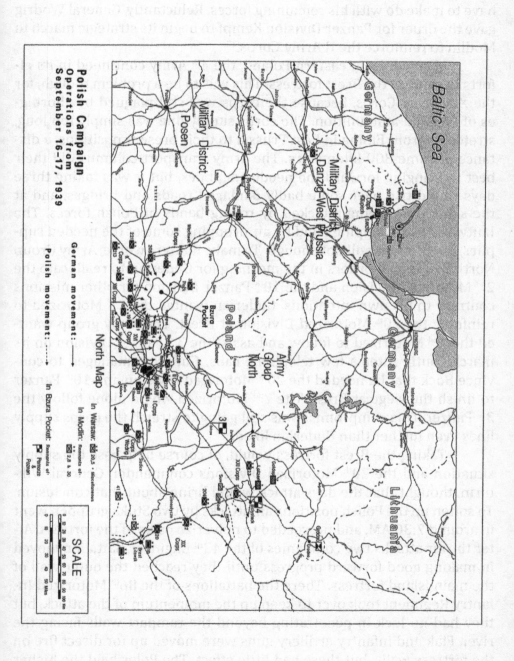

Polish Campaign
Operations from
September 16-17, 1939

German movement: ➝

Polish movement: ⇢

In Bzura Pocket: ⟶

North Map

In Warsaw: Remnants of:
In Modlin: Remnants of:
In Bzura Pocket: Remnants of:

SCALE

being taken away from his command and protested that he still needed it for operations along the Vistula River. General Küchler said he would have to make do with his remaining forces. Reluctantly, General Wodrig gave the order for Panzer Division Kempf to begin its strategic march to Modlin to reinforce the II Army Corps.[27]

Meanwhile, in eastern Poland, the 4th Army continued in its efforts to capture the Brest fortress. This was to be a problem though, for the XIX Army Corps, because the corps was still plagued by shortages of fuel and ammunition. The corps supply line was simply too long, stretching from Elbing in East Prussia to their present positions, a distance of some 300 kilometers. The army transport columns did their best in bringing forward the needed supplies, but it was taking three days round trip over some badly damaged roads and bridges, and at the same time, being attacked by roving bands of Polish forces. The Luftwaffe lent a helping hand by air dropping some of the needed supplies, but this was still not enough. To make matters worse, Army Group North had issued orders in the morning for Guderian to reallocate the 2nd Motorized Division and the 10th Panzer Division for other missions contrary to his own intentions. Guderian wanted the 2nd Motorized to reinforce the 20th Motorized Division at Brest. The army group wanted the 2nd Motorized to follow and assist the 3rd Panzer Division on its march south. After a few telephone calls, Guderian managed to convince Bock that he needed the 20th Motorized Division and 10th Panzer to finish the siege at Brest. The 2nd Motorized would alone follow the 3rd Panzer. This compromise was still going to stretch the corps supply lines even further than Guderian liked.

Taking the Brest fortress would, of course help ease the supply situation and the 20th Motorized Divisions commander, General Wiktorin, thought that the days attack would bring about that conclusion. To soften up the Polish positions air attacks by two Stuka gruppen went in around 7:30 AM, and proceeded to pulverize parts of the fortress. After the air attacks two companies of the 43rd Engineer Battalion moved in making good forward progress until they reached the outer wall of the main island fortress. There the battalions of the 86th Motorized Infantry Regiment took over to keep up the momentum of the attack, but they had no luck in penetrating beyond the rampart walls facing the river. Flak and infantry artillery guns were moved up for direct fire on the fortress walls, but these had little effect. The Poles held the higher ground and could bring down accurate small arms fire on any troops attempting to cross the river itself. By late afternoon the day's assault was called off. Conferring with General Guderian, Wiktorin said that heavy howitzer support was needed to make a successful penetration. Guderian agreed and Wiktorin began setting up the next days assault.

Moving south of Brest, the 3rd Panzer Division made extraordinary progress during the day on its march on Wlodawa despite its fuel shortages. The division had been out off radio contact during the latter part of the day due to interference from electrical storms. The worried corps staff did not hear from the 3rd Panzer until late in the day. When they did, they learned that the advance guard of the division was engaged in combat with the enemy just outside of Wlodawa. Following in the wake of the 3rd Panzer, the 2nd Motorized Division moved north of Brest towards the Muchaweic River at Zabinka. Because of the lack of fuel only the reconnaissance battalion and a few other units could make it to Zabinka, leaving the mass of the division waiting some miles back.[28]

To the north of the XIX Corps, the divisions of the XXI Army Corps continued their march to the east without encountering any significant enemy resistance. Both the 21st and 206th Infantry Divisions were directed to continue their movement east, after crossing the Narew River, until they reached the Grodno – Slonim line, some 130 kilometers east of their present position.

Army Group South – 16 September

With the battle zone of the Bzura pocket growing smaller each day, the staff of Army Group South knew that it would be only a matter of days before the pocket would be finished off. In anticipation of this, two corps were designated to be placed in reserve when the battle was over. The two corps chosen, the III and X Army Corps, were to be deployed where the army group could best utilize them. The 1st, 2nd, and 3rd Light Divisions, plus the 29th Motorized Division, were also to be placed in reserve, since mobile operations appeared to be winding down.

The 14th Army was now only fighting the Poles in several disorganized groups still retreating to the south and east. Though only small units, these disparate groups still had plenty of fight in them. The XVIII Army Corps found this out during its day of fighting around the city of Lwow. Still barely holding its positions around Lwow, the 1st Moun-

[28]National Archives: T314/611/667-675; Records of the XIX Army Corps.

tain Division was put under tremendous pressure by the Poles trying to break the 1st Mountain's hold on the north part of the city. Holding the division's positions in the hills north of Lwow, Group Franek (composed of the I and II/99th Mountain Regiment and I/98th Mountain Regiment) was attacked by several groups of Polish forces over the course of the morning and afternoon. The situation had become critical at one point, when in the late morning hours, the Poles managed to push the companies of the I/99th Regiment off of one of the dominating hills. This threatened the flanks of the other two battalions holding the line. Colonel Franek immediately moved the just arrived II/98th Mountain Regiment to cover the group's east flank, while reforming the units of the I/99th for a counterattack. At 2:00 PM, the attack went in and after much bloody fighting the battalion regained the heights. The quick reaction of Colonel Franek and the timely arrival of the II/98th Mountain Regiment had stabilized the group's positions for now. But the 1st Mountain Division was still in desperate need of reinforcements. The Poles would certainly strike again on the 17th.

Meanwhile the 1st Mountains forces holding the line at the Grodeck Lakes had noticed a considerable easing of pressure against them. This was because the Poles were now moving en masse towards the northeast to escape the German forces pursuing them form the west. General Kienitz, recognized this from the intelligence reports and saw that if the Poles were to gain the forest north of Jaworow and Lwow they would threaten the 1st Mountain Divisions rear and could possibly breakthrough and reinforce the enemy forces holding Lwow. To prevent this, he ordered both the 7th and 44th Infantry Divisions to step up their march rate to prevent the Poles from reaching the forest. In this both divisions achieved at least a partial success. The 7th Infantry Division had captured Jaworow by midday and had kept its advance guard force, Group Muhl, holding its positions 15 kilometers east of Jaworow. For the rest of the day the division poured artillery fire on groups it could observe crossing the Jaworow – Lwow road. The 44th moved into positions just north of the 7th Infantry to support its operations on the 17th. The corps other division, the 45th, was still cooperating with the 28th Infantry Division in blocking the remnants of the Polish Army of Krakow moving any further south. This was apparently successful as the division noted that the Poles were now moving precipitously to the north and the 45th Division followed them. By late in the day, the 45th had surrounded a substantial enemy force in a forest just north of

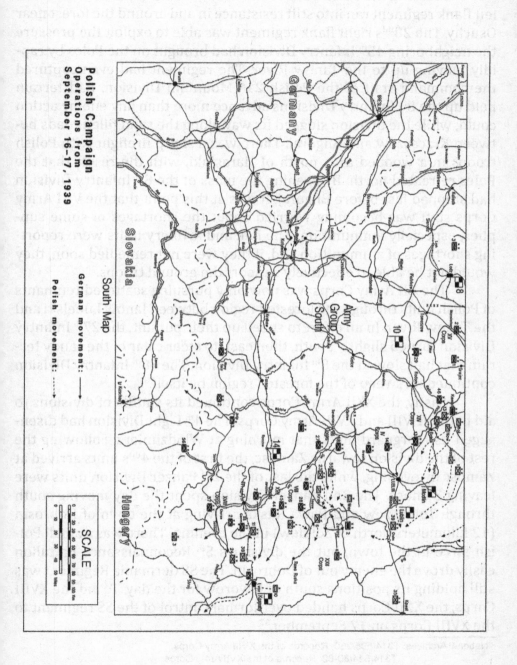

Polish Campaign
Operations from
September 16–17, 1939

South Map

German movement: ⟶

Polish movement: ----->

Germany

Slovakia

Hungary

Army Group South

SCALE
0 10 20 30 40 50 60 Miles
0 10 20 30 40 50 60 km

Lubaczow and made preparations to clear them out the next day.[29]

Pressing the Poles back to the north, the 28th Infantry Divisions left flank regiment ran into stiff resistance in and around the forest near Osuchy. The 28th's right flank regiment was able to exploit the pressure the neighboring 45th Infantry Division had brought on the Poles by rapidly moving up to the Tanew River. The regiment had even captured the command staff of the Polish 21st Mountain Division. Bad terrain held up the 8th Infantry Divisions advance more than any enemy action could, while the division slogged its way along the sand filled roads between Krzceszow and Bilgoraj. There was a sharp firefight with Polish troops in a wooded area north of Harasiuki, with the result that the Poles retreated north. By evening the mass of the 8th Infantry Division had stopped just before Bilgoraj. It was at this point that the VIII Army Corps staff was becoming worried about the shortages of some supplies, especially ammunition. The flak and artillery units were reporting shortages of ammunition and, if they were not remedied soon, they would not be able to effectively support the ground troops.[30]

The VII Army Corps was now only pursuing scattered remnants of Polish units through the forested region between Janow Lubelski and the Tanew River. In an effort to speed up their pursuit, the 27th Infantry Division turned slightly south, then east, to steer clear of the sandy terrain that had slowed the 8th Infantry Division. The 68th Infantry Division continued its sweep of the forested region by itself.[31]

Lastly, the XXII Army Corps continued its shuffle of divisions to aid both the VIII and XVIII Army Corps. The 4th Light Division had disengaged its rearguard units that morning at Wlodzimierz. Following the rest of the division towards Zamosc, the first of the 4th's units arrived at Zamosc by evening, while the last of the 2nd Panzer Division units were leaving Zamosc. The 2nd Panzer Division spent the day moving south through Tomaszow and Rawa Ruska arriving at the town of Dobrosin (12 kilometers north of Zolkiew) in the evening. There was a small Polish force in the town, but the division's 5th Reconnaissance Battalion easily drove the enemy out of Dobrosin. The SS Germania Regiment was still holding its positions south of Jaworow for the day. To aid the XVIII Corps, the XXII Corps handed over formal control of the SS regiment to the XVIII Corps on 17 September.[32]

[29]National Archives: T314/595/260; Records of the XVIII Army Corps.
                    T314/644/80-82; Records of the XVII Army Corps.

[30]National Archives: T314/366/1016; Records of the VIII Army Corps.
[31]National Archives: T314/343/199-200; Records of the VII Army Corps.
[32]National Archives: T314/665/63-64; Records of the XXII Army Corps.

The 8th Army continued its pressure on all sides of the Bzura pocket to bring about its rapid collapse. But the Poles bravely battled the Germans on all sides and even managed to launch a counterattack against the 18th Infantry Division, bringing that divisions advance to a dead halt. Despite this, General Blaskowitz was confident, that with the reinforcements in the form of the 3rd Light, 1st Panzer Divisions and the XV Army Corps, he would be able to bring about the complete destruction of the Poles in the next few days. It was readily apparent during the days advance by the X Army Corps that the Poles had abandoned the Bzura River line. Only having to engage rearguard units, the 17th and 30th Infantry Divisions crossed the Bzura en masse and by evening reached the Kutno – Bedlno rail line. The corps had also established ground contact with the III Army Corps north of Kutno, thereby preventing any likelihood of the Poles attempting a breakout out of the pocket to the west.[33]

To the right of the X Army Corps, the divisions of the XIII Army Corps also made successful penetrations across the Bzura River. Reinforced by the late arriving 16th Infantry Regiment[34] , the 10th Infantry Division forced bridgeheads across the Bzura with the 16th Infantry Regiment on the left and the 41st Infantry Regiment on the divisions right flank. Using early morning fog as a cover, both regiments slipped some troops across the river. Then after a prearranged artillery fire on the Polish forward positions, they drove the Poles back. By noon both regiments were well established and were waiting to move forward, while the engineers built the temporary bridges so that the divisions heavy equipment could be brought across the Bzura.

The 24th Infantry Division had also made good progress in crossing the Bzura with the exception of the 31st Infantry Regiment. After crossing the river, the regiment had not moved very far when, it came under heavy artillery fire from the direction of Zduny. The Germans found out that there was a large Polish armored train sitting on the Kutno – Lowicz rail line pouring fire into the 31st Regiment's area, disrupting any chance of further advance until it was dealt with. At first none of the other German forces could get close because the train was well protected by its own machine guns and a screen of armored vehicles. Lieutenant General Olbricht, the division's commander, came up

[33]National Archives: T314/441/960; Records of the X Army Corps.
[34]The 16th Infantry Regiment (from the 22nd Air Landing Division) had been flown in by air transport from Oldenburg the previous few days via Sagan, thence to Lodz. The regiment had arrived without any motor vehicles or horses so all of its heavy weapons and equipment had to be hauled by its men on its march to the frontline.

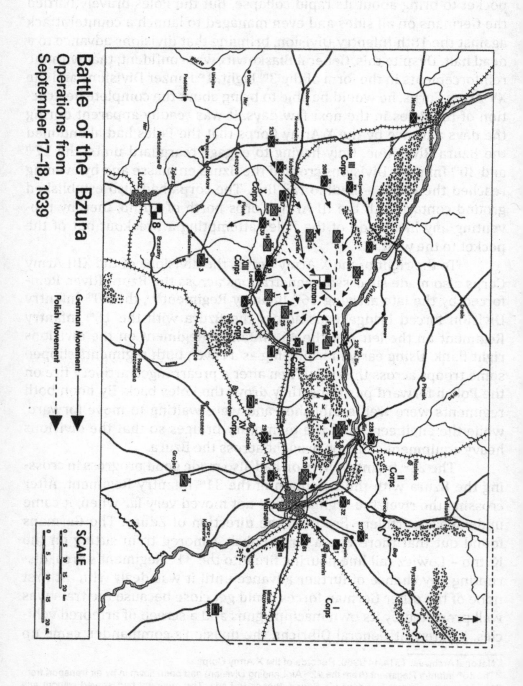

Battle of the Bzura
Operations from
September 17–18, 1939

German Movement ▼
Polish Movement ▼

SCALE

0 5 10 15 20 km
0 5 10 15 20 mi.

and conferred with the 31ˢᵗ's commander on what could be done. Both wanted heavy artillery to bombard the train, but none were available at this time. They both decided to use one of the divisions anti-tank companies, as it would have the penetrative power and range to disable the armored vehicles, and then take a shot at the train itself. A company, commanded by Lieutenant Bauer, was brought up and placed itself in a position close enough to fire on the train and the Polish armored cars. It wasn't long before the lieutenant had maneuvered some of his guns close enough to damage several of the armored cars, then the train's locomotive and artillery cars. Encouraged by the results the infantry moved in and captured the whole train after a brief firefight. Both the divisional and regimental commanders were impressed by Lieutenant Bauer's handling of his guns and he was highly praised in their reports. After having cleared this impediment to the divisions advance, the whole division had moved forward to the Studwia area by nightfall.[35]

The XI Army Corps faced one of its toughest days fighting in the campaign against some tenacious Polish resistance. After securing bridgeheads across the Bzura River in the early morning hours, the 18ᵗʰ and 19ᵗʰ Infantry Divisions moved out of their lodgments on both sides of Kompina. The 18ᵗʰ Infantry Division had only advanced a couple of kilometers when the Poles launched a counterattack at the seam between both divisions. The Poles easily broke through the frontline part of the 18ᵗʰ Division causing the division to have stop and plug this hole before the enemy reached its rear area and bridgeheads. The division turned its right flank regiment, the 54th, back towards the Bzura and in the ensuing fight barely stopped the Poles from reaching the river. The 19ᵗʰ Infantry Division moved slowly forward with its two lead regiments, the 73ʳᵈ and 74ᵗʰ, coming against stiff resistance by the Poles. To cover its left flank against the same attack that threatened the 18ᵗʰ Infantry Division's flank, the 19ᵗʰ Division moved its 59ᵗʰ Infantry Regiment over to its left flank. Because of the slow advance of the 19ᵗʰ Infantry Division, the 1ˢᵗ Panzer Division's follow up crossing behind the infantry division was delayed. Only a few of the 1ˢᵗ Panzer's units had made it across the Bzura by days end. The 4ᵗʰ Panzer Division and the SS Leibstandarte Regiment had also edged forward a little in a days hard fighting. Much of this delay was due to the Poles rapid transfer of units from the west side of the pocket to the east side. This heavily weighted the enemy forces the Germans had to face on that side of the pocket.[36]

[35]National Archives: T312/37/7545352-7545354 & 754550-5501; Records of the 8ᵗʰ Army.
[36]National Archives: T314/477/41-44; Records of the XI Army Corps.

On the western flank of the pocket, the III Army Corps continued to chase the retreating Polish forces. The 50th Infantry Division had advanced a reconnaissance unit as far as Gostynin. But Polish forces proved to be too strong in the area to try and seize the town proper, so the unit withdrew to await the rest of the division. The 208th Infantry Division was prepared to move a reinforced infantry regiment into Kutno, but this was delayed allowing the X Army Corps time to move up its 221st Infantry Division to coordinate an assault from both sides of the city.[37]

Pushing its XIV and IV Army Corps east of the Vistula, the 10th Army had the capture of Lublin in its sights. The capture of this important road junction would force the Polish Group Anders even further to the east making their attempt to escape to the south even more difficult. Leaving a small detachment to guard its temporary bridges across the Vistula River at Pulawy, the 13th Motorized Division formed a special group to make an advance down the Pulawy – Lublin road to support the IV Corps advance and to guard its left flank against the approaching Poles from the north. This group advanced to and past Kurow and encountered no Polish forces. The IV Army Corps also had little or no contact with Polish forces in its advance on Lublin.[38]

Army Group North – 17 September

Unbeknownst to the German Army, a new problem was about to be presented to the OKH and the field armies steadily advancing into Poland. All the plans drawn up by OKH and the army groups were based on the assumption that the German Army would have to invade and occupy all of Poland. However, the army was never informed (belatedly by Hitler for security reasons) of the secret protocols signed by Germany and the Soviet Union in late August 1939. In the treaty, once the German invasion had gotten underway, the Soviets would invade Poland from the east, proclaiming that they were only "protecting their fraternal brothers in Byelorussia and the Ukraine". Both countries had already agreed in the secret protocols on what territory each would control and where the demarcation line would generally run once Poland was conquered. So, on the morning of September 17th, when the Führer headquarters informed OKH of the Russian invasion, this brought about several problems that Halder and the OKH staff would have to solve rather

[37]National Archives: T312/37/7545313-5314; Records of the 8th Army.
[38]National Archives: T314/216/859; Records of the IV Army Corps.

quickly.

First, with the German and Russian forces rapidly closing toward each other OKH would have to inform all its ground forces when and where they might encounter Russian forces in order to prevent any friendly fire incidents. Second, the German forces could not just turn around and march back to the demarcation line. The best march route would have to be determined since the road and rail network had been damaged by the last two weeks fighting. Lastly, there were lots of captured war material and other civilian assets that the Germans wanted to try and retain once the fighting was over. Unfortunately, some of this was now going to be in Russian territory and it would have to be determined what could or could not be brought back. Over the next several days though, OKH came up with a suitable plan to withdraw its forces to temporary halt lines until all the ground forces had reached the permanent demarcation line. In this way, the withdrawal would be tidier and measured and would cause the least amount of confusion.

In the early morning hours, OKH relayed by telephone to the headquarters of Army Group North that Soviet forces had crossed over into Poland on its eastern border. All of the army groups forces that were close to the Polish - Russian border were made aware of the possibility of coming into contact with the advancing Russians. To prevent any firing on Russian troops, OKW issued an order that the army groups (including air units) were not to exceed the line running through Wlodawa – Brest – Kaminiec Litowski – Bialystok – Lyck. Since the 4th Army would be the first German troops the Russians would encounter, special emphasis was made to General Kluge that all efforts should be made to avoid any conflict with the Russian forces. The 4th Army's troops were told to display the swastika and Balkan cross on all vehicles so that the Russian forces would not misidentify them as Poles and attack them.

When General Guderian received news of the Soviet invasion, he had two immediate concerns. First, most of his forces were well over the demarcation line, which meant his forces would be more than likely, the first to make contact with the approaching Russians. After having informed all the divisions, he and his staff worked out a withdrawal plan that would minimize contact with the Russians. Second, and most important, Guderian wanted to capture the Brest fortress before the arrival of the Soviets. The XIX Corps had invested a lot of its effort (and blood) to capture the fortress. He did not want to ask his troops to give up now and leave its capture to the Russians. With this in mind, he emphasized in the orders to both the 20th Motorized and 10th Panzer Divisions that the fortress needed to be taken before the end of the day. And in this they did not disappoint him. Taking up their attacks from where they had left off the previous day, both divisions renewed with vigor their assaults in the early morning hours. The 20th Motorized Division quickly captured the airfield with several aircraft intact. The II/ 76th Infantry Regiment penetrated the citadel on its west side taking some 500 prisoners. Attacking the east side of the fortress, the 10th Panzer also quickly gained access to the inside of the fortress and, by 11:00 AM, had linked up with the 20th Motorized units coming from the other direction. The fight was all but over, except for some mopping up in the city and fort. What the Germans had captured in material amounted to; 1,400 soldiers, 21 artillery pieces, 3 flak guns, 60 machineguns, 1,200 rifles and 7 armored vehicles. Wanting to keep a minimum number of troops in the city, Guderian ordered the mass of the 10th Panzer Division to the north of the city and left only two battalions of the 20th Motorized Division to garrison the city until the arrival of the Russians.

Meanwhile, the 3rd Panzer Division was still in a fight for Wlodawa. Some of the divisions other units though, had bypassed the town and had advanced further south towards Chelm. Another battlegroup from the 3rd Panzer had driven down the east side of the Bug River past Tomaszowka and had eventually reached the outskirts of Opalin. Both advances were called to a halt by 5:00 PM, however, after receiving word of the Russian invasion. General Schweppenburg, the divisional commander, had been instructed by corps headquarters to halt any further advances south and to hold his position for now. It was just as well because he had to recall several tank units back to reinforce the units still holding the Wlodawa – Tomaszowka area. The Poles had launched several attacks at the bridges crossing the Bug with the aim off cutting off the 3rd Panzer Division from the north. It was touch and go for the defenders for a while, but the recalled tank units arrived just in time to help repel the Polish attacks.[39]

Still driving east, the 21st Infantry Division crossed the Bialystok – Bielsk highway in the morning hours without encountering any significant Polish forces. By the afternoon, the division had marched its set goal for the day, the Grodek – Michalowo line 22 kilometers east of Bialystok. The corps other division, the 206th Infantry, did not gain much ground this day because of its attempt at trying to cordon off the units of the Polish Suwalki Cavalry Regiment movement to the east. The 206th Infantry Division was only partially successful as that some 1,200

---

[39]National Archives: T314/611/676-681; Records of the XIX Army Corps.

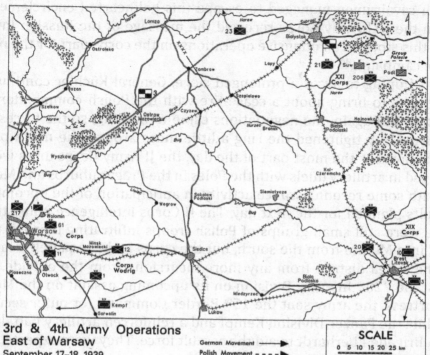

**3rd & 4th Army Operations
East of Warsaw**
September 17–18, 1939

SCALE

German Movement →
Polish Movement - - - →

0 5 10 15 20 25 km
0   5   10   15   20 Mi.

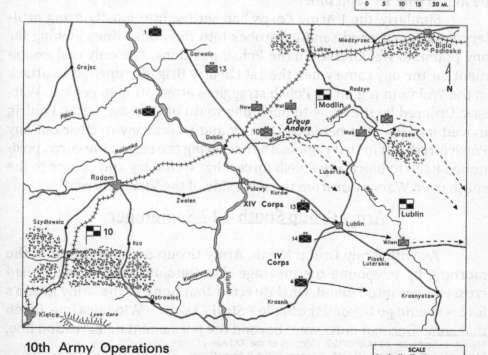

10th Army Operations
September 17–18, 1939

German Movement →
Polish Movement - - - →

SCALE
0 5 10 15 20km
0   5   10   15   20 Mi.

Polish cavalrymen managed to escape this halfhearted encirclement. When the XXI Army Corps received the message of the Russian invasion, this stopped all offensive operations on the corps part for the rest of the campaign.[40]

Hoping to avoid a prolonged siege, General Küchler continued his efforts to bring about a cease-fire with the Polish commander in Warsaw. But again, the negotiations came to nothing, so the forces of the 3rd Army tightened the ring a little more around the north part of Warsaw. For the most part of the day, the II Army Corps units were engaged in artillery duels with the Poles in the Praga suburbs and Modlin with some reconnaissance activity in anticipation of the upcoming assaults planned for the next day. The II Corps intelligence noted that there were still small groups of Polish troops infiltrating through the lines into Modlin from the south, but the corps had adequately sealed off the Praga district from any more incursions from the outside. To assist the 228th Infantry Division on its upcoming assault on the Modlin fortress, the army sent the 15th Border Command for outer security while the Panzer Division Kempf and a reinforced artillery battalion from Brigade Eberhardt to aid the assault force. They were expected to be in place by 19 September.[41]

Similarly, the I Army Corps had settled into mostly firing artillery into the city and sending probes into the Polish lines looking for any potential weaknesses in the Polish positions. The only real excitement for the day came when the 1st Cavalry Brigade repelled an attack in the Wolomin region by Polish stragglers attempting to get into Warsaw. Ordered by the army to positions south of Warsaw, Corps Wodrig moved into the area between Otwock and Luskarzew to clear out any Polish forces left in that region. After securing the region the corps positioned itself to block any Polish forces that would try and escape to the south from Warsaw or from the west side of the Vistula River.[42]

Army Group South – 17 September

As with Army Group North, Army Group South received in the morning by telephone the message that Russian military forces had crossed over into Poland. OKH directed that none of the army group's forces should go beyond the Skole – Stryj – Lwow – Wlodawa line. Given that some German units were beyond the permanent demarcation line,

[40]National Archives: T314/660/122; Records of the XXI Army Corps.

[41]National Archives: T314/81/246; Records of the II Army Corps

[42]National Archives: T314/34/450-451; Records of the I Army Corps and T314/750/50; Records of Corps Wodrig

the army group's staff prepared phase lines for which each army could make an orderly withdrawal to. It was obvious that the 14th Army's forces in and around Lwow and as far north as Cholm would be the first to make contact with the advancing Russians. Special instructions were passed on to General List's staff to be distributed down to the divisions on what conduct was expected when the ground troops made contact with the Russians.

At the Bzura pocket, fierce fighting continued. Overall the 8th Army noted that despite the stiff resistance by the Poles reported by its divisions, intelligence indicated that the Poles were disengaging their forces along the west and southwest sides of the pocket. This indicated to General Blaskowitz that the Poles were going to regroup for a breakout attempt either towards the Polish capital or north across the Vistula River between Wysogrod and Modlin. This presented an opportunity for the 8th Army to bring about a more rapid collapse of the pocket from that side and, with this in mind, Blaskowitz wanted the commanders of the III, X and XIII Army Corps to press the enemy even harder, while the XI and XVI Army Corps were to expect renewed assaults on their frontlines by the Poles.

Only having to deal with weak enemy rearguard units, the 50th Infantry Division easily drove past the Trebki – Gabin road. The advance of the 50th Division was now becoming more of a pursuit now that the Poles were rapidly falling back. The 208th Infantry Division found itself in a tougher battle, however, trying to push past Polish rearguard units centered on the town of Trebki. This held up the divisions advance for the rest of the day.[43]

There was a noticeable lack of resistance before the X Army Corps advance as the 17th Infantry Division rapidly moved through Zychlin and Luszyn while the 221st Infantry Division had captured Pacyna. An indication that the pocket was starting to collapse was that many of the captured Polish soldiers were now wearing civilian clothes in an effort to escape detection by blending into the general population. The German soldiers captured just a week ago were being liberated from their captors. For the most part, they said they had been well treated by the Poles. Meanwhile, the 30th Infantry Division was taken out of frontline duty and put into the army reserve. This division had taken the initial brunt of the Polish from 9th – 12th September and was now deemed not fit for any further offensive operations.[44]

[43]National Archives: T314/37/7545314; Records of the III Army Corps.
44   National Archives: T314/441/960; Records of the X Army Corps.

To try and cut off parts the Polish forces that were retreating on its front, the XIII Army Corps was ordered to make a sharp turn to the right to join up with the 1st Panzer Division advancing westward in the vicinity of Wicie. Around midday both divisions had executed the turn and began driving east. Both divisions reported that they had captured or destroyed many formations of Polish troops fleeing to the north. Apparently, the Poles had not anticipated the Germans change of direction, believing that the 10th and 24th Infantry Divisions would continue to move directly north. With this move, the Poles were being driven directly back upon the XI and XVI Corps creating a mini kesselschlacht. Because of the compression of the collapsing battlefield, the 18th Infantry Division was ordered to hold its positions just across the north bank of the Bzura River east of Lowicz while the 19th Infantry Division continued its advance into the pocket. The Poles fought hard to slow the 19th's northward advance, but could do little to stop it. Pressing the pockets eastside, the 1st Panzer Division made significant gains pushing the Poles further west towards the Bzura River. The 4th Panzer Division had turned east to pursue enemy Polish forces moving east past Wyszogrod along the Vistula River. The 4th Panzer however, found itself under assault in its rear by Polish units that had infiltrated during the night as they tried to escape towards Warsaw. The 4th Panzer had to laager its battlegroups to keep unit cohesion in the face of the unexpected hordes of Poles that were also coming at them from the east. Adding to its problems the division was running low on ammunition and fuel. It was hoped that the SS Leibstandorte Regiment would provide some relief to the beleaguered division as it moved north behind the division.[45]

Having been warned that Russian forces would be approaching from the east, General List would now have to push his troops harder to capture the city of Lwow. Like General Guderian and Brest to the north, he did not want to just abandon the siege around the city and leave it to the Russians to take at their leisure. The 1st Mountain Division had spent a lot of its effort and blood to capture Lwow and it might have a demoralizing effect on them, as well as the other German units around the city. Also, he wanted to finish off the wandering pocket of Polish forces along the lower Wieprz. Bringing an end to these operations would enable General List to safely bring the 14th Army forces back behind the demarcation line to avoid any clashes with the Soviet army.

While the 44th and 45th Infantry Divisions continued their drive the Polish forces north of Jaworow, the 7th Infantry Division prepared to

---

[45]National Archives: T312/37/7545354 and 7545501; Records of the 8th Army.

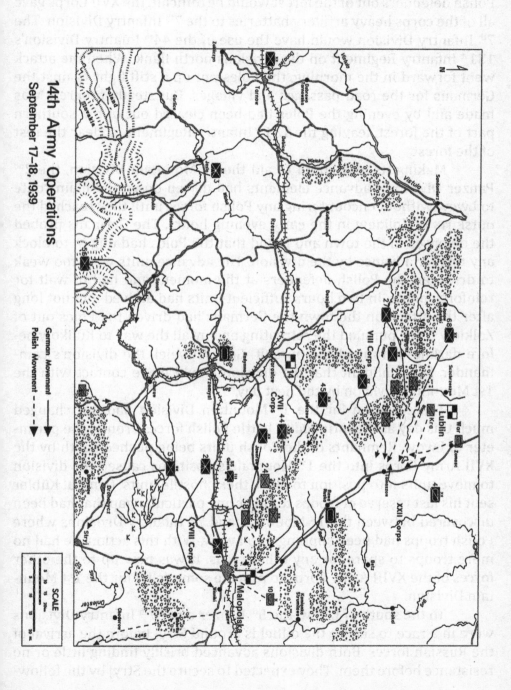

14th Army Operations
September 17-18, 1939

German Movement
Polish Movement - - - - -

SCALE

force its way through the forest above Janow. Knowing that driving the Polish defenders out of the forest would be difficult, the XVII Corps gave all of the corps heavy artillery batteries to the 7th Infantry Division. The 7th Infantry Division would have the use of the 44th Infantry Division's 131st Infantry Regiment on the divisions north flank. When the attack went forward in the morning, the Poles put up a stiff fight against the Germans for the road passages and villages. But steady progress was made and by evening the Poles had been cleared out of the southern part of the forest, leaving the 131st Infantry Regiment to clear the rest of the forest.

Making its way south to aid the 1st Mountain Division, the 2nd Panzer Division's advance elements had driven down the main route to Lwow without encountering any Polish forces until they reached the outskirts of Zolkiew in the early evening hours. The Germans probed the defenses in the town and found that the Poles had dug in to block any further advance by the division. The advance units were too weak to drive out the Polish defenders at the moment and had to wait for reinforcements. In two hours sufficient units had arrived and not long after the attack on the town the Germans had driven the Poles out of Zolkiew. They pursued the retreating enemy all the way to Kulikow before darkness stopped the pursuit. General Veiel, the division's commander, felt confident that the division would make contact with the 1st Mountain Division by the next day.[46]

The situation for the 1st Mountain Division had not changed much this day as it continued to battle Polish forces around the perimeter of Lwow. Remnants of the Polish units being pushed south by the XVII Army Corps into the 1st Mountain's positions caused the division to move units into position to block these hostile units. General Kübler sent his last reserve of troops to cover one particular gap that had been discovered between the 1st Mountain and 7th Infantry Divisions where Polish troops had been slipping into Lwow. With this action, he had no more troops to spare for any other crisis. It was now up to the other forces of the XVIII Army Corps to provide some relief for the 1st Mountain Division.

To the south of Lwow, the 5th Panzer and 57th Infantry Divisions were in a race to secure the oilfields around Stryj before the arrival of the Russian forces. Both divisions advanced briskly finding little or no resistance before them. They expected to secure the Stryj by the follow-

---

[46]National Archives: T314/573/333; Records of the XVII Army Corps.

ing day.[47]

Both the VII and VIII Army Corps continued in their efforts to pin down the remnants of the Pole's Lublin Army, but were not having much success this day. Leading the way, the 8th Infantry Division first captured the town of Bilgoraj in the morning hours then drove steadily east against little or no enemy resistance. The 27th Infantry Division moved up behind the 8th Infantry Division slowed not by any enemy action or terrain, but by the rear service units of the 8th Division. Having lost total contact with the Poles to its front, the 68th Infantry Division forged ahead looking for any sign of the Lublin Army's north flank. Only the 28th Infantry Division had any substantial contact with the enemy when, the Poles made a stand at Jozefow 27 kilometers east of Bilgoraj. The Poles put up a good fight, but the Germans determined assault on the town forced the Poles to retreat into the forest east of Jozefow. The only hope of rounding up this enemy group now would be determined by the ability of the 4th Light Division setting up blocking positions along the main road between Zamosc and Tomaszow and the 2nd Panzer's force south of Tomaszow to pin them down long enough so both the VII and VIII Corps could crush them from the west.[48]

The IV Army Corps continued its solitary pursuit of enemy forces to the east. Assuming the Poles would abandon Lublin without a fight, the IV Corps assigned the task of taking the city to the 7th Machinegun Battalion. However, the Poles were not going to give up Lublin quite so easily, for when the 7th Machinegun Battalion approached the west side of the city it came under heavy fire. Estimating the size of the Polish defenders to be about that of a regiment, the 7th Machinegun requested some assistance from the nearby 14th Infantry Division. The division sent its 101st Infantry Regiment and upon arrival, together with the 7th Machinegun Battalion, it drove into the southwest section of the city securing that section by the evening hours. When both units renewed their attack the next morning, they found that the Poles had abandoned the city and had retreated to the east.[49]

Army Group North – 18 September

The Poles seeming lack of will to negotiate the surrender of Warsaw was becoming more and more frustrating to the Germans. At

---

[47]National Archives: T314/595/261; Records of the XVIII Army Corps.
[48]National Archives: T314/343/200; Records of the VII Army Corps and T314/366/1017; Records of the VIII Army Corps
[49]National Archives: T314/216/945; Records of the IV Army Corps.

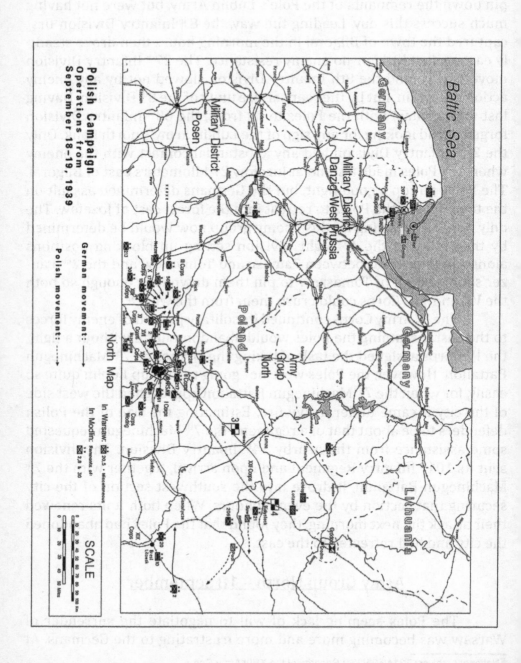

Polish Campaign
Operations from
September 18–19, 1939

German movement: ⟶

Polish movement: ⟶

North Map

In Warsaw: 20,5 · Miscellaneous
In Modlin: Remnants of:– 2,8 & 30

SCALE

the next proposed time, the Polish negotiators failed to show up. It was now becoming apparent to General von Bock, OKH and Führer headquarters that the Poles were playing for time now that the Russians had invaded eastern Poland. Hitler issued a message to OKH and to General Bock that if the Poles were not willing to negotiate either a cease-fire or surrender in Warsaw, he would order an immediate attack on Praga. General Brauchitsch himself did not think that the time was right to launch any attacks into Praga or Warsaw, because the Poles had time to fortify the city, which would make any assaults into these urban areas a costly affair. He wanted more time to bombard the city by heavy artillery and air attack. Brauchitsch thought that it would be prudent to take the fortress Modlin first. General Bock wanted the assaults on Warsaw to start before 21 September using only the 1st, 11th and 12th Infantry Divisions while keeping the 32nd, 61st and 217th Infantry Divisions in reserve. However, OKH did not foresee any attacks taking place before 25 September because of the situation on the Bzura. The German high command wanted a concentric attack on all sides of Warsaw and this could not take place until the Bzura pocket was finished off. Hitler was in agreement with OKH and wanted to see what the Soviets might do as they neared the Polish capital. He also agreed with Brauchitsch's view of bringing up more firepower in the form of heavy artillery and Luftwaffe bomber *gruppen.* So, for the time being Warsaw was to be left alone.

Meanwhile the 3rd Army tightened its ring around Warsaw. For the I and II Army Corps, the routine of a siege was now setting in. Combat activity was just reconnaissance patrols and the harassment shelling from both sides. But the corps commanders knew that once the orders to attack into Warsaw arrived they would have to be ready, so both corps staffs worked diligently on what attack plans would be followed. Particular attention was paid to the corps rear areas to make sure the roads and bridges were properly repaired and maintained so that the constant flow of supplies could be provided once the attack was underway.

The 228th Infantry Division resumed its assault on the Modlin fortress by trying to force its way in on the Nowy Dor side. The initial attack had to be postponed several times in the morning because of the ground fog. Finally, around 11:00 AM the fog lifted and the assault went in, but it was soon brought to a halt as the German infantry became too entangled in the Poles forward positions. Polish resistance was great and their artillery fire disrupted any forward movement. The division desperately tried to locate the various enemy artillery positions to silence them with counter battery fire, but it was hopeless. The Poles had concealed their batteries too well. Until the Germans could locate these artillery positions any further attacks would be fruitless. Observing the attack, von Bock thought that the division had not sufficiently prepared for the attack and that it also lacked the strength to take on the fortresse's well-prepared defensive works. He recommended that at least another division or two of the "first wave" type be brought up to take over the main assaults when available.[50]

The XIX Army Corps received another message from Army Group North emphasizing the importance of not letting any of its divisions move further east or south. General Guderian could not ignore this second message. He wanted the 3rd Panzer Division to make physical contact with the 2nd Panzer Division, but given the army groups order and the corps present situation he would have to recall the 3rd Panzer Division anyway. By mid-morning the 3rd Panzer Division had already moved several kilometers south capturing the towns of Chelm and Luboml in firefights along the way. It was about this time that General Schweppenburg received the orders to halt any further movement south and was to hold his present positions. This effectively brought to close offensive operations for the XIX Corps for the campaign.[51]

Army Group South – 18 September

The army group headquarters received a revised set of maps from OKH detailing where the new demarcation line would be. OKH emphasized that all the army groups forces should be moved behind the demarcation line as soon as possible. Further, securing the Skol – Stryj oilfields were still to be carried out. OKH had issued a bulletin setting the time and type of assaults planned for Warsaw, tentatively set for 25 September, the earliest date when all the forces would be in place. OKH wanted all the assault forces, with their support units, ready by that date.

Wanting to go over the future plans for both the 10th and 8th Armies, von Rundstedt visited both of the respective field headquarters. At the 8th Army's headquarters, the field marshal discussed with General Blaskowitz about closing the Bzura pocket and what units would be

[50]National Archives: T314/34/451-452; Records of the I Army Corps and T314/81/247; Records of the II Army Corps.
[51]National Archives: T314/611/682-685; Records of the XIX Army Corps.

needed for the siege of Warsaw. Both agreed that the XIII and III Army Corps would be used as the major offensive forces to destroy what was left of the Bzura pocket, while holding back the X Corps for defensive purposes. Moving on to Reichenau's headquarters, both Rundstedt and Reichenau were in agreement about leaving the XVI Army Corps in position to hold the east side of the Bzura pocket while at the same time the XV Corps would clear the area of any remaining enemy troops between the Bzura and Warsaw. The XI Army Corps would generally stand on the defensive. When the pocket was finally finished off the motorized and panzer divisions would move south and southwest of Warsaw and await their next deployment.

It was now clear to General Blaskowitz and the 8th Army staff that the end was near for the fighting in the Bzura pocket. The army had captured some 40,000 Poles thus far and there could not be many Polish soldiers left to put up a fight. The pursuit of Polish forces on the III Corps side of the pocket had turned into a rout. Units of the 3rd, 50th and 208th Infantry Divisions were now just gathering hundreds of prisoners and tons of abandoned equipment as they steadily marched east. Not wanting to detail too many of its combat troops just to guard the ever-increasing numbers of prisoners, the corps brought up the Netze Brigade to handle guarding the prisoners of war. By the end of the day, the Netze Brigade had set up several holding pens in and around the towns of Gostymin and Straelce.[52]

Spearheading the advance into the pocket for the X Army Corps, the 17th Infantry Division also faced little or no resistance against a rapidly disintegrating Polish army. The division might have driven all the way to the Vistula River, but it was halted at the Sochazew – Sanniki road about mid-day because other German forces had already reached the divisions objectives.[53] The situation was similar for the 10th Infantry Division's advance into the very center of what was left of the Poznan Army. The division's regiments had marched forward facing little resistance with the exception of small pockets of Polish troops making last stands here and there. While advancing and taking hundreds of prisoners along the way, the men of the 10th Infantry were struck by the violence of the previous days Luftwaffe attack had wrought on the hapless Poles. The division's staff particularly noted the devastation on the Polish columns that were caught out in the open. Wrecked vehicles, carts and dead horses were everywhere, twisted up equipment and lots

---

[52]National Archives: T312/37/7545314; Records of the 8th Army.
[53]National Archives: T312/37/7545564-5565; Records of the 8th Army.

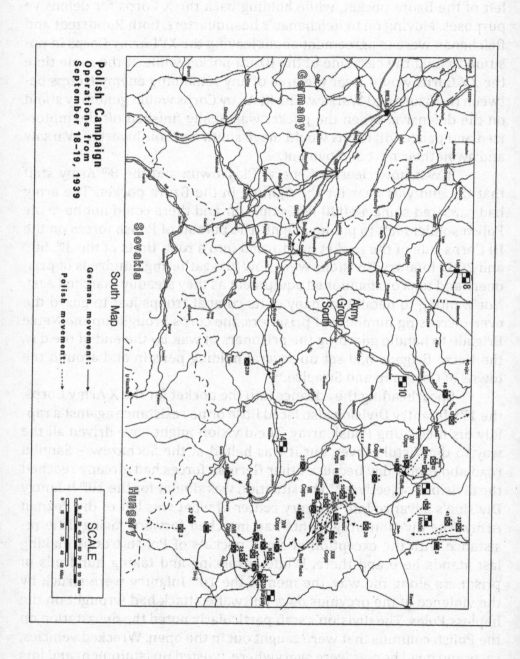

Polish Campaign
Operations from
September 18–19, 1939

German movement: ⟶

Polish movement: ⤍⤍⤍

South Map

SCALE

of ammunition boxes were scattered all over. By noon the division had reached its days objective, but the lead units continued their march until they reached the Vistula River around 5:30 PM. The flanking divisions, the 17th on the left and the 19th on the right had already stopped after linking up with the 10th Infantry Divisions forces. On the banks of the Vistula the Germans found what was left of the remaining Polish artillery, broken and smashed from the Luftwaffe's attack from the previous day. It was here that the 10th Division encountered the last and largest group of enemy soldiers still fighting on. The 85th Infantry Regiment had initially bypassed the town of Brzozow in its haste to reach the Vistula River. When a following artillery battery was moving through the town it was violently attacked by Polish troops who had hidden themselves in the buildings. Many of the batteries troops were either killed or wounded in the ensuing melee. The 85th Regiment had to send back some troops to subdue the Poles, but attacking the well-entrenched enemy proved to be difficult. A battery from the II/10th Artillery Regiment was brought up to blast the Poles into submission. Even with that the Poles still hung on through the night. It would be the next day before the Germans had cleared the town in some vicious close quarter fighting. This showed the Germans that some Polish units were still willing to fight to the death rather than surrender.[54]

Before the 19th Infantry Division could begin its final advance into the pocket, its 73rd Infantry Regiment had to fight a desperate defensive action against Polish troops that were trying to escape out of the pocket. The focus of the Polish attack was at the town of Delk Ruszki. The Poles attacked with the support of some armored cars, and after a seesaw battle for the town, the enemy was beaten back with the aid of the divisional artillery. After firmly securing Delk Ruszki, the division moved forward only to become entangled in a forest north of Mlodziezyn. The Poles were firmly entrenched and it took the rest of the day to ferret them out. By the time the division started to move again, the 10th Infantry Division had moved across its front, thus bringing an end to its drive into the Bzura pocket. North of the 19th Infantry Division, the 1st Panzer Division had stopped offensive operations and had set up a defensive line to slow down the number of Polish troops infiltrating out of the pocket. Likewise, the 4th Panzer Division was over its previous days crisis, but several Polish groups had escaped through the division's lines during the night. During the day, the 4th Panzer managed to close most of these gaps. It was up to the XV Corps to intercept

---

[54]National Archives: T312/37/7545501-5504; Records of the 8th Army.

any of the Poles who had gotten through during the night.[55]

However, the divisions of the XV Army Corps found that fighting through the thick trees and bogs in the Kampinoska forest was not an easy task. To secure the area between the forest and Warsaw the 1st Light Division marched from its positions, just west of Warsaw, to the north about noon, the forward elements of the division arrived at the banks of the Vistula River at Lomna cutting the main road and rail line between Modlin and Warsaw. Other elements of the division had turned east to link up with the 31st Infantry Division. It was at Palmiry that the 1st Light found several freight cars and warehouses full of munitions, which were promptly seized. The 29th Motorized Division's drive into the forest itself was slow, but steady. Only the infantry could move forward with any surety while the armored cars and artillery were strictly limited to road movement. This meant that the infantry had to carry out the attack unsupported. Even with this, the 29th Motorized managed to struggle up to the Vistula River near Polsk by the end of the day whilst warding off several of the Polish groups that had escaped from the Bzura pocket. The 2nd Light Division had faced the same problems during the day, but it too managed to reach the Vistula River. Both the 29th Motorized and 2nd Light Divisions now faced what they knew would be a long night of attacks by the Poles trying to break through their lines to escape the pocket.[56]

On the 10th Army's central front attempts to intercept and destroy the remnants of the Modlin Army continued. The Poles had abandoned Lublin to the Germans when they realized they were about to be cut off by elements of the IV Army Corps. In order to cut off the Poles further east, the IV Corps would have to seize the important road junction at Krasnystaw. The corps advance, however, was slowed throughout the day by encounters with ever-larger groups of Poles performing rearguard actions. The hope of capturing Krasnystaw and its bridges across the Wieprz River was dashed for the day. The 4th Infantry Division would have to make greater effort the next day if they were to cut off the Poles.[57]

The main concern for the 14th Army continued to be the eradication of the Polish forces holding Lwow and the large group caught between the VII, VIII and XXII Army Corps. The Poles launched multiple attacks against the 1st Mountain Divisions positions on the north part of Lwow from the early morning hours of the 18th until late morning. All of

---

[55]National Archives: T312/37/7545388; Records of the 8th Army.
[56]National Archives: T314/550/265-267; Records of the XV Army Corps.
[57]National Archives: T314/216/944; Records of the IV Army Corps.

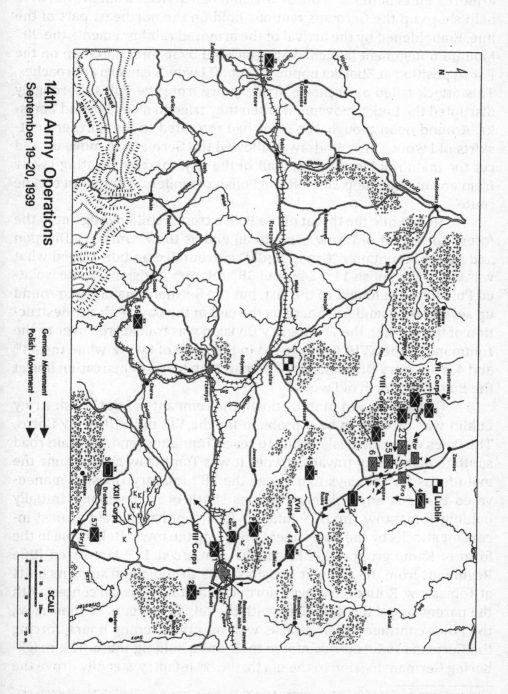

14th Army Operations
September 19-20, 1939

German Movement ➡
Polish Movement ➡ (dashed)

N ↑

SCALE
0 5 10 15 20km
0 5 10 15 20 m.

the assaults were bloodily repulsed. Much to the relief of the division, armored units of the 2nd Panzer Division had arrived from the north to help shore up the Germans tenuous hold on the northeast part of the line. Emboldened by the arrival of the armored reinforcements the 90th Mountain Regiment launched an attack led by its first battalion on the Polish position at Zboiska hoping to cut off Lwow's eastern approaches. This attack failed as accurate artillery fire from the Poles thoroughly disrupted the tanks' movement when they tried to move beyond Zboiska. Around noon though, the Poles had retreated to the northern outskirts of Lwow. This withdrawal, allowed the Germans to move up and cut the main road leading east out of the city, thereby isolating Lwow from any outside help and left the Polish defenders without an escape route.

Meanwhile the threat of the Polish troops still holding out in the forest northwest of Lwow came to an end as the 7th Infantry Division and the 1st Mountain's "Group Rudki" surrounded and destroyed what was left of the Polish 11th, 24th, and 38th Infantry Divisions. Some isolated Polish troops fought to the last, but the Germans managed to round up several thousand prisoners by the end of the day. With the destruction of this pocket, the 7th Infantry Division was transferred over to the command of the XVIII Corps to aid in the siege of Lwow, while the 44th and 45th Infantry Divisions were to march up to the demarcation line at the Bug River north of Lwow.[58]

Containing and pinning down the remnants of the Polish Army Lublin was proving to be a problem for the VII and VIII Army Corps. The Poles were obviously trying to reach Tomaszow and the main road south to make a run towards Lwow. It was Tomaszow that became the main focus for the days fighting as the 28th Infantry Division maneuvered to block any Polish incursions south of its positions. Initially holding Tomaszow, the I/7th Infantry Regiment barely held against incessant attacks by the Poles intent on taking the town. Help came in the form of Kampfgruppe Rothkirch (the reinforced 11th Motorized Rifle Regiment) from the 4th Light Division. After dropping off some its units at Tomaszow, Rothkirch moved north to maintain physical contact with the parent corps, the XXII. Even with the reinforcements at Tomaszow, the Poles continued their attacks well into the evening hours, forcing the Germans to further reinforce their units holding there. The neighboring German division to the north, the 8th Infantry, steadily drove the

---

[58]National Archives: T314/595/261; Records of the XVIII Army Corps and T314/343/201; Records of the VII Army Corps.

Poles back towards the east. The Poles tried to break the seam between the 8th and 28th Infantry Divisions, but failed. The 8th Infantry Division had shifted its reserve 38th Infantry Regiment south and this stopped any further efforts by the Poles along this part of the line.

Cutting off any escape routes to the north, the VII Army Corps advance was slowed by the Poles deft use of the terrain. The Poles had made good use of the forested area through which the corps had to advance by downing trees and placing high explosive booby traps along the narrow roads. But the corps' biggest problem stemmed from the bottleneck of the supply columns that had developed at the bridge over the Tanew River at Harzsiuki. Poor traffic control allowed the horse transport to get mixed with the motor transport snarling the traffic for miles. Without their proper share of rations the advance elements of the corps had to stop and wait until the situation in the rear had been solved.[59]

Army Group North – 19 September

Army Group North received from OKH the information for setting up the second demarcation line. All troops were to be behind this line by the evening of 20 September. The new demarcation line would run from Pisia (south of Johanissburg) to the Narew River, then Zambrow to the Bug River, then along the Bug south to Jaroslaw through Stryj and then to the Hungarian border. Other information in the message emphasized the need for bridging equipment for the upcoming assault on Warsaw. In this case, Army Group North staff reassured OKH that there was plenty of that. As to the actual attack date set for the assault on Warsaw, 22 September, Bock found that Army Group South would not be ready for its initial attacks until 25 September. Bock was not pleased with this, as he wanted to start the attacks as soon as possible. He knew that every day's delay would allow the Poles time to better organize their defenses in the city. On the other hand, Bock and the army group staff wanted to bring back some of the heavy artillery batteries with the 4th Army to help with the upcoming assault on Warsaw. Redeployment back to Warsaw would take several days with the distance they would have to travel and parts of the rail line were still damaged. The Luftwaffe informed Bock that more time was needed to properly prepare the airfields for the air units that were to support the attacks. So, Bock and the rest of the ground forces would have to wait.

---

[59]National Archives: T314/367/683-684 and 699-700; Records of the VIII Army Corps.

In the meantime, Bock, the army group staff and the 3rd Army had drawn up a general plan of attack for the upcoming assault on Warsaw. There would be a one-hour artillery preparation fire on all known enemy strong points and artillery positions. Four assault groups the size of one regiment each, reinforced with flamethrowers, infantry and anti-tank guns, would make the initial attacks. For further support, groups of armored vehicles were to be brought up if further firepower was required. The first attack group was to move into the Praga suburbs north of Struga Street. The second group would drive into the city between Struga and Marki Streets. The ultimate goal of both these groups would be to seize the upper bridge over the Vistula River. The third assault group would drive down both sides of Wanver Road until it reached the middle bridge over the Vistula. Lastly, the fourth group would move south of Wanver Road to seize the third and fourth lower bridges. Bock added his own emphasis in the war diary that "only pinpoint artillery fire from the heavy guns was to fire on known enemy positions. No drum or rolling fire should be used. Assault troops should be well equipped with infantry guns and flak guns to deal with enemy strongholds. Concentration of units should be maintained and no piecemeal attacks." The 3rd Army was already coordinating with the 1st Air Fleet on what would be the best targets for the dive-bombers. The only thing the Luftwaffe was concerned about was the weather. The air fleet staff informed the 3rd Army staff that they should be aware that if the weather turned bad the ground units would be on there own.

Turning to active operations for the day, there was very little to report. For the I and II Army Corps facing the Polish forces in the Praga suburbs, the only activities were the artillery shelling and probing attacks. More important to both the corps staffs were the problems facing them in the projected attacks. Both staffs meet with General Küchler during the day to discuss how to tackle any tactical problems that might arise during the battle. What concerned the I Corps staff the most was the security of its rear area and its problem of caring and feeding of the enormous number of prisoners being held around Minsk Mazowiecka. Dr. Drey, the I Corps chief medical officer, expressed the concern that there was a potential of disease breaking out amongst the POW's and that it could spread to their own troops. This, combined with the upcoming assault would stretch the ability of the medical staffs of both corps and army to care for both. Küchler, though, felt confident that the army could handle the situation by drafting the local medical personal (and this was done subsequently).

Much to the relief of the 228th Infantry Division, the Panzer Division Kempf had begun moving into positions around the west part of Modlin, relieving that part of the line from the infantry division. With this reinforcement, it would now be easier for the Germans to hold the Poles in place around the fortress. The 15th Border Command had also taken over rear security behind both divisions enabling both divisions to concentrate all their forces against the Modlin fortress. With both these divisions and the non-divisional forces at their disposal, the II Army Corps felt confident that it had the forces to take the fortress.[60]

South of Brest-Litovsk, the 3rd Panzer Division had settled into a defensive mode, fighting off various Polish groups that were trying to infiltrate their lines. Not only had the division captured large numbers of prisoners, but also were having to deal with the massive amount of refugees fleeing the approaching Russian forces. The divisions, under orders by corps headquarters, were simply turning them back. The Germans had more than enough refugees already to have to deal with that were already west of the Bug River. Overall the number of POW's taken by the XIX Corps had slowed considerably during the day indicating that there were few Polish forces left in the region and that they had, for the most part, fled south. All the corps was waiting on now was the arrival of the Russians.[61]

Army Group South – 19 September

With organized resistance effectively over in the Bzura pocket, the 8th and 10th Armies assessed the total number of enemy prisoners of war captured in the pocket at about 120,000. For weapons and equipment, the Germans estimated total was as follows: 300 artillery pieces, 3,500 horses, 30 armored cars, 3 aircraft, 1 armored train, 4,450 wagons and several thousand rifles and machineguns. The one draw back to the German success was their inability to stop the several thousands of Polish troops that had slipped through the eastern side of the pocket, allowing the Poles to add significant reinforcements to the Warsaw garrison. The units effectively destroyed in the pocket from the Polish order of battle were the 4th, 9th, 14th, 15th, 16th, 17th, 26th and 27th Infantry Divisions and parts of the 31st and 35th Infantry Divisions. Some eleven regiments from the 1st, 2nd, 3rd, 5th, 7th, 10th, 11th and 24th Infantry Di-

---

[60]National Archives: T314/34/452-455; Records of the I Army Corps and T314/81/248-252; Records of the II Army Corps.
[61]National Archives: T314/611/686-689; Records of the XIX Army Corps.

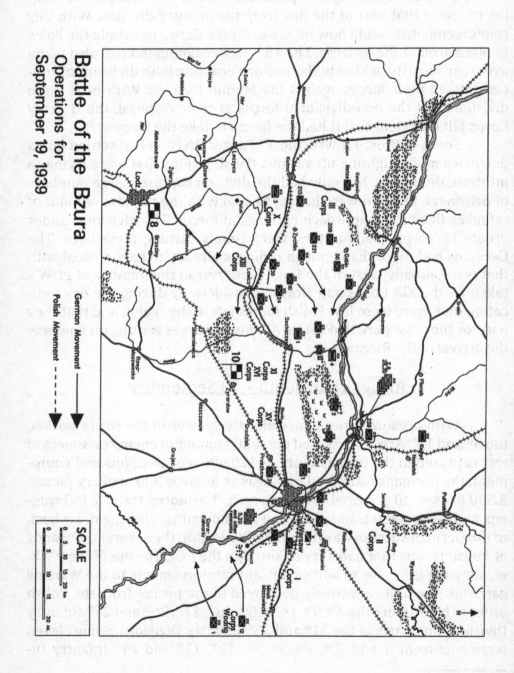

Battle of the Bzura
Operations for
September 19, 1939

visions were identified as well. Parts of the Wielpolska, Podolska and Nowogrodska Cavalry brigades were eliminated in the pocket. General Blaskowitz himself had nothing but praise for the divisions of the 8th Army, for their resilience on the defense against the initial Polish attack and for the offensive work preformed by all the units under his command. The quick assessment of the situation and the rapid redeployment of the German forces were key to the destruction of the Polish forces in the pocket.

With the elimination of the Bzura pocket, the army group could now focus its entire attention on the assault on Warsaw. A new date for the assault to begin was set for 25 September if the necessary heavy artillery and engineer units were brought up in time. The army group's plan was to begin the movement of the necessary divisions by 21 September. Control of the assault forces were to be under the control of the 8th Army with two corps headquarters, the XI and XIII. Five infantry divisions were to be moved into positions around Warsaw. The 17th, 18th, 19th, 24th and 31st Infantry Divisions were chosen as they were deemed to be in the best shape after the fight for the Bzura pocket. For artillery support the 8th Army would have its own artillery with the addition of the corps artillery of the III and X Army Corps as well as the 614th Artillery Regimental staff. The 10th Army would provide the 605th and 634th Heavy Artillery Battalions and the 627th Artillery Regimental Staff from the XV Corps, the II/54th, II/60th, II/93rd and II/115th Heavy Artillery Battalions from the XVI Corps, the 624th Heavy Artillery Battalion from the IV Corps and the II/56th Heavy Artillery Battalion with the 49th Artillery Regimental Staff from the XIV Corps. The 14th Army would provide the 610th, 617th and 623rd Regimental Artillery Staffs with the 629th, 605th, 631st and 641st Heavy Artillery Battalions. For engineer support the 8th Army would use its own assets with the addition of the 60th Engineer Battalion from XIV Corps, the 62nd and 48th Engineer Battalions from the XVI Corps, the SS Engineer Battalion from the XV Corps and the 51st Engineer Battalion with the 617th Engineer Regimental Staff from army group reserve. The army group took the flamethrower troops from the divisions of the 8th and 10th Armies that were not being deployed before Warsaw and placed directly under the command of the above engineer battalions for additional support. The plan was to have all these units in place by the evening of 24 September.

The staff of Army Group South once again emphasized the need for close cooperation with the Luftwaffe and to coordinate all ground efforts with the 3rd Army attacks coming from the Praga side of Warsaw.

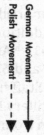
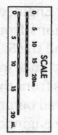
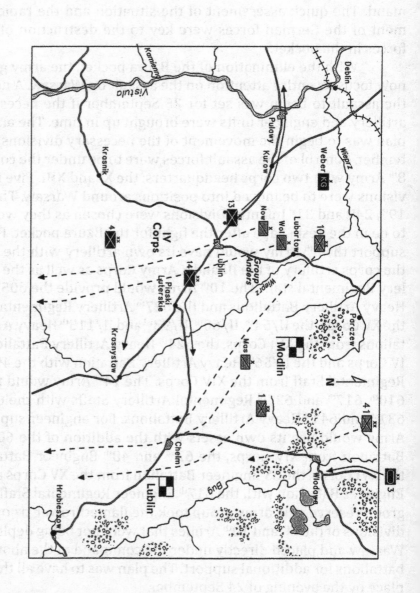

10th Army Operations
September 19-20, 1939

Of particular importance to Rundstedt and Manstein was that the latest intelligence on Polish morale in the city was that it remained high and that they would put up a spirited defense. The one thing both generals wanted to avoid was a long siege. A prolonged siege would give the other Polish forces in the field heart to fight on and might encourage the Allies to launch a sustained offensive on Germany's still vulnerable western frontier. In this relation, OKH already had several divisions from both army groups slated for movement to the western front. The recent Saar offensive launched by the French Army, gave pause to Hitler, Halder and the OKH staff. They realized they had better reinforce the western front in case the Allies tried to launch a more serious offensive. Some of the divisions nominally slated for movement were the motorized divisions of Guderian's XIX Corps and the infantry divisions of the III and X Corps. Other divisions would follow predicated on how much longer it would take to subdue the other Polish forces in the field and how serious matters might become on the western front.

Turning to active operations in the field, the IV Army Corps continued its push east to intercept the remnants of the Army Modlin and Group Anders. But the tables were turned on the 4th and 14th Infantry Divisions as they found that the Polish forces they sought to stop were much stronger than anticipated. Both divisions were under constant attack by the enemy, forcing the divisions to form some sort of defensive barrier against these assaults. What contributed to both divisions' problems was that both were already considerably strung out and this allowed large groups of Poles to slip through their defensive cordon. The corps desperately needed reinforcements. With the Bzura battle over, General Reichenau hoped to switch some of his free divisions to the south to aid this beleaguered corps in the next few days.[62]

With the arrival of the 7th Infantry Division taking over the 1st Mountain Divisions positions north of Lwow, The XVIII Army Corps could now make a proper plan of attack on the Lwow itself. Slating the assault to begin as early as 21 September, General Beyer wanted a simultaneous concentric attack made by all three divisions, the 7th Infantry Division from the north, the 2nd Mountain Division from the south and east and the 1st Mountain Division from the west. Two pieces of news lent urgency to accomplishing this as soon as possible. A communiqué arrived via the 14th Army headquarters that Hitler had directed that the XVIII Corps leave Lwow to the Russians as soon as they arrived. At the same time, the 2nd Mountain Division had encountered the

---

[62]National Archives: T314/216/946; Records of the IV Army Corps.

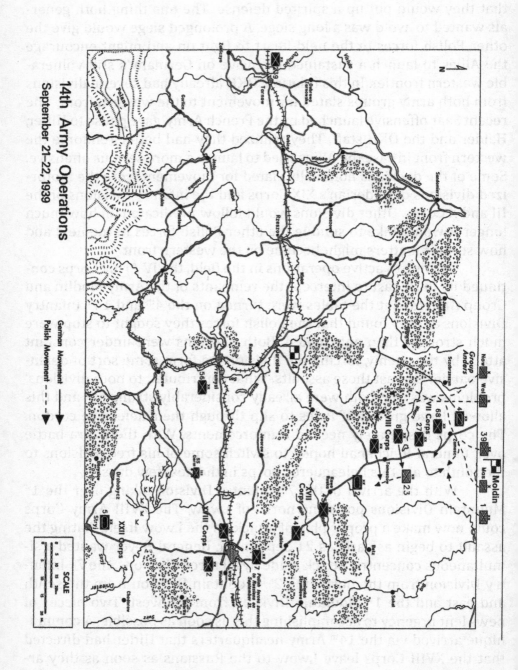

14th Army Operations
September 21-22, 1939

German Movement →
Polish Movement - - - →

N ↑

SCALE
0 5 10 15 20m
0 5 10 15 20 24 km

Note: Based on the wartime Records of the 14th Army Group

advance guard of the Russian forces arriving just east of Winniki that morning. General Beyer was very reticent to just hand over the city to the Russians after having fought so hard to get to this point. Over the next two days Beyer would have to build up his forces for the final assault, while at the same time holding off the Russians long enough for him to take the city.[63]

The days actions for the Tomaszow pocket were at the north end at Zamosc, where the Poles were trying to halt the Germans advance and at the south end at Tomaszow the Poles were attempting to force their way south out of the pocket. At Zamosc, two Polish battalions attacked the small German force holding the town, but all attacks were repulsed by well-timed artillery fire that broke up each attack. Units of the 2nd Motorcycle Battalion, then holding Zamosc, counterattacked after being reinforced by a company of the 4th Light Division's engineer battalion. They captured a Polish colonel, one of the battalion commanders and several hundred prisoners. At the same time, the Poles had launched several attacks against the positions of Gruppe Rothkirch (the reinforced 11th Mounted Rifle Regiment) just north of Tomaszow. These assaults lasted all day, but the regiment managed to beat them all back with, again timely artillery barrages breaking up each attack. Another threat that appeared during the day was that the Poles had brought part of the Zamosc – Tomaszow road, some 10 kilometers north of Tomaszow, under artillery fire. This action threatened the supply and communications line to units to the north. Determining that the shelling originated from a section of forest just west of Tarnawatka, the 4th Light Division's 9th Reconnaissance Regiment sent its armored car reconnaissance battalion to clear it out. Once the battalion had moved in, the shelling stopped. Apparently, the Polish artillery had abandoned its positions once they saw the armored column approaching.

Whilst the 4th Light Division was heavily engaged with the Poles on the east and south side of the pocket, both the VII and VIII Corps faced little or no opposition to their front as they collapsed the pocket from the north and west. The Poles had decided to concentrate all their forces at Tomaszow to affect a breakthrough. But all the efforts came to naught because of the stout defense of the 4th Light Division.[64]

With the XVIII Corps heavily engaged with the siege of Lwow, operational control of the 5th Panzer, 56th and 57th Infantry Divisions in the Stryj region added an extra burden on this corps command. To help

[63]National Archives: T314/595/262; Records of the XVIII Army Corps
[64]National Archives: T315/230/196-197; Records of the 4th Light Division. T314/345/203; Records of the VII Army Corps. T314/367/685 and 701; Records of the VIII Army Corps.

alleviate this strain, the 14th Army sent the XXII Army Corps headquarters staff to take over command of the 5th Panzer, 56th and 57th Infantry Divisions. Since the XXII Corps had already relinquished control of the 2nd Panzer and 4th Light Divisions, the army felt it could be better used in this capacity.[65]

<u>Army Group North – 20 September</u>

To the disappointment of General Bock, the army group received orders from OKH that there would be no ground attack on Warsaw on their front. There was a fear on the part of Hitler and the general staff that a ground assault on Praga would produce too many casualties and that it would be safer to bombard that part of the city by aerial and artillery attack. It was explained to Bock that these would induce the city to surrender in one week. Of course, Bock completely disagreed with this assessment. Bock wired Brauchitsch that abandoning the ground attack on Warsaw now would only encourage the Poles to greater resistance. There were also ongoing attempts by the Poles to break out of the capital. The commander of Army Group North was afraid that the Poles might attempt a large-scale attack to link up with the approaching Russian forces and that his troops would not be strong enough to stop them. But Bocks protestations fell on deaf ears at the army high command. He would have to follow orders.

Further complicating matters, the new instructions from OKH on the locations of the new fallback and demarcation lines were unclear to Bock and his staff. The Russians were already claiming areas that were still behind the agreed demarcation line that was controlled by the Germans. Bock did not want a hasty retreat by the 4th Army that would leave behind any captured war material much less their own equipment (such as temporary bridges and broken-down vehicles). Further clarification on the temporary line was relayed to Army Group North that evening from OKH. The line would run down the Pissa River, then the Narew River until the Vistula following that river until the San River, along the San until Przemysl. From Przemysl the line would run to Chyrow and finally to the Uzoka Pass. This still meant that the 4th Army would have to make haste in its withdrawal to get behind the new temporary line. However, Bock would not be rushed. He ordered General Kluge, the 4th Army commander, to take his time, while avoiding any incidents with the advancing Russian forces. In this Kluge was

[65]National Archives: T314/665/73-77; Records of the XXII Army Corps.

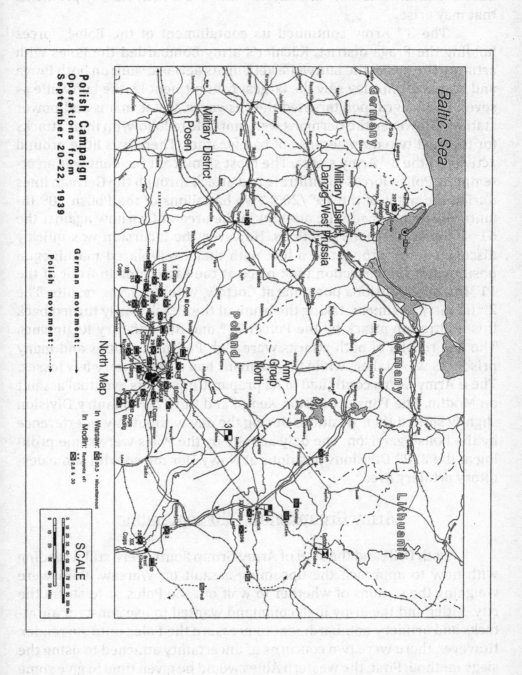

handling the Russians well, as his forces were already in active negotiations with the Russians at Bialystok and Brest to avoid any problems that may arise.

The 3rd Army continued its containment of the Polish forces holding the Praga district. Küchler's army bombarded the Poles with artillery fire, while the Luftwaffe kept up its aerial assault on both Praga and Warsaw. This day saw the largest commitment by the Luftwaffe as several Stuka gruppen targeted the gasworks, water mains and power stations. However, the Germans were not able to follow-up their attacks for the next two days because of bad weather. There was little ground activity in the 3rd Army's area. The most significant incident was an attempt by Polish forces to infiltrate and attack through the German lines during the night of the 19th/20th. Two battalions of the Polish 28th Infantry Regiment made the attempt in the area of Grochow against the 61st Infantry Divisions positions. However, the incursion was quickly discovered and brought to a halt with their well-placed machinegun positions. A similar action took place at the same time in front of the 11th Infantry Divisions positions at Goctow, with the same results. The 2nd Infantry Regiment, taking the brunt of the attack, easily turned back this infiltration attack by the Polish 21st and 36th Infantry Regiments. The end results of both attacks were high Polish casualties and many prisoners were taken, while the Germans had suffered very few losses. The II Army Corps continued in its preparations for its eventual assault on Modlin. The Panzer Division Kempf and the 228th Infantry Division slightly shifted their positions during the day without any interference by the Polish garrison. The only activity by the Poles were some probing at the 228th Divisions positions at Nowy Dor mixed with some desultory artillery fire.[66]

Army Group South – 20 September

Both OKH and the staff of Army Group South were still wrestling with how to approach the upcoming assault on Warsaw. Both were weighing the options of whether to wait out the Poles or to storm the city. Hitler and the army high command wanted to use constant air attacks and artillery bombardment to pressure the Poles unto surrender. However, there were two concerns of uncertainty attached to using the siege method. First, the western Allies would be given time to give some

---

[66]National Archives: T314/81/252-254; Records of the II Army Corps. T314/34/455-458; Records of the I Army Corps. T312/31/7539509; Records of the 3rd Army.

sort of direct or indirect aid and this could bolster the Poles morale to hold on longer. The second concern was the approaching Soviet forces from the east. Even though both the Germans and Russians had made written agreements as to the division of Poland once the fighting was over, Hitler, the foreign office and the military did not fully trust their new partners. And even with these concerns, the Army Group South staff was, for now, very much for the siege method. The army group staff wanted to avoid the excessive casualties that would be brought about if a ground assault occurred. However, General Rundstedt and his staff well knew that time was not on their side and that provisions for a ground assault would have to move forward. The final decision was entirely at the discretion of Hitler and the high command.

There were several concerns that the army group considered most important if an assault was ordered. First and foremost was the matter of keeping casualties low as possible for the attacking troops. The staff used as a comparison the battle for Madrid in the latter stages of the Spanish Civil War. There, the defenders (the Republicans) had a considerable advantage in the number of troops available, an easily defensible urban area and their morale had stood very well. To the staff the situation they faced now was very similar. If an attack were to be made, it would require the use of only first wave divisions and lots of heavy artillery, plus the close cooperation of the Luftwaffe. The staff felt confident that the last two requirements would be more than adequately filled. It was the infantry troops morale that worried them if the assault should become bogged down. The more casualties the assault troops suffered, the more their morale would decline. The first list of units to be moved east had also arrived from OKH. Listed were the III Army Corps headquarters, the 3rd, 17th and 30th Infantry Divisions. All the aforementioned units were to be readied for rail transport within five days.

Turning to the field operations, the 14th Army had achieved a major success in forcing the capitulation of the Polish forces that were in the Tomaszow pocket. On the north side of the pocket, the 27th Infantry Division easily rounded up the remnants of the Polish 6th and 23rd Infantry Divisions, while the 68th Infantry Division had run into much tougher resistance in the forest north of Radka. Its progress was slow until a regiment from the 27th Infantry Division turned to assist the 68th by moving into the rear of the forest. When this happened, the Polish resistance quickly collapsed. Adding to the 68th's discomfort, units of the 4th Light Division that had been moving in from the east had fired

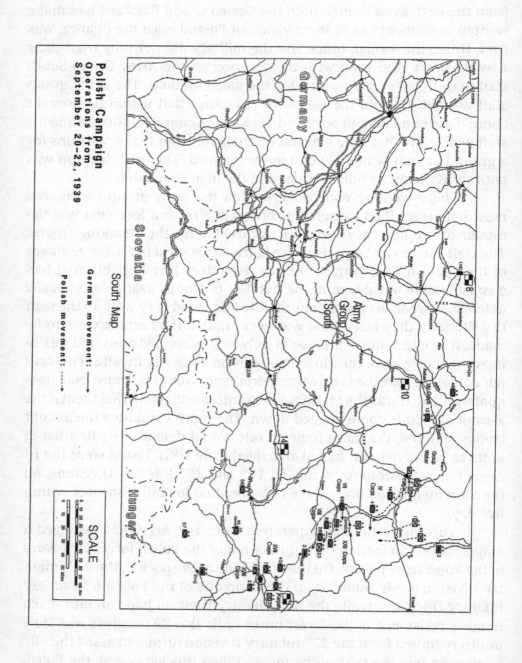

Polish Campaign
Operations from
September 20-22, 1939

South Map

German movement: →
Polish movement: ·····→

SCALE

0 10 20 30 40 50 Miles
0 10 20 30 40 50 60 70 80 90 km

Germany

Slovakia

Hungary

Army Group South

Group Weber

BRESLAU

XIV Corps

VII Corps

IV Corps

VIII Corps

XXII Corps

XVII Corps

XII Corps

upon the 196th Infantry Regiment. It was only after a couple of hours and some wounded soldiers later that the 4th Light had realized their mistake. By the end of the day, the VII Corps had estimated they had rounded up about 13,000 prisoners bringing about an end to the fighting on their side of the line.

On the VIII Corps front facing the pocket, the Poles were desperately hanging on and had even managed to launch some spoiling attacks against the Germans. In the morning hours, the 28th Infantry Division had to repel several attempts by the Poles to break out of the encirclement to the south. Some of these attacks even included tanks from what was left of the Polish Warsaw Mechanized Brigade, but even with this support all the attacks failed. By mid-day the division had gone over to the offensive and, with the support of Group Rothkirch, was able to mop up the remaining Polish troops including the commander and staff of the Polish 6th Infantry Division. The 8th Infantry Division had also encountered stiff resistance in the morning hours, but then a general collapse and surrender by the evening hours. By the end of the day the corps had reported that it had taken about 15,000 prisoners, numerous artillery pieces and large quantities of war material over the previous two days fighting. Lastly, the 4th Light Division held its defensive positions for the day allowing only a few small groups of Polish cavalry to infiltrate to the east through their cordon. The highlight of the 4th's day was when they captured the command staff of Army Lublin attempting to break out of the pocket.[67]

To the south the siege of Lwow was about to reach its conclusion, though not to General Beyers satisfaction. The XVIII Army Corps commander was still making plans for a final assault on the city for 21 September. The Poles themselves were trying to break the German hold on the city's northern perimeter in the morning hours. All attacks on the 1st Mountain Divisions positions were firmly rejected. The 1st Mountain then tried to press the Poles to gain better jumping off positions for the next days attack, but very little ground was gained. However, even if the Germans had gained any further ground it would have been for naught. At about mid-day a direct command from the Führer himself had been transmitted through the 14th Army to the XVIII Corps stating, "that the friendly forces around Lwow were to remain on the defensive and to hold their positions. Once the Russian forces had arrived in force, the corps would hand over their positions to the Russians. The

---

[67]National Archives: T314/343/204; Records of the VII Army Corps. T314/367/685-686 and 701; Records of the VIII Army Corps.

corps would then move all of its forces back to the demarcation line at the San – Vistula Rivers." A direct command from Hitler could not be ignored. So, with great reluctance he ordered the corps to go over to the defensive and to await the arrival of the main Soviet forces.[68]

With its failure to stop the mass of the Polish forces moving south the previous day, the IV Army Corps was given a new mission. They were to move across the Wierpz River and seize the city of Chelm before the Russians had a chance to take it. Tasked to take the city, the 14th Infantry Division had moved up by mid-morning and had established a bridgehead across the river, while the 4th Infantry Division drove towards Krasnystaw to cover the corps southern flank. It was in the afternoon that the 14th Infantry Division ran into heavy resistance from the Polish 10th Infantry Division, slowing the divisions advance the rest of the day. This had not been anticipated, as the Germans intelligence had not detected this large Polish force moving across the IV Corps front. This meant that it would be another one or two days before the 14th Division would have the chance of capturing Chelm.[69]

<u>Army Group North – 21 September</u>

With the reduction of Army Group North's role in taking Warsaw reduced to a mere defensive one, Bock and the army group staff turned to other matters at hand. Negotiations with the Poles in Warsaw on allowing which diplomats could leave the capital was handled by General Küchler and his staff. The Poles wanted some 1,500 diplomats and ambassadors to be allowed to leave, but Küchler would only allow 800. This is how many the Germans could handle in one day to verify their credentials.

Bock continued to fret over the captured war material that his forces would have to abandon if they followed the set dates and lines prescribed by OKH. Not only would the Russians get Polish material and supplies they would also get some of some of their own materials that could not be moved in time. In this case Bock urged General Kluge to delay his forces movements behind each demarcation line as much as possible without openly antagonizing the Russians. Especially frustrating to Bock was the delay for setting the assault date on Warsaw. Now it seemed that Hitler and the high command were worried about the perception of the war was having in America. General Stülpnagel

[68]National Archives: T314/595/262; Records of the XVIII Army Corps.
[69]National Archives: T314/216/946-947; Records of the IV Army Corps.

had relayed to Bock that Hitler and OKH wanted to see how meetings in the American congress about the war might affect weapons exports between America and other European countries. Bock thought all of this was patently ridiculous and had nothing to do with the prosecution of the campaign. This would only give the Poles more time to shore up their defenses in Warsaw.

The Germans assessment of the Poles morale in Warsaw was still unchanged from the previous few days. Polish morale remained high. What greatly aided the army group's intelligence assessment were their interviews with several of the diplomats that were processed out of the city. This greatly clarified the picture of what was going on in the city. The Germans learned that most Polish governmental agencies had already evacuated the city and that the civil government was in the hands of Mayor Stazynski. They also learned that General Walerian Czuma, the commander of the Warsaw military forces had been wounded several days earlier and that he had been replaced by General Rommel. Some diplomats had noted an increase in the number of machinegun nests and barricades erected in the past week. To help keep order in the city the government had formed citizen defense companies to act as auxiliary police. Overall the diplomats reported that there was a general calm amongst the citizens of Warsaw and that there were few signs of panic.

Militarily, there was little activity. There was no activity by the Poles at the Fortress Modlin save that 500 defectors from the fortress that had been captured west of Modlin. The defectors said that the Poles were going to gather a force to try and breakout and reach Warsaw in the next twenty-four hours. The Germans dismissed this as the Poles were seen to be too weak to make such an effort. At Praga the Poles made several probing attacks during the night of 20/21 September against the I and II Corps. All of these were easily contained and beaten back. Lastly, Corps Wodrig was still in the process of rounding up stray Polish troops southeast of Warsaw in and around the town of Aleksandrow. According to a Polish staff captured a few days earlier said that these were mostly troops from the 13th Infantry Division. After the division had crossed the Vistula River around 11/12 September, some of the division's troops had been cut off from the main body when they had attempted to move north to Warsaw. When the division found the Germans were too strong around Warsaw the division was forced to retreat to the south leaving some of its units cut off by the advancing Corps Wodrig.

Army Group South – 21 September

With the sole responsibility of taking Warsaw left to Army Group South, the army groups command staff worked out the finer details of how this would be accomplished. Since the 8th Army had already been assigned the task of controlling the corps and the divisions for the assault, the area of the 8th Army's operations zone had to be established, the method of attack and time of attack. The frontage the 8th Army was to cover started just north of Warsaw in a line running from the Vistula River at Lomianki to Latchorzow just west of Warsaw to Raszyn and from there to Wilanow and the Vistula River just south of the city. The 10th Army was to take control of the Modlin – Kaminoska Forest area west of the city relieving the 8th Army forces that were currently holding these positions. The 10th Army also took over all the positions south of the city leaving the 8th Army free to concentrate all its forces on Warsaw.

In preparation for the final assault the 8th Army would first have to eliminate the outer forts that ringed the city. The staff expected the fight for these field works to be difficult, but with the proper mix of artillery and infantry they were expected to fall in two days. Once the outer ring had been broken the assault on the city itself would be divided into two main groups. The north group, the XI Army Corps, would concentrate its main effort along the Modlin – Warsaw road with a secondary thrust moving in from Powazki. The south group, The XIII Army Corps, would make its main effort along the Warsaw – Wilanow road with a secondary effort up the Warsaw – Siuzewiec road. Both groups would work there way to the center of Warsaw, eventually capturing all of the bridges along the Vistula to prevent any reinforcements coming from Praga. Diversionary attacks were launched on the west side of Warsaw to divert Polish attention from the main attacks. The army group emphasized the importance of using an all arms approach to the battle, especially the use of infantry guns to reduce field works and machinegun nests. Some of the targets that the Luftwaffe was targeting to destroy before the initial assaults were the telephone exchanges, the electric and gas works and water works. Lastly, to ensure that civilian casualties were kept to a minimum, wherever they were encountered they were to be moved quickly to the rear as time and circumstances would allow. The follow-up troops would then hold the civilians until they could be handed over to the military police or security units. The day for the assault had not been set yet, but the 8th Army's forces were to be ready by the 23rd.

In preparation for the upcoming assault the 8th Army began shifting some of its divisions into position. The 10th Infantry Division moved to Zyradow to take over the 31st Infantry Divisions positions directly south of Warsaw, while the 213th Infantry Division had begun movement to take up positions south of Modlin. Most disconcerting to the army was the outer forts had not been fully occupied by the Poles in the previous days. But now reconnaissance had indicated that they were all now fully manned and additional field works and barricades had been erected covering all the roads leading into Warsaw. The 8th Army's intelligence staff estimated that some 20,000-30,000 Polish troops were occupying this outer ring of defenses.

With most of the 10th Army's divisions shifting to accommodate the 8th Army around Warsaw there was little action on its part. The 29th Motorized and 2nd Light Division began their movement that would place them north of Warsaw to block the Warsaw – Modlin road. All the other motorized divisions were moving south of Warsaw to begin entraining to be sent west when rail transport became available. Only the army's IV Army Corps was continuing any offensive action past the Wieprz towards Chelm. Both the 4th and 14th Infantry Divisions had marched east about a half a day when orders had arrived from the army to turn back and return to the newly set demarcation line. This effectively ended any more offensive actions for the 10th Army for the campaign .

The large Polish force that had tangled with the IV Corps the previous two days had now run into the forces of the 14th Army. This force, consisting of the remnants of Army Modlin and Group Anders, at first tried moving east and then south to avoid the Germans, while attempting to reach Lwow. However, once the Poles had realized there were massive Russian forces blocking their way to the east, the Poles had no choice but to take their chances against the Germans by moving south again. This is when they ran into the VII Corps. The VII Corps itself had not anticipated encountering any more major enemy formations as its divisions made their way back to the demarcation line. The first sign of trouble came in the morning hours when the 4th Light Division reported it had been attacked by Polish formations from the northwest. At first General Schobert and his staff thought the 4th Lights command was exaggerating the seriousness of the situation. The 4th Light had, in the previous week and a half (the corps felt), overestimat-

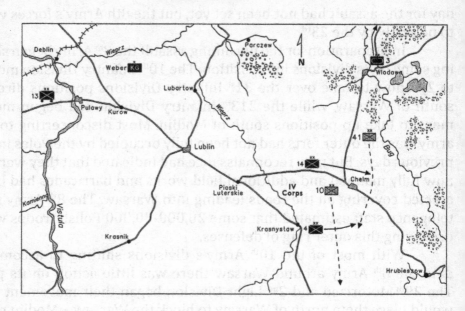

10th Army Operations
September 21–22, 1939

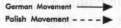
German Movement ———▶

Polish Movement – – –▶

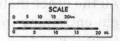
SCALE

0 5 10 15 20 Km

0 5 10 15 20 Mi.

ed the threat the Poles were to their own forces and were distrustful of this report. However, before long another report from the 27th Infantry Division changed their minds. The divisions 40th Infantry Regiment had come under attack around Labunie by a Polish force of two battalions with the support of some artillery and cavalry. Adding weight to the seriousness of this threat, the VIII Corps reported they had also come under attack along their eastern flank. To meet this threat the VII Corps suspended all movement by the 27th and 68th Infantry Divisions to the west. Both divisions were to hold their present positions until the corps could assess the situation and what measures should be taken. By mid-day the corps decided to take action against the Poles with a limited attack. The 68th Infantry Division would move towards Zamosc while the 27th Infantry Division would cross the Zamosc – Tomaszow road and act against the Polish forces to its north. Both divisions had only moved forward a few kilometers when both were halted by a stubborn Polish defense. Meanwhile the 4th Light Division, which had been ordered to continue its march west, was still under attack by portions of Group Anders. To assist the division the VIII Corps sent units of the 27th Infantry Division, which enabled the 4th Light to finally extract itself from the front line. Eventually a regiment (the 169th) of the 68th Division took over the positions vacated by the 4th Light. By dusk the 27th and 68th Infantry Divisions had made little progress against the Poles. It was the corps decision to wait until the next day to launch any further attacks. The 28th Infantry Division would be heavily reinforced to be the 'hammer' while the 68th Division would hold its positions to act as the 'anvil'.[70]

For the rest of 14th Army's divisions, they remained in their positions for the day. General List, like Bock at Army Group North, wanted to take his time before moving the army's divisions back behind the demarcation line. He wanted time to recover as much of the their own damaged equipment and captured enemy material so none would be left for the Russians. In this the Russians were going to oblige. Except at Lwow, the Russians forces had not arrived in force before the 14th Army giving List and the army the time they needed.

Army Group North – 22 September

There was very little combat activity to report on the part of the army group. The most significant incident of the day was the death of Lieu-

---

[70]National Archives: T314/343/205; Records of the VII Army Corps.

tenant General Werner Fritsch.[71] Fritsch, the commander of the 12th Artillery Regiment, was killed while participating in operations with the 48th Infantry Regiment making security sweeps south of Warsaw. His column had been ambushed by some Polish stragglers at the crossroads of the town of Zacisze. General Bock made sure that word of his death was communicated throughout the whole army command this day.

Hitler himself had visited the front to watch some of the artillery and air attacks during the day. The 3rd Army had set up an observation post at a church at the town of Glinki, some five kilometers east of the Praga district. While at the 3rd Army headquarters Bock appealed to the Führer again for a ground attack on Praga itself by the 3rd Army. However, Hitler rebuffed any ideas of that sort and that the 3rd Army would continue its artillery bombardment of the Praga district. In relation to this, the 3rd Army had cancelled any further *stuka* attacks against both Praga and Modlin, because some of the bombs had fallen on some of its own troops. Küchler felt that his troops might become demoralized if this went on too long. The Luftwaffe would still continue its assault beyond the immediate front line.

Reports of the effects of the artillery and air attacks were having on the Poles in Warsaw had been coming in through by word of Polish deserters. The numbers of deserters were increasing each day. The Polish deserters said that some shortages of food and water were now becoming apparent. The Luftwaffe propaganda leaflets were having some effect as their own officers told the Polish soldiers that they would be executed upon surrendering to the Germans, but the leaflets promised they would be treated well. Polish troops were also being told that the French had launched attacks against the Germans on the western front and that relief would come soon. But, to the deserters there had been no evidence of that in the last few days, giving them more incentive to desert.

Finally, the 4th Army headquarters staff was ordered by OKH to be moved to Frankfurt-am-Main within the week. The 206th and 23rd Infantry Divisions had already moved back to East Prussia for redeployment. Following these divisions, the 2nd and 29th Motorized and 3rd Panzer Divisons were to be moved to the western front as soon as the

---

[71]General Fritsch had been commander in chief of the German Army in 1938, but was dismissed by Hitler. Fritsch had long opposed Hitler's expansionist policies. Faced by trumped up charges of homosexuality by Himmler he voluntarily left his post. He still wanted to serve in the army so he was allowed to assume command of his old artillery regiment, the 12th at the beginning of the war. With his death, the army gave Fritsch an elaborate and public funeral after the campaign, much to Hitler and the Nazi's displeasure

corps had arrived back in East Prussia.

Army Group South – 22 September

While the preparations for the Warsaw assault continued unabated, General Rundtstedt and his staff had noted that there were still large bodies of Polish troops hiding in the area between Modlin and Warsaw, particularly in the Kampinoska Forest. The Germans feared that their continued presence could be a threat to their besieging forces rear and that they should be eliminated before the actual assault began. To clear them out, the task was given to the 10th Army, which had nominal control of this area. General Reichenau, the 10th Army commander, handed over this task to the XV Army Corps, which in turn tasked its two divisions, the 29th Motorized and 2nd Light, to finish the job. For further support the army group ordered the 24th Infantry Division to place itself between the 18th Infantry Division and the XV Corps so as to give support to either as required. The 18th Infantry Division itself was to consolidate its own positions and made preparations for the upcoming assault on Warsaw.

Turning to the siege preparations, all the heavy artillery batteries were now in place. Shelling of targets, mostly the outer fortified positions, would begin the next day. Once the operations at Modlin and the Kampinoska Forest were brought to a conclusion, operational control of the XI and XV Army Corps and the SS Leibstandarte Regiment, as well as the 19th Infantry Division, were to be handed over to the 8th Army. All the above units were to support the 8th Army's assault on Warsaw, except the XV Corps, which would seal off the Poles southern part of the Modlin bridgehead on the Vistula River. The 10th Army would pull out the XVI Corps with the 1st and 4th Panzer Divisions from Wysogrod – Vistula area, moving them south of the 8th Army's operational area. Reinforcing its own ideas of how to proceed with the assault, the army group had received a message from OKH (and approved by Hitler) on its own set of orders and guidelines to follow during the siege. First and foremost, Army Group North was not to launch any kind of ground assault from its side. Only the artillery bombardment would continue. This did not sit well with Manstein and Blumentritt as they had anticipated the ground assault on Praga would tie down Polish troops, keeping them from reinforcing Warsaw's western defenses. Army Group North was to carry out demonstrations of a ground attack. However, Manstein and Blumentritt knew this would not fool the Poles for long.

OKH had set a tentative date of October 3rd that the city should be in their possession. It was by this date that the Russians were anticipated to have fully drawn up to the demarcation line placing them only 100 kilometers away. There was still a fear on the part of the Führer and OKH that some form of Communist government might overthrow the present government and appeal for aid from the Russians. The sooner they had taken Warsaw the less chance this would happen. In all other aspects, the OKH and Army Group South were in agreement on the attack plans. The date for the ground assault was still set for 25 September.

With its orders to clear out the remaining Polish troops between Warsaw and Modlin, the XV Army Corps set about its task. Reconnaissance had indicated that there was a large concentration of Polish troops in the area of Palmiry and the 29th Motorized Division was given the mission of clearing out these enemy forces. The division's 71st Motorized Infantry Regiment launched an attack out of Janowek at 9:00 AM, moving north until the regiment had made contact with the Poles in Palmiry. When the regiment attacked into the town proper they easily captured it, taking some 200 Polish troops in the process. The Germans pursued the rest of the retreating Poles to Lomna where, upon finding no more enemy troops, called an end to the day's operation. In capturing Palmiry the Germans discovered why the Poles had concentrated there. A search of the town turned up a large stockpile of ammunition. The Poles would certainly have used this to supply any breakthrough attempts to either Modlin or Warsaw.[72]

The only other large field operation taking place was with the 14th Army's VII and VIII Army Corps. The VII Corps 27th Infantry Division was making preparations for another day of fighting, but the Poles had seemingly disappeared before the division during the night. However, around noon the Poles once again appeared to the 27th's front and launched several attacks against its positions, especially against the 40th Infantry Regiment holding the Labunki area. The VII Corps headquarters sent out its air reconnaissance element to assess the situation and found a large Polish force traveling south down the Zamosc – Tomaszow road. Since the Poles were moving away from their forces anyway, the 27th Infantry Division was ordered to make limited attacks against the Poles, and then withdraw.

What ensued during the afternoon was confused state of affairs between the 27th Infantry Division and the VII Army headquarters. By

---

[72]National Archives: T314/550/276-277; Records of the XV Army Corps.

3:00 PM, the 27th had not moved at all. General Schobert, the corps commander, asked General Bergmann why his division had not moved. Bergmann replied that he had received no orders at all that morning! Since there was too little time left in the day for the division to do anything, Schobert ordered the 27th to hold its present positions. Around 5:00 PM, the corps received yet another message from the division saying that the division was moving back six kilometers to a more defensible line. This was against what General Schobert had intended. He wanted the 27th to stay where it was so that it might cooperate in an attack with the VIII Corps the next day. Since it was too late in the day to turn the division around, General Schobert approved of the move. But, at 6:30 PM, the corps received yet another message that the division was moving forward again! By now, Schobert and his staff were getting very exasperated with General Bergmann and his division. All the operations that VII Corps had planned were now completely thrown out of kilter. At this point Schobert had lost any confidence in the 27th's ability to follow orders and consequently cancelled any further offensive moves for the next day. It was just as well. The VII Corps received orders from the 14th Army late that night that the whole army was to start a general withdrawal to the demarcation line the next day.[73]

Immediately to the south, the VIII Army Corps had a quiet morning. Like the VII Corps, the Poles renewed with vigor attacks on both the 8th and 28th Infantry Divisions in the afternoon hours. The 28th Infantry Division, which had spent the morning resting and reorganizing, was attacked around 4:00 PM, northeast of Tomaszow. The division easily beat off these attacks. The 8th Infantry Divisions position, however, became a little bit more precarious because of the strange movements of the 27th Infantry Division. Late in the day a Polish force had moved into a forested area north of Wiepyrzow and Tarnawacki, endangering the divisions northern flank. The division sent in one battalion, the III/38th, to clear the forest and reestablish a link with the 27th Division. The battalion retook the forest, but the Poles tried to retake the forest in a series of attacks the rest of the day. The Poles failed and the battalion held its positions that evening and all through the night.[74]

[73]National Archives: T314/343/206-208; Records of the VII Army Corps.
[74]National Archives: T314/367/687 and 702-703; Records of the VIII Army Corps.

Army Group North – 23 September

While awaiting the assault on Warsaw to begin, the army group attended to other matters at hand. The 4th Army's units continued their movements back to East Prussia without any problems. At first all the divisions were going to move back to their original prewar cantonments. However, OKH and General Brauchitsch were still uneasy about the Russians intentions once they had reached the Reichs border and demarcation line. In case the Russians infringed on the Reichs territory, the army wanted the proper forces to counter them. It was ordered that the majority of the motorized divisions be retained in East Prussia until such time that other units could properly secure the new borders. Once this had been accomplished, OKH would give notice to the army group that it should be ready for redeployment to the western front.

Meanwhile, consultations with Army Group South over the anticipated attack on Modlin continued. Bock suggested a simultaneous attack on the north and south sides of the fortress under the uniform leadership of the II Army Corps. Army Group South responded saying that they wanted to bring the assault on Warsaw to its proper conclusion first before turning its attention to Modlin. This meant that the assault on Modlin could be as late as October 3rd or 4th. Bock knew that this would give time for the Poles to reinforce their positions at Modlin, which would mean more time and effort in taking the fortress. It would also delay the transfer of troops that might be needed to counter any offensive moves by the Allies on the western front. With all this in mind, Bock asked and received permission from OKH to take Modlin himself with what forces he could gather, with the provision that he leave adequate forces around Praga to assist in the main assault on Warsaw.

Assessing its twin missions, Bock and the army group staff worked out what forces could be spared at the Praga front and what would be needed against Modlin. The forces then before Modlin at the moment were deemed inadequate for what was required. The 32nd Infantry Division was then chosen to beef up the assault forces. The 217th Infantry Division was deemed adequate to hold the front line at Praga by itself. The 3rd Army and II Corps were informed of the plans and both adjusted their plans accordingly. The II Corps now planned to have the 32nd Infantry Division carry out the main assault on Modlin Forts II and III while Panzer Division Kempf would launch secondary attacks on the fortresses northwest line with its main focus on Fort Number I. The 228th Infantry Division would remain on the defensive on the east

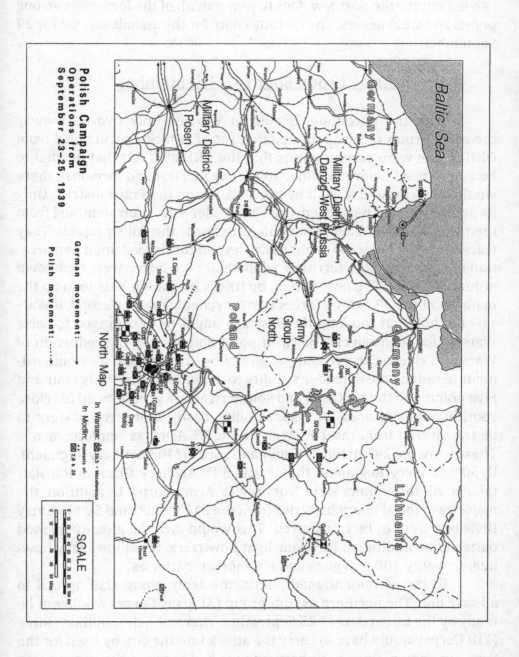

Polish Campaign
Operations from
September 23-25, 1939

North Map

Baltic Sea

Germany
Military District Posen
Military District Danzig-West Prussia
Poland
Army Group North
Germany
Lithuania

German movement:
Polish movement:

In Warsaw:
In Modlin: Remnants of:

SCALE

side of Modlin unless there was a rapid collapse of Polish resistance. In the meantime, intensive reconnaissance of Modlins positions was to be carried out for the next few days to pinpoint all of the fortresses strong points and weaknesses. The tentative date for the assault was set for 29 September.

Army Group South – 23 September

With the upcoming assault on Warsaw only two days away the army group received an updated set of 'attack instructions' from OKH. There were several points that the OKH staff felt that needed to be emphasized before the final attack began. First and foremost, there would be no ground assault by the 3rd Army on the Praga district. Only its artillery would be needed. OKH and Hitler's decision stemmed from their uneasiness of having Russian forces near the Polish capital. They feared that the Russians might move beyond the agreed upon demarcation line, seizing more territory, while their own forces were tied down around Warsaw. The best option, by OKH's reasoning, was to keep the majority of the 3rd Army's forces free for redeployment. Second, if Warsaw did hold out too long the Russians might be encouraged to seize Warsaw for themselves. The third point emphasized the reduction of Warsaw's electric, water and gas works by artillery and air bombardment to reduce the defender's ability to defend the city. Parts Four and Five pointed to the northern and southern attack groups need for close coordination and areas of responsibility. Lastly, more troops were to be transferred from the 10th Army to the 8th Army as reinforcements. These were the 24th Artillery Command staff, II/40th Artillery Regiment, II/50th Artillery Regiment, the 4th and 14th Artillery Observation Battalions. All these units were from the IV Army Corps. In addition, the majority of the artillery batteries from the 213th, 208th and 50th Infantry Divisions were to be transferred. This would give the already massed batteries an additional fifty-four light howitzers, fifty-four heavy howitzers, twenty 100 mm guns and six 'mörser' batteries.

To the aforementioned points, the army group staff agreed to all save one. The northern assault group (XI Army Corps) would not be ready by the target date of 25 September. Therefore, the southern force (XIII Corps) would have to carry the attack into the city by itself for the first day or two. Once both battlegroups had reached their secondary goal lines (the outer suburbs) the 8th Army would pause to demand the surrender of the city. If this was rejected the army would opt for an artillery and air bombardment against the rest of the city to avoid any house-to-house fighting. It would be left up to the Führer for the decision whether to carry the infantry battle into the city.

Helping the 8th Army, the army group asked for the 3rd Army's cooperation to, as much as possible, limit the military and civilian traffic across the Vistula bridges by artillery fire. This would limit the Poles in moving civilians out of Warsaw, while restricting the number of reinforcements coming from Praga. The army group staff was unsure at this point what air units would be available to support the 8th Army. The staff requested that the Luftwaffe give a list to the 8th Army's staff and to send a Luftwaffe officer from *Flieger Führer Zbv* to help coordinate the air attacks with the ground troops.

Turning to field operations, the majority of the 14th Army's divisions had begun their movement back to the demarcation line. The exception was the VII and VIII Army Corps, which were still battling with the remnants of Group Anders and Army Modlin. Both corps would try yet another enveloping attack with the VII Corps being the northern pincer and the VIII Corps acting as the southern pincer. Ultimately neither corps was able to affect the desired pocket. The VII Corps difficulty stemmed from its previous days problems with the 27th Infantry Division. General Schobert planned on having the 27th Infantry Division act as the corps main attack force forming the outer wheel of the pincer, while the 68th Infantry Division would maintain contact with the Poles holding them in place. It was not long after the divisions had begun their attack around 8:00 AM, when a report from VIII Corps stated that a large Polish force was moving west, apparently to drive a wedge between both corps at Krasnobrod and Lipsko. To meet this threat the 169th Infantry Regiment was moved to the area to setup a defensive position. However, only a small Polish force appeared before the regiment making it appear that the VIII Corps was seeing enemy forces that were not really there. By 10:00 AM, General Schobert felt both divisions had advanced far enough east to turn south and close the pockets north side. But this is where things began to go wrong. First the 27th Infantry Division said they were running short of artillery ammunition and could not advance without adequate artillery support. Even with the dispatch of extra ammunition trains to the division there seemed to be no forward movement being made by the division. At 1:00 PM, General Schobert decided to go to the 27th Division and assess the situation himself. What Schobert found after interviewing several of the regimental and battalion commanders was that the troops had lost their aggressive

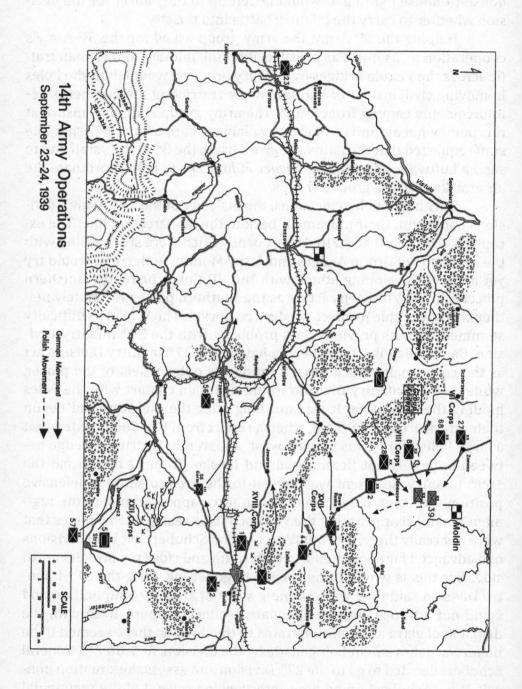

spirit. All the sub-commanders pointed to the issuance (and apparently read by all the rank and file) of the last Führer order that stated, "that no more German blood should be shed east of the demarcation line". This order, combined with the knowledge that the rest of the army was retreating, had taken any offensive spirit the division had left. General Schobert realized that he could not push this division any further, so he ordered the 27th Division to halt its advance. Besides, the 68th Infantry Division had advanced further east and had found little or no enemy forces to its front. Seeing little to be gained by any further advance, offensive operations were halted for the day.[75]

The southern pincer, the VIII Corps, did not encounter any problems as its northern neighbor during its days advance. Both the 8th and 28th Infantry Divisions moved forward without encountering much resistance from the Poles. By midday the corps commander, General Busch, had stopped the advance. The supposedly large enemy force that the VII and VIII Corps was to surround and destroy turned out to be a much smaller force than had been previously thought. Combined with the fact that the order to begin the withdrawal back to the demarcation line had arrived that morning, General Busch felt it was not worth any further effort. The only real crisis of the day came when the 8th Infantry Division's headquarters came under attack in the morning hours by a wayward Polish cavalry regiment. The headquarters staff had made preparations to move forward when, at around 8:00 AM, they came under rifle and machinegun fire. The staff immediately formed a hedgehog defense, while radioing nearby units for assistance. For some four hours the officers, officials, clerks, cooks and drivers maintained their positions using the few machineguns and rifles they had on hand. Relief came in the form of the 47th Engineer Battalion and 8th Reconnaissance Battalion, when both units broke through the Polish positions around 12:30 PM. They forced the Poles to break off their attacks and drove them away.[76]

Finally, the XI Army Corps had completed its task of clearing the remnants of the Polish forces hiding in the Kampinoska Forest. The corps rounded up nearly two thousand prisoners and significant amounts of equipment. Most curiously, the Germans found numerous dead Polish soldiers from the 29th Motorized Division's earlier sweep of the area.

---

[75]National Archives: T314/343/208-211; Records of the VII Army Corps.
[76]National Archives: T314/367/687 and 703-705: Records of the VIII Army Corps.

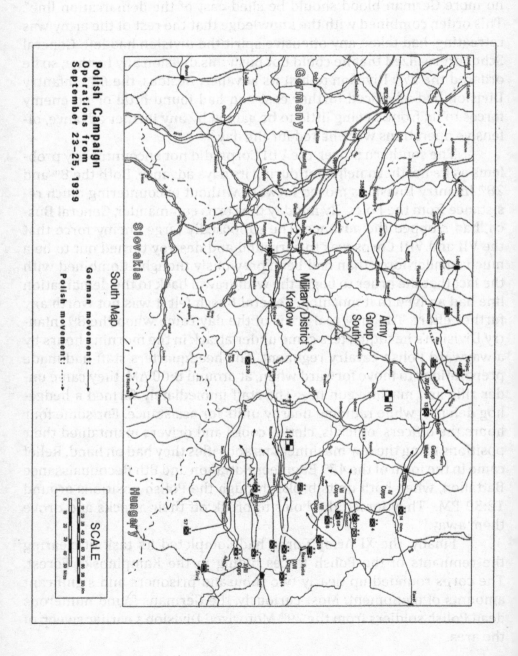

Polish Campaign
Operations from
September 23–25, 1939

South Map

German movement: →
Polish movement: ⇢

SCALE

0 10 20 30 40 50 Miles
0 10 20 30 40 50 60 70 80 90 100 km

Germany

Slovakia

Hungary

BRESLAU

Military District
Kraków

Army
Group
South

Group
Weier

Army Group North – 24 September

For the most part, the army group's activities were centered on the more mundane problems of winding down its part of the campaign. OKH had requested a schedule on handing over the non-divisional troops presently under the army group for reassignment and transport to the western front. There was a discussion on whether to move the 21st Infantry Division to Danzig for security reasons. In the end, it was agreed to leave the division at the East Prussian border near the Masurian Lakes for now. Next, the II Army Corps with its assigned divisions, was to be moved once the siege of Warsaw and Moldlin were over. Concerning the siege itself, the army group received a request from the 8th Army for additional artillery crewmen to help man their guns. With the intensive bombardment, some of the 8th Army's batteries needed some relief at different times of the day. Still under discussion was the 3rd Army's ability to aid the 8th Army's effort in the upcoming assault. Both armies' staffs were still working out the details to avoid any friendly fire incidents. Lastly the assault on Fortress Modlin was reset to begin on 28 September, but this date was still dependent on how the assault on Warsaw was progressing.

The only notable field actions were at Nowy Dor and with the 10th Panzer Division. At Nowy Dor the Poles launched weak attacks on the 217th and 228th Infantry Divisions positions. These were easily repulsed. Of note, when Polish prisoners were interrogated after the attacks, they stated that the fortress had plenty of ammunition, but was short of all other provisions. For the 10th Panzer, there was a 'friendly fire' incident between the division's reconnaissance battalion and advancing Russian cavalry near Widowla. However, the situation did not escalate, as officers on both sides were able to quickly bring the firing to a stop without any casualties on either side.

Army Group South – 24 September

Once again emphasizing the salient points for the upcoming assault on Warsaw, the staff of Army Group South sent a detailed message to OKH outlining what they considered would lead to a successful conclusion. First was the ability of the assault forces to form its pincer movement by penetrating into the city from the north and south along the Vistula River. Seizure of the bridges across the river was vital to prevent the Poles from fleeing into the Praga district. Next, once the ground assault was started, the army group staff requested that the 3rd Army restrict its artillery fire to specific parts of Warsaw so it would not fall on the attack routes laid out for its own troops. Lastly a staff officer from the 3rd Army would be sent to the 8th Army to provide a liaison with the 3rd Army in case of any coordination problems between the two armies. Unfortunately, late in the day a message from the 3rd Army stated that some of its forces deployed north of Praga were to be redeployed to help with the Modlin siege. This meant that the north flank attack on Warsaw would not have as great as support as had been planned.

At the same time, the Army Group South staff sent a message to OKH asking to clarify certain points on the handling and treatment of civilians in the battle zone. The army group was certainly aware that with such an intense air and artillery bombardment in a city crammed with civilians there would be enormous civilian casualties. Rundstedt and Manstein were aware that too many dead civilians would not look good in the eyes of the world. They had to balance this with the required firepower that would be needed for the troops support. Unless told by the high command, they were going to allow the 8th Army to use all the weapons at their disposal. Another question was "should the battle continue with the assault without consideration of the casualties to one's own troops". The army group was worried that the frontline troops morale might suffer if they started taking to many losses with little to show for it.

Lastly, the army group wanted to put greater restrictions on what targets the Luftwaffe wanted to bomb and what type bombs to use. This was somewhat related to keeping civilian losses low. The Luftwaffe on its part wanted a free hand to bomb what targets they saw fit, including any targets the army might pick. But in the end the Luftwaffe agreed to keep to primarily military targets and to restrict its use of incendiary bombs. The incendiaries would only be used as a last resort if Polish resistance had not been broken by 3 October. In summary Rundstedt and Mainstein wanted to take the city as quickly as possible with minimal casualties. To that end they wanted the execution of the attack to be as ruthless as their forces could allow under the above circumstances.

In keeping with the above, the army group staff passed along an outline of "attack principles" to General Blaskowitz as a guide on the upcoming assault. First, the outline emphasized concentration of forces; firepower and speed were of prime importance. Also, artillery fire was not to be wasted on unimportant targets. In between assaults a systematic attritional fire was to be utilized to keep the enemy occupied. Next were specific guidelines for the artillery. First and foremost, the artillery batteries were to be utilized under any command that was deemed to need them the most. Artillery batteries were to get as close as possible to the frontline and close cooperation with the ranging units were essential to this end. But, close cooperation with the lead assault troops was essential.

In relation to the above, the air reconnaissance units would play an important role in locating enemy units and targets. The air reconnaissance units would need to get the necessary information to the frontline troops in a timely manner. As to the dive-bomber and bomber groups, they would be used to help cordon off and isolate parts of the assault troops flanks. And, like the artillery, the air units would keep up a steady bombardment during the pauses in the ground action to keep the Poles off balance. For the infantry, they would use by and large "stosstrupp" tactics. Organization during the upcoming assault would have to be flexible enough to reflect the changing tactical situation in the battlefield environment. The assault troops were to avoid moving up the main streets of the city to avoid the spreading effect of their fire and the enemies. The smaller side streets were to be used concentrate the firepower of the assault troops. The soldiers in the assault columns had to understand their tasks, especially the NCO's since they were critical to keeping the lower ranks moving forward. Finally, security of the flanks was of the utmost importance. The follow-up troops were to secure and maintain the integrity of the flanks at all times so the assault troops could maintain the main effort. If all of the forgoing guidelines were followed the army group staff felt that the seizure and final surrender of Warsaw would be assured well within the time frame allowed. As to active field operations there was little to report. Both the 10th and 14th Armies were steadily withdrawing their units to the demarcation line. There was little contact with the advancing Russian forces.

Army Group North – 25 September

The 8th Army began its preliminary attacks on Warsaw's outer fort ring with the 3rd Army contributing artillery fire where needed. The army group noted that the assault seemed to be going well. The plans for the assault on Modlin by II Corps continued apace. There were some discussions between the II Corps staff and the army group staff about some minor points on the corps attack plan, such as concentration of

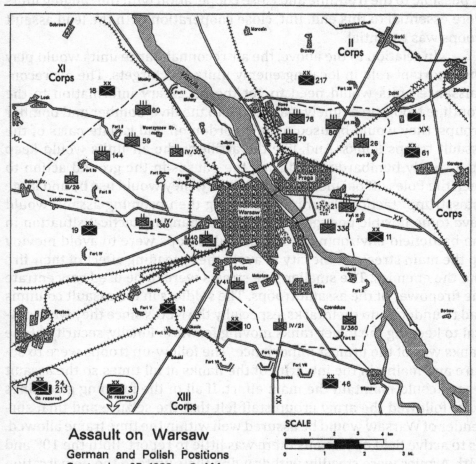

Assault on Warsaw
German and Polish Positions
September 25, 1939 – 8 AM

SCALE

Frontline - - - - - -

artillery fire and where the main weight of the ground assault should be directed. The II Corps wanted to attack on the eastern side of the fortress, but Bock and the 3rd Army resolutely turned down this idea, as it would dilute the concentration of the artillery. The 228th Infantry Division was deemed not suitable for any further offensive action. To help beef up its offensive firepower the 3rd Army said they would provide an extra flak battalion to the II Corps assault units. Flak guns had proven to be effective against Polish bunkers in the previous weeks fighting. The 3rd Army requested and got the Luftwaffe to provide dive-bomber attacks on the first days assault. With this additional help, the II Corps felt this would be enough to break the Polish defenses.

One minor point came up about the retention of the XIX Corps in East Prussia. Many of its units were in need of spare parts and the depots in East Prussia did not have many of the requisite parts. At first General Guderian requested that his divisions be allowed to move back to Germany proper to get what was needed. However, OKH deemed it more important to have the XIX Corps stay where it was. The high command was still nervous about the approaching Russians. The corps' problem was solved when the army's quartermaster was able to send the necessary components from Germany to East Prussia in a timely fashion.

Army Group South – 25 September

Having set the firm date of 26 September to begin the final ground assault on Warsaw, the Germans picked up the intensity of the aerial and artillery bombardment against the cities defenses. To gain better positions to break into the outer fortress ring, General Blaskowitz gave permission to the 10th and 18th Infantry Divisions to make footholds in the Polish positions. General Cochenhausen, the 10th Divisions commander, set the 41st Infantry Regiment just west of the Warsaw – Piaseczno road, with the goal of taking Fort Number VIIa due north of its position. The 21st Infantry Regiment in its position between the 41st Regiment and the Warsaw – Rakow road would advance parallel with the 41st, moving up to the suburb of Ochota. The 85th Infantry Regiment would remain in division reserve. The time for the assault was set for 9:00 AM.

However, even before the attack had begun the I/20th Regiment had already taken out some of its first objectives. The battalion would have been faced with having to cross a wide-open field before even getting close to the Polish positions. The crossfire would be murderous for any of the German troops attempting to get to the emplacements. To prevent this, before dawn the battalion sent an assault group from the 2nd Company of the 20th Regiment, under the command of Lieutenant Geßner, to silence the guns in the Polish forward positions. After successfully penetrating the Polish lines, Captain Henneberg followed directly behind with the rest of the company and some engineers. In only about two hours the company had not only cleared out all the bunkers, but had also lodged themselves in a row of houses north of the emplacements. The 20th Infantry Regiment had already reached some of its goals long before the 9:00 AM start time.

The 41st Infantry Regiment had a much tougher fight on its hands. First, the regiment had to clear the Polish forward emplacements, then fight their way through the town of Mokotow. At 9:00 AM, the attack went in with the regiment quickly clearing the emplacements just to the south of the town. Once the regiment had pushed into Mokotow proper the assault slowed to a block-by-block struggle. The Poles had well fortified the streets and city blocks. The 41st was aided by some of the divisional artillery that had worked its way up to clear terrain on the west side of Mokotow. The divisional artillery commander was able to direct accurate fire from a tower at the civilian airport at Okecie. Still many of the streets were heavily mined and it took considerable time for the *pioniere* of the 60th Engineer Battalion to clear each street. Still the assault teams struggled forward methodically clearing each block. One particular block that proved to be difficult to clear was one held by the students of the Warsaw War Academy in the center of town. The Germans had nothing but praise for the bravery and tenacity in the defense of their position. By dusk most of Mokotow had been cleared, but the regiment faced another day's fighting before clearing the rest of the town before moving on to Warsaw.[77]

With the 20th Infantry Regiments successful push forward the 31st Infantry Division was able to exploit that regiments success by going over on the attack with its frontline regiments, the 12th and 17th. Both regiments were able to push the Polish defenders back right up to the Warsaw suburb of Czyste. On the 10th Infantry Division's right the 46th Infantry Division maintained its positions as its commander felt his troops were not ready for an attack.

On the northern sector, the 18th Infantry Division achieved its goal for the day. The 54th Infantry Regiment successfully seized Fort

[77]National Archives: T312/37/7545504-7545508; Records of the 8th Army

Number I in a quick strike, while the neighboring 51st Infantry Regiment captured Fort Number II after a much more pronounced struggle. The gains were well worth the cost, as the division had gained a much better position for its final assault into the city itself. The 19th Infantry Division maintained its positions as General Schwantes, the division's commander, was satisfied that his own attack positions were more than adequate.[78]

Having arrived the day before, Hitler and Generals Kietel, Halder and Brauchitsch were escorted to the frontline to see some of the day's fighting. Earlier in the day this group attended a meeting at General Reichenau's headquarters where they were briefed on the previous weeks Bzura battle and its results. After the presentation Hitler and the group of generals moved on to the 8th Army headquarters where General Blaskowitz gave an overview of the plan to take Warsaw. Blaskowitz explained that the XIII Corps would begin its main assault on Warsaws southern perimeter at 8:00 AM on the 26th, while the XI Army Corps would start its assault on the north side of the city the next day at 8:00 AM. Telling the Führer about the days action by the 10th Infantry Division, Hitler expressed the desire to see the results. After visiting the 10th Infantry's headquarters and being briefed by the division's commander, he was shown where the assault troops had initially broken through the emplacements and the town blocks where heavy fighting had taken place. The Führer was very impressed by what the troops had accomplished.[79]

Meanwhile the 14th and 10th Armies continued their withdrawal to the demarcation line. The Poles did not try to interfere nor were there any reported incidents with the Russians. The army group estimated that it would be another few days before all of the 10th and 14th Armies' divisions were behind the demarcation line. Also in preparation to move some of its divisions to the western front the 29th Motorized Division and the SS Liebstandarte Regiment were relieved by the 213th Infantry Division and the 2nd Light Division area was handed over to the 221st Infantry Division.

Army Group North – 26 September

The 8th Army began its formal attack on Warsaw as planned, with the 3rd Army contributing its artillery fire to aid in the assault on

---

[78]National Archives: T312/37/7545374-7545375 and 7545389; Records of the 8th Army.
[79]National Archives: T312/37/7545282-7545289; Records of the 8th Army.

the city. The coordinating fire went well as the 8th Army reported at the end of the day that their troops had made significant gains. With no problems in that area, the army group attended to other details in its command area. One was to make sure there were adequate bridges at the key crossings on the Vistula River at Danzig, Graudenz, Mewe, Thorn and Plock. These would have to be maintained by the new area command 'Oberbefehlshaber der Ost'. The army group wanted to make sure that the bridges they left were structurally sound to ensure that supplies and troops could be moved safely across them. The new command wanted the army group to build more bridges especially at Danzig, but Bock said that since the army groups command and staff was moving to the west soon there was no time for their engineers to be engaged in such work. The East Command was on its own as far as the army group was concerned. Another issue related to the bridges was what to do with the ones in the soon to be Russian occupied zone.

Some command changes were also taking place before the army group was to be moved to the western front. The XIX Army Corps was placed under the direct command of Army Group North in case of any incursions over the demarcation line by the Russians. The 4th Army and 21st Infantry Division were detached from the army group's command. The 4th Army would make its preparations to move to the western front, while the 21st Infantry Division would remain in the area until the border situation was more settled.

One other problem that came up during the day that greatly disturbed General Bock himself was how the surrender of Warsaw itself would be handled. Bock expected to receive the surrender of the city for his own armies since he felt they had contributed more to the fall of the city than Army Group South. However, as he found out, this was not to be. In the afternoon two Polish officers showed up with a flag of truce at the 217th Infantry Divisions front line with the purpose of starting a dialogue that would lead to a possible ceasefire and surrender. In a letter signed by General Rommel the Poles were asking for a 24-hour ceasefire and setting up of formal negotiations to surrender the city. This information was dutifully passed up through the chain of command to army group headquarters. When Bock sent a message to OKH on how to proceed, he shortly received a message back from Colonel Greiffenberg, the OKH's chief of operations, stating that all negotiations were to be handled by Blaskowitz's 8th Army. Bock immediately raised his objection to Greiffenberg and Halder about leaving the negotiations solely to the 8th Army. But it was to no avail. Halder said it

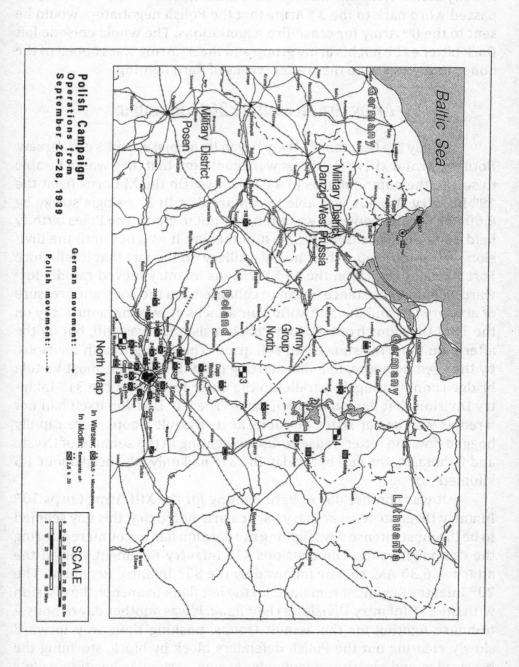

Polish Campaign
Operations from
September 26-28, 1939

North Map

German movement: ⟶

Polish movement: ⟶

In Warsaw: 🔲 20,5

In Modlin: 🔲 2,8 & 30

🔲 20,5 = Miscellaneous

Remnants of:

SCALE

0 10 20 30 40 50 60 70 80 90 100 Miles

0 10 20 30 40 50 60 70 80 90 100 Km

had already been decided that the 8th Army would take the surrender of the city alone. With this finality, the commander of Army Group North passed word back to the 3rd Army that the Polish negotiators would be sent to the 8th Army for cease-fire negotiations. The whole episode left Bock bitter as he felt his army group and the 3rd Army was robbed of the honor that was due to them after weeks of hard fighting.

Army Group South – 26 September

Today the German 8th Army began its formal assaults on Warsaw. Both the XI and XIII Army Corps were confident that they would be able to secure the outer suburbs in a day or two. On the XI Corps front the 19th Infantry Division was able to capture Fort III in a single stroke by 6:00 AM. Fort IIa however, was a tougher nut to crack. The Poles bitterly held on to their positions for most of the day. It was not until the division had concentrated their heavy artillery on the fort that it fell. Once Fort IIa had been taken the 19th Divisions infantry moved rapidly forward as Polish resistance began to collapse from the constant pressure of artillery fire and the Luftwaffe's air attacks. It was the same story on the 18th Divisions front. At first Polish resistance was stiff, but by the afternoon most resistance had collapsed. This brought both divisions, by the evening hours, to a line starting from the northernmost Vistula bridge running roughly parallel to the outer rail line to the 31st Infantry Divisions left flank outside of Czyte. The 31st Division itself had not fared as well as her sister divisions as its assault troops were rapidly bogged down in bitter house-to-house fighting in the suburbs of Czyste and Ochota. By the end of the day the 31st had only advanced about 1.5 kilometers.[80]

It was another day of hard fighting for the XIII Army Corps 10th Infantry Division. It's war diary particularly noted that this day seemed to be the most intense days fighting the division had encountered during the campaign so far. The divisions 41st Infantry Regiment started the attack at 6:30 AM, shortly followed by the 85th Infantry Regiment. The 20th Infantry Regiment remained on the left flank to anchor the division with the 31st Infantry Division's right flank. It was another day of house-to-house fighting for the assault troops, pushing their way forward slowly, clearing out the Polish defenders block by block, storming the barricades and clearing minefields. At one particular location cadets from the Polish military academy had placed some light artillery pieces

---

[80]National Archives: T314/477/63-64; Records of the XI Army Corps.

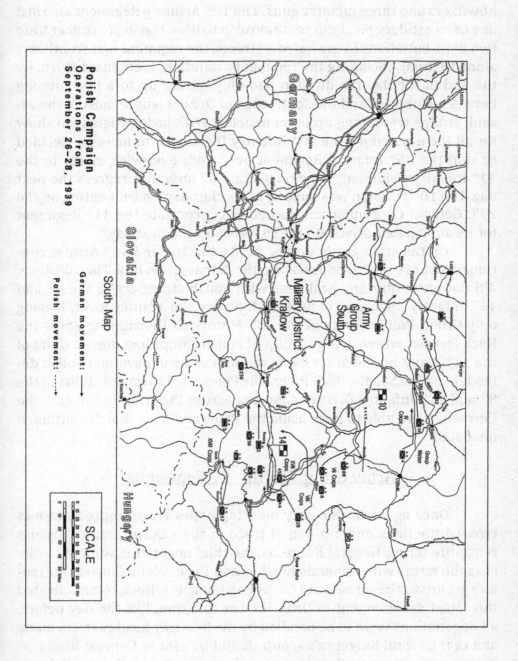

into cellars they had converted into bunkers. Besides the infantry casualties they incurred in taking the cellars, the Germans also lost three howitzers and three infantry guns. The 10th Artillery Regiment also lost one of its artillery pieces in some close in battles. Having to concentrate two of its battalions in the narrow streets, the regiment lost six officers alone that day, including the regiment's adjutant, Lieutenant Horn. By the end of the day the division had only moved up to a line running between Mokotow and the south edge of Ochota where most of the assault troops were hung up on minefields. With little progress to show for all the days effort, the 10th Infantry Division's commander decided to shift the 85th Infantry Regiment over from Rakowiec, closer to the 41st Infantry Regiment, to help facilitate its forward progress the next day. The 10th Division was looking at another day's hard fighting on the 27th. General Cochenhausen wanted to concentrate the 41st Regiment for its anticipated drive into the city's center the next day.[81]

On the army group's other fronts, the 10th and 14th Armies continued to move their troops back to the demarcation line. The 10th Army did not encounter any problems with Polish stragglers as the 4th and 14th Infantry Divisions moved back across the Vistula River, leaving only Group Weber (units of the 13th Motorized Division) to cover the Kock fortress where a large group of Polish troops had dug in. Units of the 14th Army, on the other hand, ran into some determined Polish defenders on the Szum – Bach River. The Poles tried to impede units of the 8th and 27th Infantry Divisions moving across the river. In the end, the Germans were able to push aside the Poles and their march continued unabated.

Army Group North – 27 September

Once again, in the early morning hours Polish representatives crossed the lines under a flag of truce in the I Corps area to discuss cease-fire terms. General Kutrzeba, the chief negotiator, wanted to discuss the terms with Generals Külcher and Bock. While General Kutrzeba's group was being held at I Corps headquarters, Bock communicated this latest development to OKH. He was told that, like the day before, all negotiations were to be handled by the 8th Army headquarters alone and that General Kutzebra's group should be sent to General Blaskowitz's headquarters. With that settled, it was arranged that the I Corps

---

[81]National Archives: T312/37/7545508-5509; Records of the 8th Army.

chief of staff, Colonel Weiss and a suitable escort would take General Kutrzeba's group to 8th Army headquarters.

One interesting sidelight to this was that while the Poles were waiting at I Corps headquarters, the Poles discussed with some of the I Corps staff the conditions in Warsaw itself. What the Germans heard was that their artillery and air attacks had inflicted considerable damage on the city's infrastructure. There were high losses in the civilian population and, because of the lack of drinking water, most of the population had turned to gathering water from the Vistula River bringing with it the danger of sickness and disease.

By noon, the army group and 3rd Army were informed of the city's surrender and that a cease-fire had come into effect. However, it still took awhile for some of the Polish defenders in Praga to get the news. In the afternoon, there were still sporadic attacks and artillery fire in the I Corps area by Polish forces. All these attacks were easily repulsed and the artillery fire did little damage. What greatly concerned the army group and 3rd Army was what to do with the huge influx of prisoners they were about to receive. The 3rd Army was told they were to handle any of the Polish troops coming out of Praga. With some estimated 40,000 Polish troops expected to surrender the only thing General Küchler and his staff could do was to move this mass of prisoners north of the city where there was enough open space to accommodate them. It would take a couple of days before the Germans could build enough pens to hold them and sort them out for demobilization.

Meanwhile the 3rd Army still had its siege operations underway at Modlin. The II Army Corps had scheduled its final assault on the fortress to begin on the 29th, but the actions of the Poles in the fortress changed all that. On the night of the 26th and 27th, the 32nd Infantry Division had moved to the north front of the Polish fortified line, while at the same time Panzer Division Kempf had moved into the Zakroczym area on the northwest side of the fortress. To support both divisions an additional five non-divisional heavy artillery battalions had been emplaced behind the 32nd Division and three heavy artillery battalions were behind Panzer Division Kempf. The formal assault was planned to start on 29 September on the contingency that all the artillery preparations were ready. On the morning of the 27th, the 94th Infantry Regiment reported seeing a white flag at Fort III. The divisional commander ordered the regiment to take advantage of the situation and seize the fort without firing a shot. At the same time artillery was called upon to bombard Fort II to induce its surrender. Upon learning of these de-

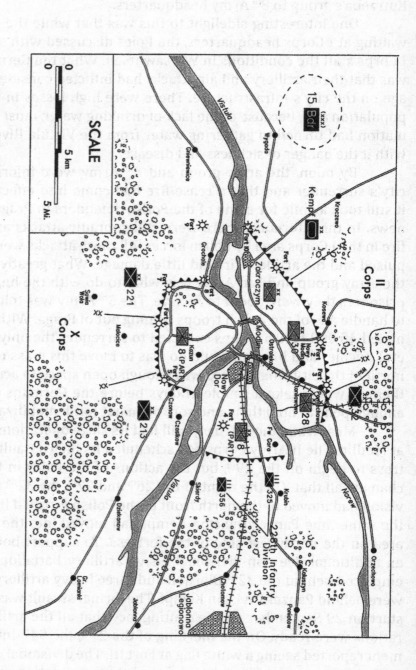

Siege at Fortress Modlin

German and Polish Positions
September 27, 1939

SCALE

0 — 5 km

0 — 5 Mi.

velopments, the II Corps advanced the timetable for the attacks for the Panzer Division Kempf and the 228th Infantry Division. Unfortunately, the white flag proved to be a ruse, for as the 94th Regiment approached Fort III it came under heavy fire. Even with that some of the regiments units had managed to work their way around the fort and gain access to the town of Pomiechowek before darkness. The Panzer Division Kempf had not attacked as planned, because the division claimed that all of its units were not in place. It would attack the next day.

On the east side of the fortress the 325th Infantry Regiment of the 228th Infantry Division had attacked and penetrated the enemy lines in the area of Gora farm. During the entire day air attacks were carried out by elements of General Richtofen's air corps in and around the Modlin area. By the end of the day the II Corps felt confident that from the days progress that Polish resistance would collapse in another day or two.[82]

Army Group South – 27 September

The 8th Army was preparing itself for another day's hard fighting when, word had arrived from the 3rd Army that they were holding a Polish delegation seeking terms for the eventual surrender of Warsaw. Since the 8th Army had been designated as the force to which the Poles were to negotiate their surrender, it was quickly arranged for the I Corps to escort the Polish group to 8th Army headquarters at Grodzisk. As this was being done General Blaskowitz ordered all units to suspend offensive operations and hold positions until further notice. The Polish group arrived shortly before 9:00 AM, with General Kutrzeba and his aide, Lieutenant Praglowski heading the delegation. It did not take long for General Blaskowitz and General Kutrzeba to negotiate the necessary protocols for the cease-fire.[83] Once the terms were agreed upon the final terms of surrender would be settled on the next day. The Germans would have to meet with the Polish military authorities to work out the final delivery of Polish troops and their equipment. They would also have to meet with the civilian authorities to assess the needs of the civil population since much of the cities services had been wrecked from the days of artillery fire and air bombardment. The official cease-fire came into effect at 12:45 PM. All of the 8th and 3rd Army units were informed and General Kutrzeba was escorted back to Warsaw to inform the Polish command so word could be passed to all of the Polish units

---

[82]National Archives: T311/200/1014-1022; Records of Army Group North.
[83]See Appendix D for the full document.

in Warsaw and Praga. To help induce the Modlin fortress to surrender the Germans asked the Poles to send one of their own officers to inform them that Warsaw had surrendered and that further resistance would be futile. The Poles flatly refused this request, saying that it was up to the local commander to decide how he wanted to proceed. It was realized by General Blaskowitz that with the surrender of the city they were going to have a huge number of prisoners to care for. During the negotiations Kutrzeba informed the Germans that the Polish garrison consisted of around 120,000 troops. The German intelligence had underestimated the number of enemy soldiers and plans had to be made to where to hold them and how to feed them. But all these details would be worked out in good time. For the 8th Army the campaign was over, culminating with the largest Polish force to surrender to any other German army during the campaign.

As to the rest of the field armies of Army Group South, the 14th Army continued its withdrawal to the San River line. There still were some minor skirmishes with Polish forces, but they had no effect on the withdrawing forces.

Army Group North – 28 September

With the surrender of Warsaw, the army group was able to turn its full attention to bringing an end to the siege at Modlin. The II Army Corps had issued orders the previous night for all of its units to continue the assault across the entire fortress line to bring about a rapid collapse of resistance. For the main attacks, the 32nd Infantry Division would take out Fort III while the Panzer Division Kempf would take Fort I, effectively unhinging the Polish defenses. However, at 10:00 PM on the night of the 27th, a Polish officer came through the lines to negotiate a meeting between the two parties for the terms of surrender. A meeting was held at midnight on the road between Jablonna and Nowy Dor. There the Germans gave the Poles their terms and wanted a response by 6:00 AM. The early morning hours of the 28th passed with no response from the Poles. In accordance to their prearranged plans, the 32nd Infantry Division and Panzer Division Kempf resumed their assaults on Forts I and III. Panzer Division Kempf launched its attack on Fort I with elements of the SS Deutschland Regiment supported by the SS Reconnaissance Battalion leading the way. The SS troops took the fort only after a hard fight then advanced on to the edge of Zakroczyn. On the 32nd Divisions side the 94th Infantry Regiment was able to take

Fort III by envelopment from the rear.

At 7:30 AM the Germans received by radio a request from the Poles for another meeting for negotiations. A cease-fire was agreed upon and a meeting was arranged for 2:00 PM. Both parties would meet at the same location where the first negotiations were held. At the appointed time the Germans meet the Poles and transported them back to the meeting hall in Jablonna. It was here that the Polish representative, General Zehak and the II Corps commander, General Strauss, worked out the final surrender terms. After the terms were agreed upon another meeting was arranged for the formal signing of the surrender of Modlin. This would take place the next day at 8:00 AM. The next morning Generals Zehak and General Thommee, the fortress commander, promptly arrived on the agreed upon time and place. After some discussion on some of the minor points of the surrender terms, on which the Poles needed clarification (mainly the treatment of the wounded) the final documents were signed.

At 12:00 PM 29 September, the 32nd Infantry Division, with its commander Lieutenant General Böhme at its head, marched into the fortress to take possession. After disarming the Polish troops and treating the wounded, the Polish garrison marched out to be taken to the prisoner of war camps. The Germans took stock of what they had captured. It was 18,854 Polish troops (1,070 officers, 3,192 non-commissioned officers, 14,592 enlisted men) and 5,755 horses. In materials they counted 12,000 rifles, 192 light machineguns, 180 heavy machineguns, 43 mortars, 21 howitzers, 14 anti-tank guns, 105 artillery pieces, 5 armored vehicles, numerous personnel vehicles and ammunition-food supply stocks. Moreover, a further 4,000 men and 160 officers were taken from Forts I and III that had been isolated during the fighting.[84]

With the surrender of the Modlin fortress the army group turned to the business of redeploying forces to the west and securing the new demarcation line. Placing overall control of East Prussia under the 3rd Army, the 1st and 21st Infantry Divisions were to remain along the Narew River to back up the divisions already holding the demarcation line. Both divisions would remain under the control of the XXI Corps. Holding the rest of the line the 206th Infantry Division remained in the Ostrolenka-Lomza area, the 217th Infantry Division would be moved east of Warsaw and the 228th Infantry Division would remain north of Modlin. The I Army Corps two divisions, the 11th and 61st would stay

---

[84]National Archives: T311/200/1014-1022; Records of Army Group North.

east of Warsaw and the Lötzen and Goldap Brigades would hold their positions east of the Masurian Lakes.

Army Group South – 28 September

The final negotiations for the surrender of Warsaw were settled in the morning hours. At 1:15 PM, the formal surrender took place with General Kutrzeba signing for the Polish forces and General Blaskowitz signing for the Germans. One of the final conditions that the Poles insisted on were that their soldiers be released as soon as possible from the POW camps and returned to the civilian population. Another stipulation was that all the officers be treated honorably and that they could retain their swords. To these General Blaskowitz had no objections. The honor of taking formal possession of Warsaw was left to General Cochenhausen's 10th Infantry Division, which would take place the next day. In the meantime, the Polish authorities would be responsible for the security of the city and its civilian population. The surrender and processing of the Polish garrison troops began in the evening. It would take three days before all of the Polish soldiers had been marched out and processed. With the surrender of Warsaw and Modlin the last of the large Polish field formations were eliminated. All that were left were small isolated pockets of Polish troops scattered around the countryside. The occupation forces would mostly round these up. OKH wanted to move most of the infantry and motorized divisions to the west as soon as possible once the rail transport became available. General Halder especially wanted to have as many of the frontline divisions moved to the western front as possible to discourage the Allies from launching any attacks.

Chapter 6

Combat Operations 29 September – 6 October
The Consolidation

Army Group North – 29 September

    With the final demarcation line set, the 206th Infantry Division, the Lötzen and the Goldap Brigades were given the task of guarding the line separating the Russians and Germans north of Warsaw. While each force was to hold some 50-60 kilometers of line, both General's Brauchitsch and Bock felt that as long as there were first wave divisions nearby, they were deemed adequate to hold this area. The only concern was for the area the Goldap Brigade would have to hold. On one side the territory was occupied the Russians, who were still considered hostile, and on the other side the Lithuanians. However, General Brand felt that the two regiments of the Goldap Brigade were more than up to the task to hold the area, so no additional forces were sent.

Army Group South – 29 September

    With the fall of Warsaw, the 8th Army began the dispersion of its units to the west and southwest of the city to grant better lodging for the troops. Most of the artillery troops remained though, in case of any trouble from the Poles. The only combat action to speak of came from the 10th Army's area. The 27th Infantry Division tangled with remnants of Group Anders east of Janow-Lubelski. The 27th spent the day rounding up as many of the stray Poles as possible, as they represented a threat to the VII Corps vulnerable rear area. Also, the IV Corps reported encounters with small groups of Polish troops in the Spieczyn area. These were easily dealt with. The 14th Army, settling in its new positions behind the demarcation line, had no significant encounters with Polish forces.

Army Group North – 30 September

    The army group continued redeployment of its forces to the west, in particular the movement of the XIX and XXI Army Corps, whose

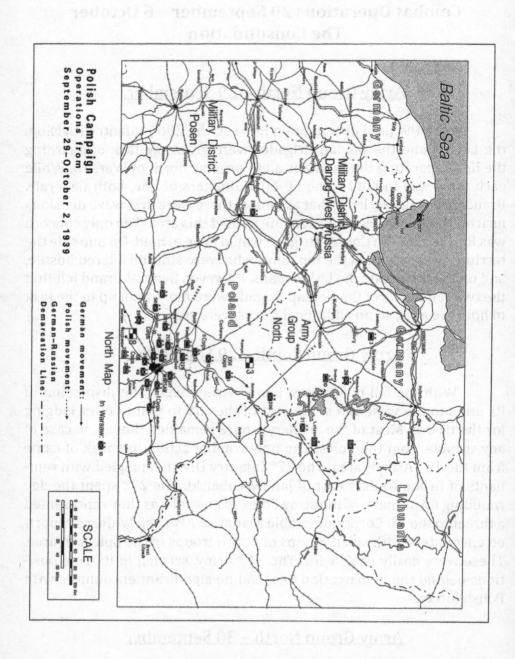

Polish Campaign
Operations from
September 29–October 2, 1939

German movement: ▸▸▸
Polish movement: ┈┈┈▸
German-Russian
Demarcation Line: ┈┈┈┈

North Map
In Warsaw: ☐ 10

SCALE
0 10 20 30 40 50 60 70 80 90 100 km
0   10   20   30   40   50 Miles

movement was to be accelerated. The XIX Corps was to be moved first as a whole force. However, there was not enough rail transport available, so it was shipped in separate sections. The only units that remained under direct command of the army group were the 1st, 11th, 61st Infantry Divisions and the 3rd Landwehr Division. When the army group's staff redeployed to the west on 3 October, these units would be placed under direct command of OKH.

Another territorial dispute arose when the Russians claimed that the town of Ostrolenka belonged to them. The local German commander easily resolved the conflict. He simply showed the Russians the orders and maps sent by higher headquarters that the town clearly fell within the German side of the demarcation line. The Russians acceded and withdrew their forces that had already occupied the town.

Army Group South – 30 September

The 8th Army made preparations to move the 10th Infantry Division into Warsaw to begin formal occupation duties. The division scheduled its march into the city to begin at 10:00 AM the next day. Meanwhile, the last significant stand by an organized Polish force was about to take place. For several days, the IV Army Corps had tangled with what appeared to be a small group of Polish stragglers during its move up to the final demarcation line. As the corps moved forward this group was steadily pushed north into the 4th Infantry Division's area. It was at this point that the Germans realized that this Polish force was much larger than had been previously realized. Air reconnaissance confirmed that this force was about the size of a division.[1] This was too large of a force to be left alone as it could threaten the security of the IV and XIV Corps lines of communication. So, the 10th Army ordered the XIV Corps to gather a battlegroup to crush the Polish force. The XIV Corps in turn, gave the task to the 13th Motorized Division. General Ott, the division's commander, would have a battlegroup formed by the next day.[2]

---

[1]This was Group Polesie, a force composed of the Suwalki and Podolska Cavalry Brigades, the 50th and 60th Infantry Divisions plus other minor units. It was commanded by General Kleeberg and contained about 18,000 men.
[2]National Archives: T312/37/7545403; Records of the 8th Army.

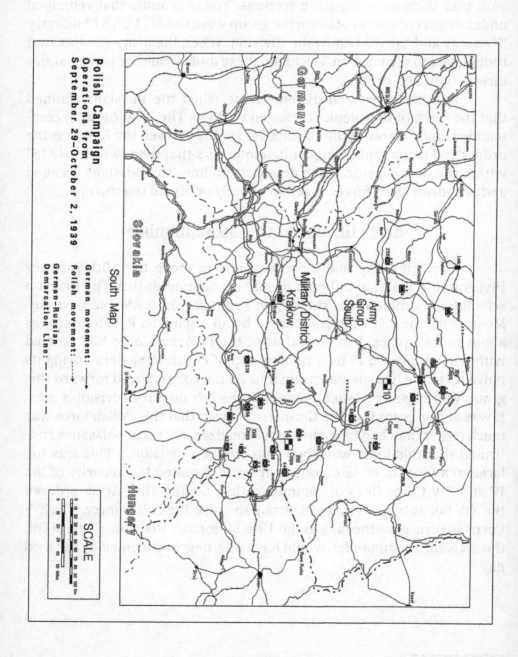

Polish Campaign
Operations from
September 29–October 2, 1939

South Map

German movement: ➝
Polish movement: ⇢
German-Russian
Demarcation Line: —·—·—

SCALE
0 10 20 30 40 50 60 70 80 90 100 Km
0 10 20 30 40 50 Miles

Army Group North – 1 October

Tomorrow, the army group was scheduled to relinquish command of its area of responsibility over to the 3rd Army. OKH wanted the army group's staff to be moved to the western front as soon as possible to form a new army group headquarters. Also, movement of the XIX Army Corps back to Germany was to be accelerated.

Army Group South – 1 October

The 10th Infantry Division marched into Warsaw around 10:00 AM. The entire division marched before the division's commander, General Cochenhausen at Pilsudski Place. Outside of Warsaw, the other divisions of the 8th Army settled into their temporary cantonments until they could be shipped west.

The 10th Army's staff began its preparations for redeployment back to Germany. The headquarters staff would be shipped to Leipzig then, in a few days, to the western front. Meanwhile, the 13th Motorized Divisions commander, General Ott, formulated his plans on how to deal with the Polish force that was moving through the Kock – Parcew area. Since intelligence had indicated that the Polish group consisted of several disparate units, their coordination for defense would not be good. Also, with the decimation of the rest of the Polish Army in the past few weeks, their morale should be extremely low. Only a mixed battalion would be sent initially to find the location and exact size of the Polish force. General Ott felt that the battalion could probably eliminate the Poles, but would reinforce the battalion if necessary. The next few days would show that the general had indeed underestimated the Poles resilience and that it would eventually take the entire 13th Motorized Division to force its capitulation.[3]

Army Group North – 2 October

The army group handed over control of its units and area of responsibility over to the 3rd Army at 4:00 PM in Allenstein. The Army Group North command was dissolved and would be reassigned to new duties in the west once they reached Berlin.

---

[3]National Archives: T312/37/7545403; Records of the 8th Army

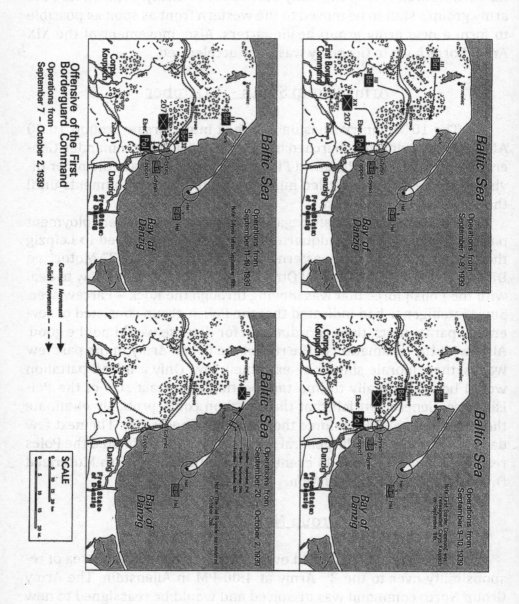

Offensive of the First
Borderguard Command
Operations from
September 7 – October 2, 1939

SCALE

German Movement →
Polish Movement --→

Army Group South – 2 October

The mixed battalion sent to investigate the Polish force around Kock soon found what they were looking for. There was a large cavalry force, greatly reinforced with artillery and combat vehicles, concentrated in a forest northeast of Kock. When the battalion reported this to the division headquarters, General Ott realized that the battalion was much too small to take on the Poles. He ordered the 33rd Motorized Infantry Regiment's commander, Colonel Fehn, to put together a large enough force to attack and destroy the Poles. The force the colonel put together consisted of the I and II/33rd Motorized Infantry Regiment, the III/93rd Motorized Infantry Regiment and one of the divisions light artillery battalions. Proceeding on to the area northeast of Kock in two columns (the 33rd on the right and the 93rd on the left), it wasn't long before both columns had run into Polish resistance. The 33rd pushed the Poles back to the lakes above Kock, making an effort to secure a bridgehead across the lakes by evenings fall. The regiment hoped to take Kock itself the next day. The III/93rd Motorized Infantry Regiment, on its part, ran into stiffer resistance. At first, the 93rd encountered no hostile forces as it moved up and through Serokomla. Once beyond it though, the Germans came under heavy attack, suffering many casualties as the Poles forced the Germans to retreat back and through Serokomla. The battalion regrouped in a forest southwest of the village and tried to retake Serokomla, but failed to do so. The Germans would have to await reinforcements if they hoped to take the village now.

Meanwhile, the 13th Division's commander was informed by 10th Army headquarters that the XIV Army Corps was to be placed under the command of the 8th Army the next day. This in no way changed its mission of eliminating the Polish forces around Kock. However, the rest of the corps would proceed to take up positions along the new demarcation line at the Bug River, leaving the division alone to battle the Poles.[4]

Army Group South – 3rd through the 6th October

The results of the previous days fighting around Kock had shown General Ott that the 13th Motorized Divisions battlegroup would have to be reinforced if the situation with the Poles was to be resolved quickly. To aid the battlegroup, the division sent the II/66th Motorized Infantry Regiment around the III/93rd's right to outflank the Poles at Serokomla.

---

[4]National Archives: T312/37/7545403 – 7545404; Records of the 8th Army.

For flank security, the I/66th Motorized Infantry Regiment was sent to the Buszisk – Charlejow area and the I/93rd Motorized Infantry Regiment around to Podlodow. The Poles, on their part, launched several attacks along the whole line, particularly at Bialobrzegi. These forced the Germans to hold their positions and were unable to make any significant offensive moves on the 3rd.

The next day, the 4th, the Germans tried to regain the initiative by concentrating their attacks on Serokomla and Adamov. Intelligence had pointed to these as being the lynchpins of the Polish line and if these were taken the whole Polish front might collapse. The 66th Regiment concentrated its attacks on Adamov and, even after a hards day fighting, was unable to take the town. To the south at Serokomla, the 93rd battled the Poles all day for possession of the town. Eventually the regiment pushed the Poles out of Serokomla, but the Polish line still held. The anticipated breakthrough of the Polish lines did not happen.

On 5 October saw the final collapse of Group Polesie. The Germans resumed their assaults at Serokomla and Adamov, certain that this would bring the breakthrough they were looking for in the previous day. The 66th finally took Adamov and thereafter broke the Polish line. The regiment rapidly moved forward, and in its advance, captured two enemy battalions. The 33rd Motorized Infantry Regiment pressed the Poles between Serokomla and Annapol, bringing about a general collapse there also. With that, the whole Polish front had become fragmented and, as the 29th Motorized Division had moved in behind Group Polesie in the previous two days, the Poles were now surrounded. By the evening of the 5th, General Kleeberg, Group Polesie's commander, had realized that his group's situation was now hopeless being that he was surrounded by German and Russian forces and was running low on all supplies. Surrender was the only option left. Kleeberg sent a representative to the 13th Motorized Division to secure a ceasefire and to negotiate surrender. General Ott made it clear to the Polish representative that only unconditional surrender would be accepted. Acceptance of the terms had to be received by 2:00 AM the next day or the fighting would continue. To add pressure to the Poles, the 29th and 13th Motorized Divisions stepped up their artillery fire on the Poles and sealed off any possible escape routes. At 4:00 AM on the 6th of October, General Ott received word from the Poles of their agreement to the surrender terms. Between 10:00 AM and 4:00 PM, the Germans took the surrender of the Polish troops, taking in some 1,255 officers, 15,605 non-commissioned officers and enlisted men, 10,000 handheld weapons, 20 guns and 5,000 horses. This brought to a close the last major combat action of the campaign.[5]

Meanwhile, the last administrative actions of Army Group South took place. The 10th Army handed over control of its area and units to the 8th Army on 3 October. Also, the army group itself handed over formal control of its area to *Der Oberbefehlsshaber Ost*. In its final report of the campaign, the army group listed its final statistics for its combat actions from 1 September through 6 October. The number of prisoners taken was listed as 523,156 men, while in weapons they captured 196,00 rifles, 7,000 machineguns, 1,401 artillery pieces, 30,135 horses, 274 aircraft, 226 horse drawn vehicles, 96 armored vehicles and 56 motor vehicles. Total losses in personnel for the army group were for officers: 585 dead, 759 wounded and 42 missing; for non-commissioned officers and enlisted men: 6,049 dead, 19,719 wounded and 4,022 missing.

[5]National Archives: T312/37/75406-7545408; Records of the 8th Army.

Appendix A

Battle for the Baltic Coast:
The Lonely Campaign of Corps Kaupisch[1]

By the evening of 4 September, the fight for the Polish corridor had come to an end. The 4th Army had rapidly cleared the lower part corridor of the three Polish infantry divisions and cavalry brigade that had been defending the region. There were still, however, substantial Polish garrisons along the Baltic coast at Gdynia, Wejherowo and the Hel Peninsula.[2] To OKH, these forces could not be left alone as they could threaten the German lines of communication across the corridor. Also, there was the possibility (at least in the minds of the German high command) that the British and French might try and land forces and supplies to reinforce the existing Polish forces. With the majority of the 4th Army's forces being redeployed to East Prussia, the only troops available were those of the 1st Border Command. Consisting mostly of borderguard regiments and one 3rd wave infantry division[3], the command had spent the first four days of the campaign securing the 4th Army's north flank during its sweep across the Polish corridor. The 1st Border Command had not thrust very far into the corridor itself, pushing the Polish border and national guard troops only about halfway across the middle part of the corridor and leaving much of the northern part untouched.

Given the order to clear the rest of the Polish forces from the coast on 5 September, General Kaupisch, the commander of the 1st Border Command, had to formulate his plan around the capabilities of his units. Using the 207th Infantry Division as his main offensive force, he would take out Gdynia first, since it represented the largest threat in the region. The border guard regiments would assist the division

---

[1]Author's Note: The reason why Corps Kaupisch's operations were not included in the main text was because it was fought completely separate from the main battles in central and southern Poland. Its impact on the campaign was minimal, but I felt it should be included in the book in some way. Hence, its own separate story.

[2]The Polish forces consisted of about 18,000 men. The largest force was at Gdynia, which consisted of two naval infantry regiments, one national guard brigade, one artillery battalion and one anti-aircraft battalion. The total garrison was about 14,700 men. At Hel, the Poles had one border guard battalion, one artillery battalion and one anti-aircraft battalion.

[3]For a complete order of battle, see Appendix F. Some of the senior German commanders did not think the 3rd Wave divisions would perform well. General Bock in his war diary constantly described them derisively as "landwehr" divisions. But, as the campaign progressed, they were mildly surprised at what they achieved during the campaign.

in sealing off and isolating the rest of the Polish garrisons along the coast and would be taken out in turn once Gdynia had fallen. OKH did send the 1st Border Command some reinforcements in the form of Group Eberhardt, which had just finished securing the city of Danzig. Eberhardt would move up from Danzig to Zoppot to secure the 1st Border Command's south flank. Also, to bolster the ground troops, the Luftwaffe promised to lend some stukas for air support when available. The 1st Border Command scheduled the main offensive to start on the morning of 6 September.

From 6 to 8 September, General Kaupisch maneuvered his units into position for the assault on Gdynia. Brigade Eberhardt had moved up to just south of Gdynia by the 5th to block off the south end. The 207th Infantry Division, along with Regiment Bothmer, moved from its positions 20 kilometers west and southwest of Gdynia, first moving north, then east to position itself west of the city. Regiment Wuth moved to due north of Gdynia to block the northern approaches and to seal of the other Polish garrisons. None of the 1st Border Command's units had run into much resistance while maneuvering into their positions, encountering only national guard and local militia units. By 8 September, the Germans reached the Polish mainline of resistance.

Now, General Kaupisch had to plan how his command would take the city itself. The southern approaches to the city were dense with urban dwellings and forest, so an advance from that direction was ruled out immediately. The western side of the city was also covered with forests, but there was a small alley of open terrain running west to east from Wejherowo to Reda. This is where the 32nd Borderguard Regiment would make its main effort. The 207th Infantry Division would make its main axis of attack with the 322nd and 368th Infantry Regiments south of the Wejherowo-Reda road to outflank the Polish defense positions along that route. The divisions other regiment (the 374th) would hold its position on the divisions south flank to maintain contact with Group Eberhardt. There was also a possible line of attack north of Gdynia, but the problem here was that the ground was swampy with only a single road to advance on making it easily defensible.[4] But the Germans felt it was still worth the effort, so units of the 32nd Borderguard Regiment, reinforced with the SS Heimwehr Battalion, would attempt an attack from that direction.

On 8 September, the 207th moved forward against the Polish defenses south of Wejherowo. The 368th Infantry Regiment made good

---

[4]To the Poles, the area was known as Mostowe Bloto. To the Germans, it was the Oxhöfter Kämpe.

progress, gaining ground all the way to Gnienowo before being halted by the Poles. The 322[5] Infantry Regiment made less progress, moving forward only a couple of kilometers. Regiment Bothmer[5] failed in its attempt to sieze Wejherowo, being stopped by the Poles effective use of terrain and mines. To the north, the Regiment Wuth crossed the German-Polish border, penetrating only as far as Piasnica, some 4 kilometers into Poland. Overall, the first day's operations were disappointing to General Kaupisch. Most of the units had not achieved their first day's objectives, however the next few days would show better results.

Over the next three days, the 207th Infantry Division struggled through the forest, pushing the Poles back slowly. The 322nd and 368th Infantry Regiments fought their way out of the forested terrain by the 10th, resting on the 11th to make preparations for the final push into the Oxhöfter Kämpe. To its north, Regiment Bothmer struggled through the narrow alley between Wejerowo and Reda, moving only six kilometers to reach Reda by 10 September. The SS Heimwehr Battalion sent two companies to try an end run on the north side of the Oxhöfter, but the Poles thwarted this, as they were able to bring enough firepower down on them to stop them. Regiment Wuth easily achieved its objective of cutting off the Polish garrisons north of Gdynia, taking the seaport of Puck on the 9th. Over the next few days, the regiment consolidated its positions, securing Corps Kaupischs[6] north flank and sealing off the Hel Peninsula.

The 12th would see one of the hardest days fighting during the campaign for Corps Kaupisch. Early in the day, the assaults of the 322nd and 368th Infantry Regiments, along with the 42nd Borderguard Regiment, gained significant ground, only stopping once they had begun receiving heavy enemy fire from the direction of Sagorsch. The Poles themselves had recognized the threat this advance represented to their ability to defend the Oxhöfter and were able to bring sufficient firepower to stop it. The Poles then launched several attacks against the Germans south flank, but the regiment holding the flank, the 368th, managed to fend off all the attacks for the rest of the day. The Poles, however, carried out more attacks into the hours of darkness. One attack in particular caused the near collapse of the German lines. Two companies of Polish infantry attacked into the seam between the 207th

---

[5]The 32nd Borderguard Regiment was referred to by its commander's name, Colonel Bothmer, throughout the original war dairy, as was the 42nd by its commander, Colonel Wuth. From now on both regiments will be called by those names.
[6]On September 9th, the 1st Border Command was renamed Corps Kaupisch, named so after the forces commander, General Kaupisch

Infantry Division and Group Eberhardt. This threw the Germans into disorder, several of the 207th's units panicked and begun a precipitous retreat. Eventually, the officers were able to restore order and stabilized the front line.

Regiment Bothmer and the SS Heimwehr Battalion once again attempted another attack into the Oxhöfter Kämpe from the north, but this one met the same fate as the first. The Germans advanced down the single road between Mrzerino and Pierwoszyno and the Poles were well prepared to stop them. After advancing over the Reda Canal the German advance column ran into heavy fire and was pinned down the rest of the day. The Germans withdrew at nightfall, stopping at a position just south of the canal. Group Eberhardt made its first formal attack south of Gdynia, gaining the high ground north of Lensitz. This gave Eberhardt an excellent platform that overlooked the Gdynia defenses.

Assessing the operations for 12 September, General Kaupisch came to the conclusion that his troops would need to rest and recuperate for several days before he would attempt another major assault. The combination of the 207th Infantry Divisions near panic and the Poles aggressive defense convinced him that it would be better to slowly grind the Poles down with artillery and air attacks.[7] Minor attacks would be carried out only if the Germans had a clear advantage. This strategy seemed to pay off as the Poles begun to give ground gradually over the next few days. Most surprising was when the Poles abandoned Gdynia to Group Eberhardt on 14 September. What the Germans did not know was that the Poles had expended much of their ammunition and had taken high casualities on the 12th. The Polish commander realized that they were not going to be able to hold the Oxhöfter Kämpe much longer. It was decided that they would hold off the Germans as long as possible, while evacuating as many troops as possible to the Hel Peninsula.

Each day, as the Poles pulled back into an ever-shrinking pocket, the Germans continued to pound the Poles from the ground, air and sea. By the 18th, General Kaupisch felt confident enough that the Poles were at a breaking point and ordered an all-out attack to start on the morning of the 19th. When the assault started the next morning, as predicted, the whole Polish front collapsed. By 1:30 PM, parts of the 207th Infantry Division had reached the Bay of Danzig at Neu-Oblusch, and by 5:00 PM,

[7] In addition to the stuka squadron (the 4th Squadron, Training Group 186, commanded by Hauptmann Blattner) brought in to assist the ground troops, the old battleship Schleswig-Holstein was sent to bombard the Poles from the Bay of Danzig. Later, the battleship Schlesien was also brought up to bombard the Polish positions along the Hel Peninsula with the Schleswig-Holstein.

had secured most of the Oxhöfter Kämpe itself. By the Germans count, they had captured some 420 officers and 12,000 NCO's and enlisted men. And even though the Poles had managed to evacuate a couple of thousand men to Hel, the Germans were confident that these troops would not substantially aid in the defense of the peninsula.

With the fall of Gdynia, the Poles were only left holding the Hel Peninsula, a small spit of land some thirty kilometers long and, at its widest, only two and a half kilometers. For the Poles, the peninsula itself would be easy to defend with many fallback positions running down its length. The problem the Poles faced was that there was little chance of reinforcement and resupply as the Germans mostly controlled the sea and skies around the peninsula. For the Germans, they were faced with advancing down a narrow strip of land with no room for outflanking the Polish positions. A seaborne landing to outflank the Poles was not possible either, as the Germans had no naval assets capable of performing such a task. Not relishing a slow grind down the narrow peninsula, General Kaupisch opted for the strategy that had previously worked before Gdynia; pound the Poles from the air and sea to wear them down. Then, only move on the ground when they had an obvious advantage.

Preparations proceeded apace. To take over the rear areas to free the rest of Corps Kaupischs troops for redeployment elsewhere, the 519th Military Administration Headquarters was set up at Berents. They would handle occupational duties. For the assault on the Hel Peninsula, a provisional attack group was formed around the 374th Infantry Regiment along with all of the 207th Infantry Division's artillery and part of Group Eberhardt's artillery. By the 21st, most of the assault forces were in place at Puck, waiting to move into its final attack positions. The jumping off positions themselves, some 3.5 kilometers east of Grossendorf, were being completed for the artillery and infantry firing positions.

In the meantime, the Kriegsmarine and Luftwaffe had started its softening up the Polish forces on the peninsula. For the next week and a half the old battleships *Schleswig-Holstein* and *Schlesien* bombarded various targets along the peninsula, particularly Hel's harbor and military installations. The Polish batteries certainly fought back the best they could. They scored some hits but did little damage against the old battleships. By the beginning of October, the *Schleswig-Holstein* and *Schlesien* had inflicted considerable damage on Polish artillery positions, flak batteries, harbor facilities and other installations. Before it was withdrawn on 27 September, Stuka Squadron Blattner had also made its contribution to the destruction; mostly targeting the rail lines and railroad facilities.

On the ground, the reinforced 374th Infantry Regiment had moved up to it's jumping off positions on the 22nd and had begun probing for weak spots in the Polish positions. On the 26th, the reconnaissance troops found one and were able to push through several companies, forcing the Poles back to Ceynowa. Pausing a couple of days to assess the new Polish defense line, the Germans attacked on the 29th, breaking through the Polish lines on the 30th and were able to seize Ceynowa that same day. The regiment was going to resume its assaults on 2 October. However, what happened the next day made what plans they made unnecessary.

Around midday on 1 October, the Poles radioed the Germans a request to open negotiations for surrender. General Kaupisch quickly arranged for a meeting to take place at Zoppot, the corps new headquarters. The Polish negotiator was picked up by sea and brought back to Zoppot. At 5:00 PM negotiations started with General Kaupisch representing the Germans and the Poles by naval Captain Majewski. By 8:30 PM both sides had accepted all items and the Polish captain was returned to Hel by boat to get final approval by the Pole's commander, Admiral Unrug. At 11:00 PM, the Poles radioed back his acceptance of the terms. With that, the battle of the Baltic coast was over. In the end, for the Germans the elimination of the Polish forces on the Baltic coast had little military effect on the entire campaign. It really became a matter of prestige for the Germans as the longer the Poles held out, it would give hope for the rest of the Polish forces. As it turned out the Hel defenders, along with the Poles at Kock, held out much longer than anyone would have expected.

Appendix B

Basic Weapons List for the German Army in the Polish Campaign

Introduction

Because many of the weapons described below have already been written about in dozens of books, I will only give a brief description and no technical details. Readers who wish to see the technical details for each weapon, I have listed several reference books in the bibliography that can be consulted for such information.

Rifles
The standard rifle of the German infantrymen through two world wars, The *Karabiner 98K* was one of the finest bolt action rifles ever produced. Even though the bolt action rifle itself was about to be surpassed by semi-automatic rifles, they were still a useful battlefield instrument.

Sub Machine Guns
The *MachinenPistole (MP) 38* was the predecessor of the famous *MP 40* machine pistol. One of the first mass-produced sub machine guns, it was a simple design and it provided additional firepower at the squad level for the infantryman.

The *MachinenPistole 34(ö)* was an Austrian produced weapon that the Germans absorbed into their inventory after the Anschluss of that country in March of 1938. A well-designed weapon like the *MP 38*, it served in many of the Austrian inducted units in 1939. By 1940 though, they were regulated to second line use for the rear area troops and security forces.

The *Bergmann MachinenPistole 34* was a weapon similar to the *MP 34(ö)*, but was produced in smaller numbers by the Germans. It was mostly used by the police and security forces of the Reich.

Machine Guns
The *Machinengewehr (MG) 34* was the main offensive weapon for the German Army squad at the beginning of the war. It had a high rate of

fire, good range, was highly accurate and was easily maintained in the field. The machine gun could be used as a light squad weapon when based on a bipod or could serve as a heavy machine gun when mounted on a tripod or other fixed mounting. It gave the Germans a definite edge at the tactical level.

Serving behind the *MG 34*, the *Machinengewehr 08/15* was a World War One era weapon, still in use in 1939. It was a bit heavy for its role, but was still a reliable weapon. It was mostly used by the second line troops such as the third wave divisions and the borderguard troops.

Mortars
The standard mortars of the German Army at the start of the war were the leichte *Granatwerfer 36* and the *schwerer Granatwerfer 34*.

The *Granatwerfer 36* was not a good weapon for the purpose it was built for. It was too heavy for its size, overly complicated and the bomb weight was light compared to other contemporary mortars. By 1941 it was out of production and being replaced by the heavier 80 mm model.

Unlike the *Model 36*, the *Granatwerfer 34*, was a much better support weapon for the infantry. It had a good bomb weight, range and was sturdy and reliable. It remained the German's standard infantry mortar for the duration of the war. Lastly, the Germans also had the *Nebelwerfer 35*, a heavy mortar intended to fire mostly smoke and chemical rounds. As it turned out, it was used more to fire high explosive rounds in support of ground troops, a task it performed well. The mortar was scaled up version of the 80mm mortar and was used exclusively by the 1st and 2nd Mortar Battalions.

Anti-tank Guns
At the beginning of the war, the Germans only had one dedicated anti-tank gun, the *37 mm PanzerabwehrKanone (Pak) 35/36*. It was a compact and easy to use gun and, compared to the tanks it had to face in the Polish campaign, had sufficient punch to deal with the opposing armor. When not being used as an anti-tank gun, they were used to supplement the infantry's firepower.

Anti-Aircraft Guns

To help protect the ground troops from opposing aircraft, the Germans provided the first wave infantry and motorized divisions with a battalion each of anti-aircraft artillery. Equipping these battalions was the *20 mm FlugzeugabwehrKanone (Flak) 30*, a reliable and sturdy gun. Its only drawback was its low rate of fire. Consequently, with little air opposition from the Poles, the guns were turned on ground targets with great effect.

Infantry Guns

The infantry gun used by the Germans was the *leichte Infantriegechütz (IG) 18*. It proved to be a steady and reliable gun and was used throughout the war. Its only drawback was its short range because of its short barrel.

The mountain infantry used a similar gun, the l*eichte Gebrigs Infantriegeschütz 18*. Essentially it was the same gun as the *Infantriegeschütz 18*, the only difference being a tubular split trail and was heavier for its ability to be broken down for pack transport.

Artillery

For the first and most of the second wave infantry divisions, the divisional artillery consisted of two types of howitzers, the *105mm leichte Feldhaubitze (FH)18* and *150 mm schwere Feldhaubitze 18*. The 105mm gun was a conventional and sturdy weapon with a useful high explosive projectile and adequate range. The 150mm piece was also a good howitzer with the same qualities of the 105mm gun. Both howitzers went on to serve the German Army for the rest of the war, a tribute to their soundness of design. Some older prewar and World War One pieces were distributed to the third wave infantry divisions and borderguard units along with Czech guns acquired the previous year. Most were the *105 mm leichte Feldhaubitze 16* and the *Skoda 105 mm Model 35* guns.

The Germans also had numerous non-divisional artillery battalions. These formations used a variety of howitzers and guns, including the aforementioned *Feldhaubitze 18* howitzers. The majority of the guns were the *schwere 100 mm Kanone (K) 18*, used in some forty-five artillery battalions. The gun was a compromise of production, using a Rheinmetal barrel and Krupp carriage. This made the gun too heavy for the amount of firepower it could deliver; it took a lot of horsepower (animal or motorized) to move the gun, not making it the most mobile of guns. Still, the gun was serviceable enough early in the war for its intended use. Next up in caliber was the *150 mm Kanone 18*. It was intended to be the standard army heavy gun. It had a good weight of shell and decent range, but its major drawback was that it had to be moved in two separate parts, the barrel and carriage. This meant a much longer set up and breakdown time, which greatly decreased the weapons time in action. Furthermore, it had a slow rate of fire, further detracting its time in action. It wasn't long before the German artillery arm was looking for a better gun.

Lastly, the Germans had three battalions of super heavy artillery that were equipped with the langer *210mm Mörser* and the *Czech Skoda 305mm Schiffs Kanone L/50*. The *210 mm Mörser* was a Krupp design from World War One that was upgraded between the wars to be more mobile gun. It could be transported in two loads, making it a cumbersome piece to set up and fire. It did however, fire a useful shell, being used to good effect at the siege of Warsaw. The *Skoda 305mm* gun was also a design from World War One intended for static warfare. Modernized by the Czechs, it was a more mobile gun, but suffered from the same problems as the 210mm mörser. Once set up though, it was a highly efficient and accurate gun. It was also used to good effect at the siege of Warsaw.

Tanks

The Germans entered the campaign using six different tanks, the *Panzerkampfwagen (Pzkw) I, II, III and IV*, along with the *Czech Pz-35(t) and the Pz-38(t)*.

The *Pzkw I*'s were tanks that were already obsolete by 1939. It was intended as a pre-war training vehicle only, but since the war had started sooner than the army had anticipated, they were pressed into service to fill the ranks of the panzer battalions. Lightly armed with only twin 7.92mm machine guns, the *Panzer I* was not much of a tank. However, it proved to be useful against 'soft' targets such as enemy infantry, trucks and other soft skinned vehicles.

The *Pzkw II* was not much better, as it was also intended as a training/reconnaissance tank for the prewar panzer divisions. Along with the *Pzkw I*'s, they made up the bulk of the armor in the panzer divisions.

The *Pzkw II* was more armored and more heavily armed with a 20mm cannon and 7.92mm machine gun, making it also a useful weapon against opposing infantry and unarmored vehicles.

The *Pzkw III*, the tank intended to make up the bulk of the panzer divisions, was a well armed and armored tank compared to many of its contemporaries. Unfortunately, the Germans only had a few dozen available for the campaign. But considering the Polish armor opposing them, this did not pose a problem. The *Pzkw III* proved to be a reliable and sturdy vehicle, soldiering on the rest of the war in various forms.

The *Pzkw IV* was only intended to be an infantry support tank in the panzer divisions. Armed with the low velocity 75mm gun, it was for direct fire support against unarmored troops. Pressed into other duties in the Polish campaign, it proved to be a versatile tank. Up gunned later in the war, it remained the mainstay of the German armored forces for the rest of the war.

The acquisition of the Czechoslovakian armory in 1939 greatly aided the Germans in filling out the panzer forces for the Polish campaign. The *Panzerkampfwagen 35(t)* was a light tank that was well built and had adequate armor, firepower and mobility. The major weakness of the *Pzkw 35(t)* (and the *Pzkw 38(t)*) was that its armor was riveted on, which left the tanks more vulnerable than a welded frame tank.

The *Panzerkampfwagen 38(t)* medium tank was a robust and reliable vehicle with the same attributes of the *Pzkw 35(t)*. For the next two years the Czech tanks would greatly contribute to the panzer forces success in the field.

Armored Cars

The *SonderKraftfahrzeug (SdKfz) 13* was a four-wheeled armored car first introduced in the early 30's to be used in the reconnaissance battalions of the motorized divisions. By 1939 they were passed on to the first and second wave infantry divisions to be used in their reconnaissance battalions.

The *SdKfz 221, 222* and *223* were the next generation of armored cars that were used by the motorized divisions in the reconnaissance battalions at the beginning of the war. These four-wheeled vehicles all had adequate firepower and armor protection to perform their duties. Their only drawback was that their cross-country ability was not good.

The family of six wheeled vehicles, the *SdKfz 231*, *232* and *263*, had much better off road capability. Sufficiently armed and armored, the vehicles also served in the army's motorized reconnaissance battalions in the first two years of the war. By 1941, they were being replaced by the newer eight wheeled armored cars.

Mention should be made of the *Schupo-Sonderwagen 21* and the *ADGZ* armored cars used by Group Eberhardt.

The *ADGZ* was an Austrian armored car that was built for police use only. When Germans inherited them, they were shipped to Danzig to give Group Eberhardt additional firepower.

The *Schupo-Sonderwagen 21* was an old design from the Reichswehr era. Produced to supplement the seven Reichswehr divisions, then passed on to the Weimar police forces, it was already outdated by 1939. Still, they performed adequately for Group Eberhardt in its battle for Danzig in the early days of the campaign.

Luftwaffe Weapons

Even though the Luftwaffe anti-aircraft battalions were only supposed to be used for warding off enemy aircraft, they were turned against ground targets for lack of any air opposition. The three main weapons of the Flak battalions were the *20mm FlugzeugabwehrKanone (Flak) 30*, *37 mm Flak 36* and the 88 mm *Flak 18 & 36*.

The 20mm gun was the same weapon that was used by the motorized and infantry division's anti-aircraft battalions and has already been discussed.

The 37mm gun was an effective weapon against low flying aircraft and was even more effective against ground targets, including lightly armored vehicles and bunkers. It remained one of the mainstays of the light flak units for the rest of the war.

What more can be said about the ubiquitous 88mm *Flak 18* and *36* guns. First used in action in the Spanish Civil War, it was given a shield and extra sights for use against ground targets. The '88' proved to be a versatile weapon during the campaign, taking out armor, concrete bunkers and a variety of other hardened targets. Its only drawback was its height, making it hard to hide once the gun was fired. The gun went on to serve the Germans well for the rest of the war, becoming the scourge of Allied armor on all fronts.

Appendix C

This after-action report[1] was submitted to the army high command from Corps Wodrig to give an evaluation on the combat effectiveness of the SS units under Wodrig's command during the Polish campaign. I wanted to include this report as an example of how the army saw the SS troops effectivness early in the war. I want to thank Leo Niehorster for translating this document.

Führungsstab z.b.V.
Abt. Ia 120/39 geh.

Corps Headquarters, D. Lochow, 25.09.39

REPORT
regarding the combat value of the SS units.

During the time that the Pz.Div. Kempf was attached to the Führungsstab z.b.V. (Special Command Staff), the following shortcomings in the combat value of the SS units appeared.

In all cases the SS Reconnaissance Battalion, (consisting of two motorcycle reconnaissance companies), failed to carry out its assigned missions. The battalion was not even able to overcome weak enemy resistance. On the contrary, when weak enemy forces were presumed to be in the area, or targeted the path the battalion following, it failed to bring back any reconnaissance results at all. This complete failure of the SS Reconnaissance Battalion resulted in severe problems for the staff and other units of the division.

It is difficult for the Führungsstab z.b.V. to assess whether the causes of the failure lay with the training or a lack of courage.

Motorized infantry units of a Panzer division are often called upon to remove obstacles and to clear the way in terrain unsuitable for tanks by rapidly attacking, and thereby opening up the way for the armored formation to advance. The SS Standarte Deutschland failed to accom-

---

[1]Translation taken from microfilm copy of document from series T 314, roll number 750, frame numbers 1001-1002.

plish these tasks. Almost always it was necessary to wait for the leading elements of the follow up infantry divisions to carry out these tasks, which they then successfully completed within a short time. Cooperation between infantry and tanks was unsatisfactory. A possible explanation might be the lack of training and experience.

Aggressiveness combined with tactically correct and practical action left much to be desired. The latter must also be said about the behavior of the SS units behind the lines against the civilian population, which was in complete opposition to those principles that the German soldiers have always stood for.

A separate report regarding this matter will be submitted.

Elements of the SS units were the only ones within the command of the corps which retreated several times before enemy attacks. The not inconsiderable casualties suffered by the SS units are probably the result a lack of training and wartime conduct.

Particularly striking was a lack of discipline, especially noticeable in march movements, improper behavior towards of noncommissioned and commissioned officers of the Army, and an exaggerated over estimation which had no basis when compared to their performance. Especially characteristic for SS units is their exaggerated or even incorrect reports, which often lead to command decisions which later proved unnecessary.

The staff cannot make any judgement regarding the combat effectiveness and achievements of the SS Artillery Regiment.

Without doubt the frequent occurrence of shortcomings in the combat value of the SS units can be, traced back in part to inadequate combat training and combat experience. The lack of discipline, the exaggerated self importance, as well as in some cases the lack of steadfastness under fire and the lack of aggressiveness cannot be explained.

Signed
WODRIG

Appendix D

Authors Note: This document was translated from the original text by Leo Niehorster.

PROTOCOL

regarding the negotiations between the German 8th Army and the representatives of the Polish Armed Forces in Warsaw for a cease fire.

Article 1

1.) The German 8th Army accepts the request by the Polish Armed Forces in Warsaw for a

Cease Fire

to enable the start of surrender negotiations of the fortress.

2.) The cease fire begins at 14:00 on 27.09.1939 for all members of both ground and air forces. It applies only for the immediate area of the fortress and the encircling troops in the east (Praga) and west (Warschau). Duration: 24 hours

3.) By 12:00, 29.09.1939, all Polish troops and military formations are to be withdrawn within the demarcation areas I - IV, as indicated in red on the accompanying 1:20,000 scale city map.
Medical facilities of the Polish Armed Forces with medical personnel and wounded outside of these demarcation areas may be left in place.

Article 2

4.) The Polish High Command guarantees
a) to maintain total law and order in the fortress, including Praga, until such time as negotiations for the surrender of the fortress are completed. All officers and civil servants of the Armed Forces and the city administration will remain at their posts. This applies also to state, community, and public services, as well as to those of the private and transport sectors;
b) that until the finalization of the negotiations for the surrender of the fortress, returning streams of refugees
aa) from Warsaw to the south, west, and north,
bb) from Parga to Warsaw,
cc) from Praga to the south, east, and north
be prevented. A withdrawal of the population from the endangered

area of the inner city which has been subjected to artillery and is on fire be supported;

c) to use of all forces available to put out the fires immediately, and to ensure the feeding of the population by using Armed Forces supplies;

d) that all political parties and miscellaneous associations cease functioning immediately;

e) to implement all necessary procedures to prevent communicable diseases and epidemics;

f) to maintain in an undamaged state all military and civilian facilities, weapons, war materials of all kinds, equipment, and documents, and to remove all blockades, explosive and destructive preparations. Where this is not possible, to assure their transfer to German troops;

g) that all German prisoners of war are to be transferred by the shortest means to the most immediate German troop commander;

h) to release all Volks and Reich Germans immediately, and to guarantee their security, accommodation, feeding, and possessions;

i) to completely assure the safety of the representatives of foreign powers and foreign citizens, as well as their possessions.

Article 3

5.) The German High Command, on the other hand, pledges itself until the finalization of the surrender of the fortress

a) to prepare the feeding of the civilian population and troops after the finalization of the negotiations;

b) to assist with medical services.

Article 4

6.) The cease fire has as its purpose to finalization of the negotiations to surrender. It can be terminated by a three-hour notification after the breaking off of the negotiations.

7.) The begin of negotiations for the surrender of the fortress is set for 09:00 on 28.09.1939. Representatives of the city administration responsible for sanitation, rations, and critical facilities are to be present at this meeting.

Place of negotiations: Rakew, Skoda Factory.

Signed at Rakow, Skoda Factory, on 27.09.1939 at 13:45.

For the Polish High Command in Warsaw
= K u t r z e b n =
Divisional General

For the Commander-in-Chief of the German 8th Army
= B l a s k o w i t z =
General der Infanterie

Appendix F
German Order of Battle

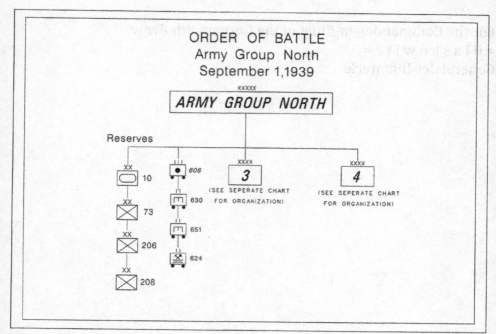

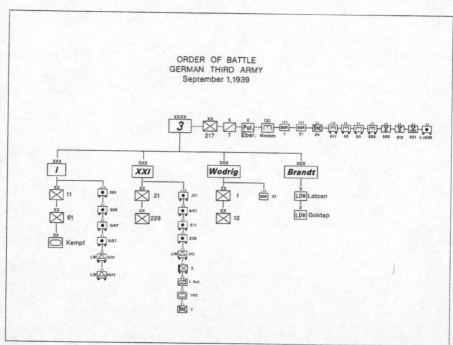

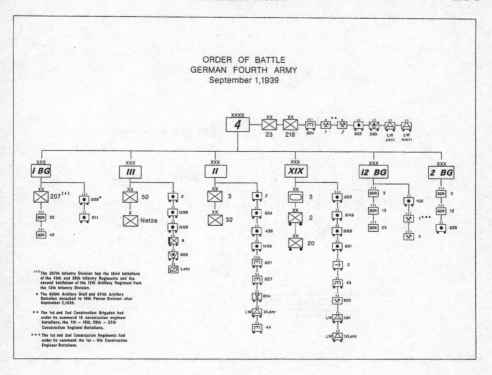

ORDER OF BATTLE
GERMAN FOURTH ARMY
September 1, 1939

(+) The 207th Infantry Division has the third battalions of the 49th and 29th Infantry Regiments and the second battalion of the 12th Artillery Regiment from the 12th Infantry Division.

* The 609th Artillery Staff and 611th Artillery Battalion detached to 10th Panzer Division after September 2, 1939.

** The 1st and 2nd Construction Brigades had under its command 18 construction engineer battalions, the 7th — 15th, 29th — 37th Construction Engineer Battalions.

*** The 1st and 2nd Construction Regiments had under its command the 1st — 6th Construction Engineer Battalions.

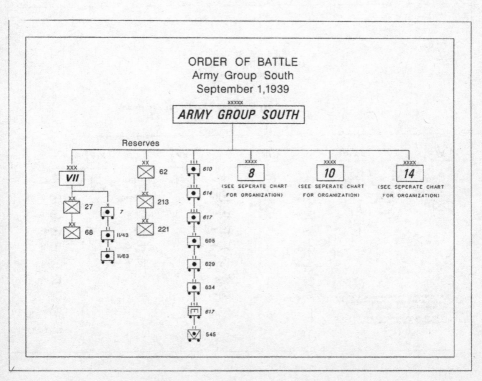

ORDER OF BATTLE
Army Group South
September 1, 1939

Case White

ORDER OF BATTLE
GERMAN EIGHTH ARMY
September 1,1939

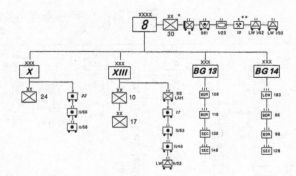

* The 30th Infantry Division stayed in army reserve
  until mid-day September 4, when it was placed
  under the command of the X Army Corps.

** The 10th Construction Brigade had under its
   command 12 construction engineer battalions.

ORDER OF BATTLE
GERMAN TENTH ARMY
September 1,1939

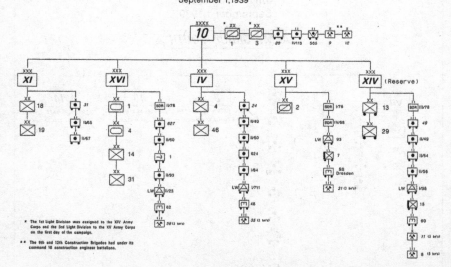

* The 1st Light Division was assigned to the XIV Army
  Corps and the 3rd Light Division to the XV Army Corps
  on the first day of the campaign.

** The 9th and 12th Construction Brigades had under its
   command 10 construction engineer battalions.

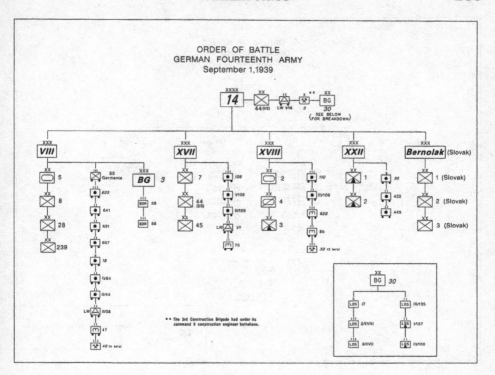

ORDER OF BATTLE
GERMAN FOURTEENTH ARMY
September 1,1939

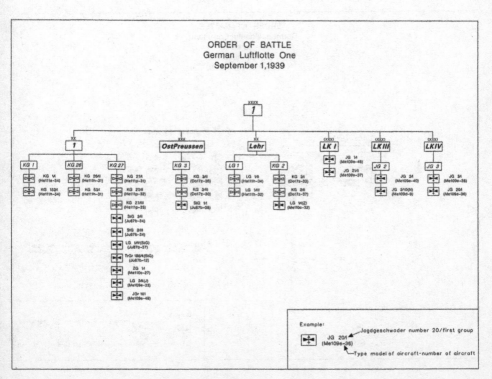

ORDER OF BATTLE
German Luftflotte One
September 1,1939

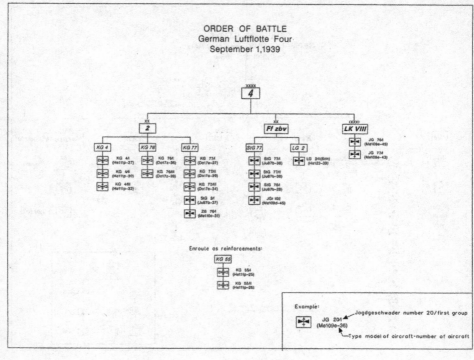

ORDER OF BATTLE
German Luftflotte Four
September 1, 1939

Enroute as reinforcements:

Example:
JG 20I (Me109e-36) — Jagdgeschwader number 20/first group
Type model of aircraft-number of aircraft

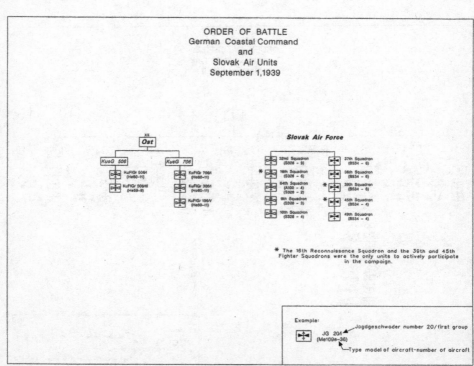

ORDER OF BATTLE
German Coastal Command
and
Slovak Air Units
September 1, 1939

Slovak Air Force

* The 16th Reconnaissance Squadron and the 39th and 45th
Fighter Squadrons were the only units to actively participate
in the campaign.

Example:
JG 20I (Me109e-36) — Jagdgeschwader number 20/first group
Type model of aircraft-number of aircraft

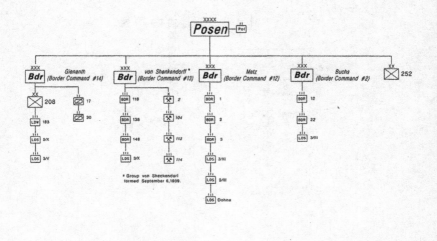

ORDER OF BATTLE
Military District Posen
September 12,1939

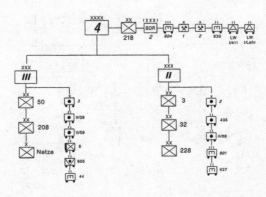

ORDER OF BATTLE
GERMAN FOURTH ARMY
September 5,1939

ORDER OF BATTLE
GERMAN FOURTH ARMY
September 16,1939

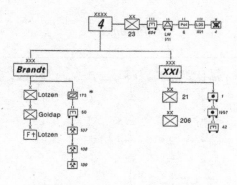

* Detached from the
73rd Infantry Division.

ORDER OF BATTLE
GERMAN TENTH ARMY
September 12,1939

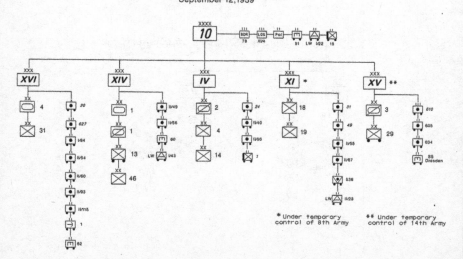

* Under temporary
control of 8th Army

** Under temporary
control of 14th Army

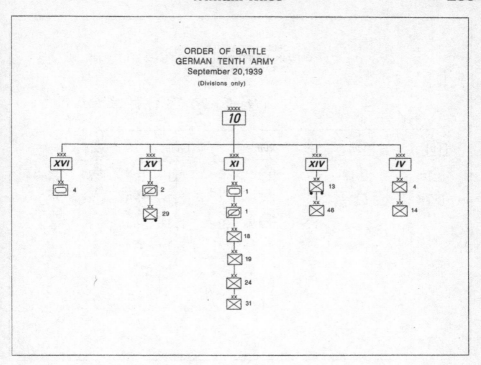

ORDER OF BATTLE
GERMAN TENTH ARMY
September 20, 1939
(Divisions only)

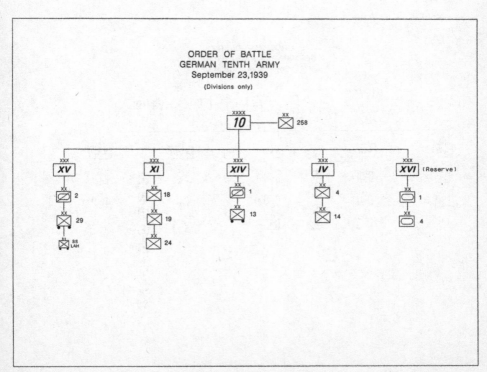

ORDER OF BATTLE
GERMAN TENTH ARMY
September 23, 1939
(Divisions only)

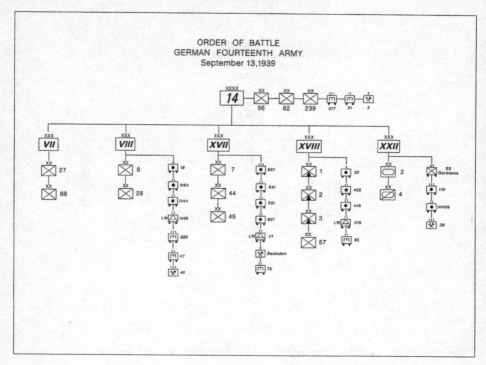

ORDER OF BATTLE
GERMAN FOURTEENTH ARMY
September 13, 1939

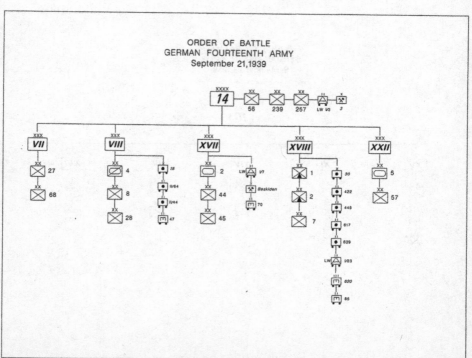

ORDER OF BATTLE
GERMAN FOURTEENTH ARMY
September 21, 1939

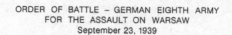

ORDER OF BATTLE – GERMAN EIGHTH ARMY
FOR THE ASSAULT ON WARSAW
September 23, 1939

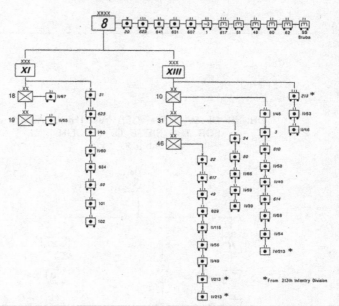

ORDER OF BATTLE – GERMAN THIRD ARMY
FOR THE ASSAULT ON WARSAW
September 23, 1939

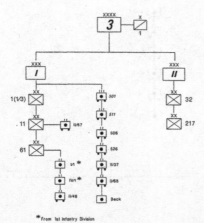

ORDER OF BATTLE – GERMAN THIRD ARMY
FOR THE SIEGE OF MODLIN
September 27, 1939

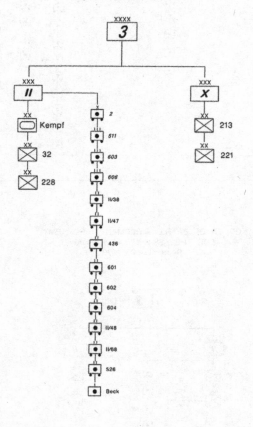

First Borderguard Command
September 1, 1939

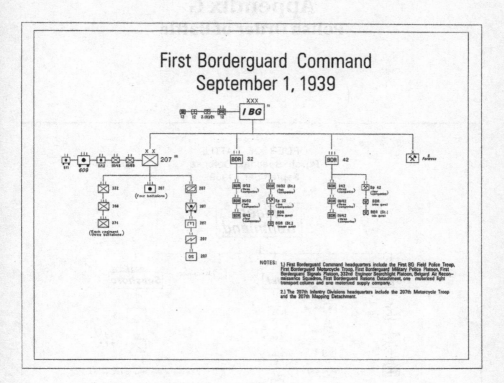

NOTES: 1.) First Borderguard Command headquarters include the First BG Field Police Troop, First Borderguard Motorcycle Troop, First Borderguard Military Police Platoon, First Borderguard Signals Platoon, 332nd Engineer Searchlight Platoon, Belgard Air Reconnaissance Squadron, First Borderguard Rations Detachment, one motorised light transport column and one motorised supply company.

2.) The 207th Infantry Divisions headquarters include the 207th Motorcycle Troop and the 207th Mapping Detachment.

Case White

Appendix G
Polish Order of Battle

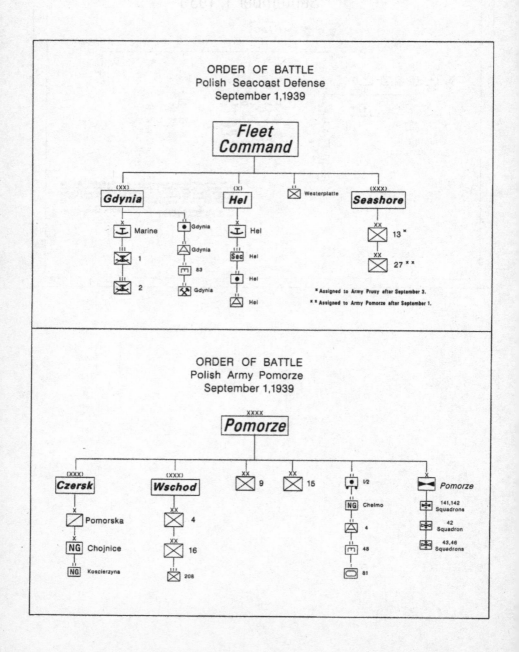

ORDER OF BATTLE
Polish Seacoast Defense
September 1, 1939

Fleet Command

(XX) Gdynia

x Marine

III 1

III 2

• Gdynia

△ Gdynia

83

Gdynia

(X) Hel

x Hel

Sec Hel

• Hel

△ Hel

III Westerplatte

(XXX) Seashore

XX 13 ×

XX 27 × ×

× Assigned to Army Prusy after September 3.

× × Assigned to Army Pomorze after September 1.

ORDER OF BATTLE
Polish Army Pomorze
September 1, 1939

XXXX Pomorze

(XXX) Czersk

x Pomorska

NG Chojnice

NG Koscierzyna

(XXX) Wschod

XX 4

XX 16

III 208

XX 9

XX 15

• I/2

NG Chelmo

△ 4

48

81

Pomorze

x 141, 142 Squadrons

42 Squadron

43, 46 Squadrons

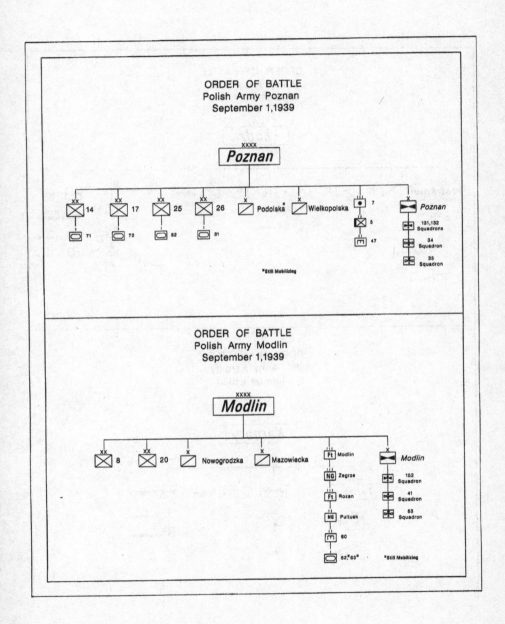

ORDER OF BATTLE
Polish Army Poznan
September 1,1939

ORDER OF BATTLE
Polish Army Modlin
September 1,1939

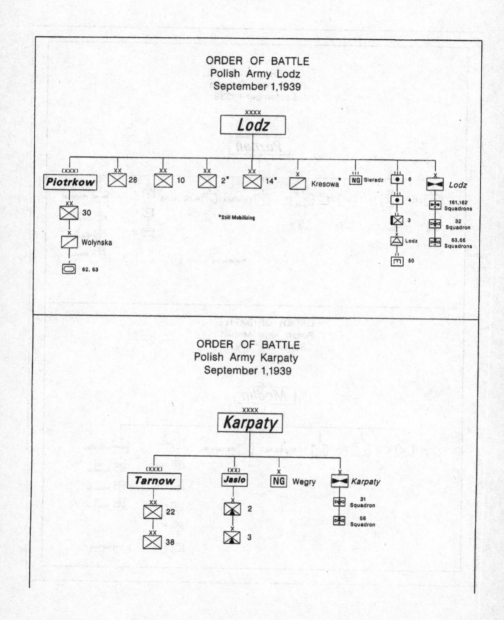

ORDER OF BATTLE
Polish Army Lodz
September 1,1939

*Still Mobilizing

ORDER OF BATTLE
Polish Army Karpaty
September 1,1939

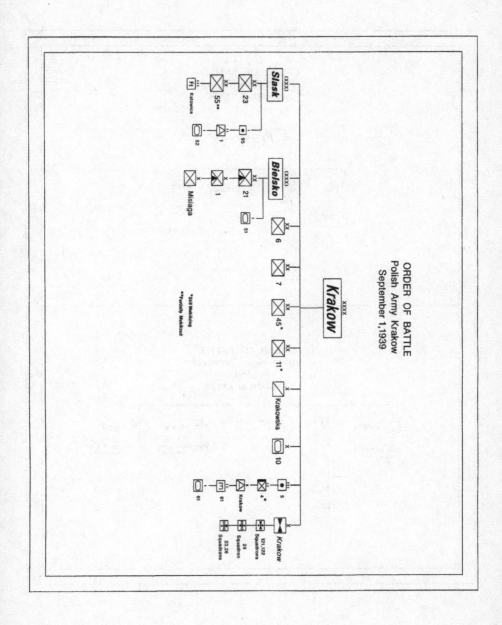

ORDER OF BATTLE
Polish Army Krakow
September 1,1939

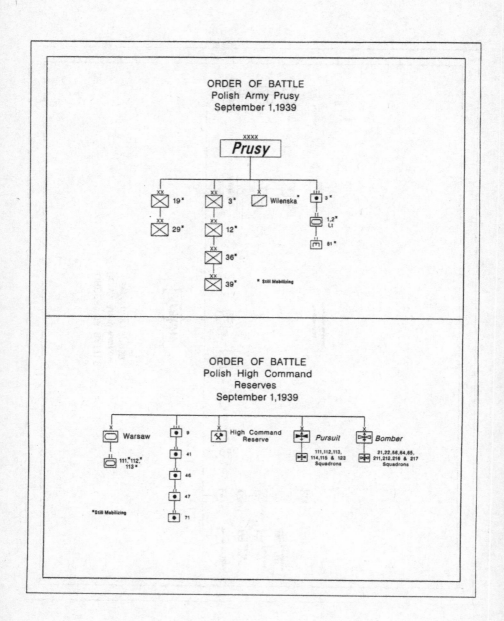

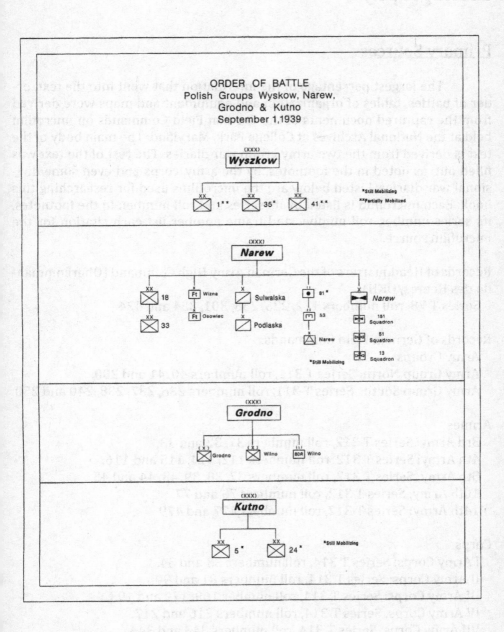

ORDER OF BATTLE
Polish Groups Wyskow, Narew,
Grodno & Kutno
September 1,1939

Wyszkow (XXX)

1 **   35 *   41 **

Narew (XXX)

18   Ft Wizna   Sulwalska   81 *   Narew

33   Ft Osowiec   Podlaska   53   151 Squadron

Narew   51 Squadron

13 Squadron

*Still Mobilizing

Grodno (XXX)

Grodno   Wilno   BDR Wilno

Kutno (XXX)

5 *   24 *   *Still Mobilizing

*Still Mobilizing
**Partially Mobilized

Bibliography

Primary Sources

The largest percentage of the information that went into the text, order of battles, tables of organization and equipment and maps were derived from the captured documents of the German Field Commands on microfilm held at the National Archives at College Park, Maryland. The main body of the text is derived from the two army group war diaries. The rest of the text was filled out, as noted in the footnotes, by the army, corps and even some divisional war diaries. Listed below are the microfilms used for researching this book. Each microfilm is listed by its series and roll number. In the footnotes, its series number, roll number and frame number list each citation for the microfilm source.

Records of Headquarters of the German Army High Command (Oberkommando des Heeres/OKH):
  Series T 78, roll numbers 122, 225, 238, 301, 354 and 424.

Records of German Field Commands:
  Army Groups
  Army Group North: Series T 311, roll numbers 40, 41 and 200.
  Army Group South: Series T 311, roll numbers 236, 237, 238, 240 and 250.

Armies
  3rd Army: Series T 312, roll numbers 31, 32 and 33.
  4th Army: Series T 312, roll numbers 112, 114, 115 and 116.
  8th Army: Series T 312, roll numbers 37, 38, 39, 43, 44 and 45.
  10th Army: Series T 312, roll numbers 75 and 77.
  14th Army: Series T 312, roll numbers 477 and 479.

Corps
  I Army Corps: Series T 314, roll numbers 33 and 34.
  II Army Corps: Series T 314, roll numbers 81 and 99.
  III Army Corps: Series T 314, roll number 169, 179 and 193.
  IV Army Corps: Series T 314, roll numbers 216 and 217.
  VII Army Corps: Series T 314, roll numbers 343 and 344.
  VIII Army Corps: Series T 314, roll numbers 366, 367, 368 and 1449.
  X Army Corps: Series T 314, roll number 441.
  XI Army Corps: Series T 314, roll numbers 477, 478 and 488.
  XIII Army Corps: Series T 314, roll number 509.
  XIV Army Corps: Series T 314, roll numbers 526 and 527.

XV Army Corps: Series T 314, roll numbers 550, 551 and 552.
XVI Army Corps: Series T 314, roll numbers 567 and 568.
XVII Army Corps: Series T 314, roll numbers 572, 573 and 582.
XVIII Army Corps: Series T 314, roll numbers 594 and 595.
XIX Army Corps: Series T 314, roll number 611.
XXI Army Corps: Series T 314, roll number 660
XXII Army Corps: Series T 314, roll number 665.
Corps Wodrig: Series T 314, roll number 750.
First Border Command: Series T 314, roll number 836.
Third Border Command: Series T 314, roll number 840.
Twelfth Border Command: Series T 314, roll number 846.
Thirteenth Border Command: Series T 314, roll number 852.
Fourteenth Border Command: Series T 314, roll number 870.

Divisions
1st Mountain Division: Series T 315, roll number 35.
2nd Light Division: Series T 315, roll number 435.
4th Light Division: Series T 315, roll number 230.
61st Infantry Division: Series T 315, roll number 1009.

Records of German Field Commands: Rear Areas, Occupied Territories and others
Military Command Danzig: Series T 501, roll numbers 230 and 231.
Slovak Army: Series T 501, roll number 296.

Records of German Field Commands: Records of the SS
SS Leibstandarte Adolf Hitler Regiment: Series T 354, roll number 609.

Maps
In addition to the maps used in the microfilm rolls, the Army Map Service maps were used for the strategic maps.
Army Map Service, Series 651: Poland – 1,000,000:1; Washington D.C. June 1946.

Secondary Sources:

Books

Axworthy, Marc Axis Slovakia: Hitlers Slavonic Wedge. New York: Axis Europa Books, 2002.

Bauer, Piotr and Polak, B. Armia Poznan w wojnie, 1939. Poznan-Wyd: Poznanski, 1983.

Bock, Fedor von (Ed. Klaus Gerbert) General FeldMarschall Fedor Von Bock-

The War Diary 1939-1945. USA: Schiffer, 1996.

Bethell, Nicholas The War Hitler Won-September 1939. New York: Holt, Rinehart and Winston, 1973.

Bishop, Chris (Ed.) The Encyclopedia of Weapons of World War II. London: Barnes and Noble, 1998.

Buchner, Alex The German Infantry Handbook. USA: Schiffer, 1991.

Chamberlain, Peter and Gander, Terry World War 2 Fact Files: Anti-Aircraft Guns; Anti-tank Weapons; Infantry, Mountain and Airborne Guns; Light and Medium Field Artillery; Heavy Artillery; Machine Guns and Mortars and Rockets. New York: Arco Publishing, 1974-1976.

Ciechanowski, Konrad Armia Pomorze. Warsaw: WMON, 1983.

Cynk, Jerzy B. The Polish Air Force at War - The Official History 1939-1943. Pennsylvania: Schiffer, 1998.

Dalecki, Ryszard Armia Karpaty, 1939. Warsaw: WMON, 1979.

Glowacki, L. Obrona Warsawy i Moldina. Warsaw: WMON,1975.

Greiner, Helmuth Die Oberste Wehrmachtführung 1939-1943. Wiesbaden: Limes Verlag, 1951.

Halder, Franz The Halder War Diaries. Washington D.C.: Washington Infantry Journal, 1950.

Hogg, Ian German Artillery of World War Two Pennsylvania: Greenhill Books,1997.

Kliment, Charles K. and Nakladal, Bretislav Germany's First Ally-Armed Forces of the Slovak State 1939-1945. Pennsylvania: Schiffer, 1997.

Lossberg, Bernhard Im Wehrmachtführungstab-Bereicht eines Generalstabsoffiziers. Hamburg: H.H. Nölke Verlag, 1949.

Madej, Victor and Zaloga, Steve The Polish Campaign 1939. New York: Hippocrane, 1985.

Michaelis, Rolf SS-Heimwehr Danzig 1939-an Ephemeral Paramilitary Formation- Polish Campaign 1939. United Kingdom: Shelf Books, 1996.

Nafziger, George F. The German Order of Battle: Infantry in World War II (2000), :Panzer and Artillery in World War II (1999), Waffen SS and other Units in World War II (2001) London, Greenhill Books (for 1999) and Pennsylvania, Combined Publishing (for 2000 and 2001).

Niehorster, Leo German World War II Organizational Series Volume 1/1 – Mechanized and Waffen SS Units (1st September 1939). Hannover: Leo Niehorster, 1998.

Rzepniewski, A. Obrona wybrzeza w 1939r. Warsaw: WMON, 1964.

Rossino, Alexander Hitler Strikes Poland. Kansas: University of Kansas Press, 2003.

Sawodny, Wolfgang Die Panzerzüge des Deutschen Reiches 1904-1945. Germany: EK-Verlag, 1996.

Shores, Christopher Duel for the Sky. London: Grub Street, 1999.

Steblik, W. Armia Krakow, 1939. Warsaw: WMON, 1975.

Thies, Klaus-Jürgen Der Polenfeldzug Ein Lage atlas der Operationsabteilung des Generalstab des Heeres. Osnabrück: Biblio-Verlag, 1989.

Vormann, Nikolaus von Der Feldzug 1939 in Polen. Wiessenburg: Prinz Eugen-Verlag, 1958.

Watt, Richard M. Bitter Glory: Poland and its Fate 1918-1939. USA: Barnes and Noble, 1998.

Wroblewski, J. Armia Lodz, 1939. Warsaw: WMON, 1975.

Zaloga, Steven J. Poland 1939- The Birth of Blitzkrieg. Great Britain: Osprey Publishing, 2002.

Internet Resources

The Internet provides a great deal of information for those who are looking for information on World War Two. There is also a lot of disinformation on the Internet, so provided below is what I consider the best websites to visit if you need information on the German Army.

World War II Day by Day: Christopher Awender, Host. A great resource for those seeking information on the German Army in World War Two. Particularly useful was the day-by-day combat actions taken from the war diaries of various units during the Polish Campaign. *www.wwiidaybyday.com*

World War II Armed Forces Order of Battle: Leo Niehorster, Host. A valuable resource for finding order of battle charts, tables of organization and equipment for the German Army in World War Two. *www.orbat.com/site/ww2/drleo/*

Feldgrau Forum: Jason Pipes, Host. This website specifically covers the German Armed Forces during World War Two (and some pre-war). Most helpful is its question and answer forum, where you can ask other members specific queries about any aspect of the Wehrmacht. *www.feldgrau.com*

Axis History Forum: Marcus Wendel, Host. Similar to Feldgrau, it covers a much more broad range of German military history, ranging from Imperial Germany to the Third Reich. In addition it delves into the Holocast and war crimes of the Third Reich. It also has a question and answer forum like Feldgrau. *www.axishistory.com*

Index

German Army Formations

Look for more books from Winged Hussar Publishing, LLC – E-books, paperbacks and Limited Edition hardcovers. The best in history, science fiction and fantasy at:

https://www. wingedhussarpublishing.com

or follow us on Facebook at:

Winged Hussar Publishing LLC

Or on twitter at:

WingHusPubLLC
For information and upcoming publications

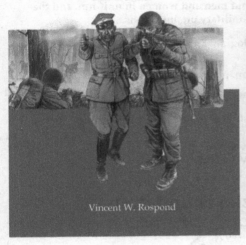

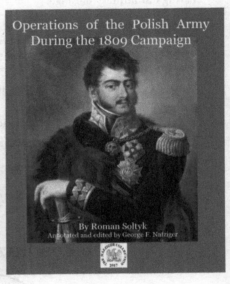

Printed in the United States